My Beloved Is Mine

דודי לי ואני לו

"My beloved is mine,
and I am his...."
Song of Songs

BOOKS BY ROLAND B. GITTELSOHN

My Beloved Is Mine
Consecrated Unto Me
Man's Best Hope
Little Lower Than the Angels
Modern Jewish Problems

My Beloved Is Mine

Judaism and Marriage

by RABBI ROLAND B. GITTELSOHN

UNION OF AMERICAN HEBREW CONGREGATIONS
New York

Library of Congress Catalog Card No. 68-54572

PRODUCED IN THE U.S. OF AMERICA

In Memoriam

F. Alexander Magoun
1896-1968

But what, after all, do thinkers need friends for? So that they can share speculations, each alternately playing benevolent authority to the other, each being the other's co-conspirator, each serving as applauding audience, and as cautioning chorus.

—Erik Erikson

Editor's Introduction

MARRIAGE REPRESENTS THE INDIVIDUAL'S CAPACITY TO GO BEyond himself to find fulfillment in life. The most sublime of all relationships, according to Judaism, is expressed in the union between man and woman. That union, however, is not as ingenuous as the one consummated in the Garden of Eden.

Judaism recognizes the complexities involved in the marital relationship. In the following pages, Rabbi Gittelsohn evaluates the complex meaning and profound significance of marriage in the light of Jewish practices and values.

According to Jewish tradition, it was expected that a period of preparation would precede the actual ceremony of marriage.

Similarly, this book is a manual of preparation directed to the couple about to be married. With the emphasis in contemporary society on intensive learning for the assurance of successful careers, it is amazing that no "education" is required for the career of marriage. Premarital conferences and discussions, in addition to the reading of literature about marriage, should be an indispensable part of the education of every couple who desires a successful, lifelong career.

It would be arbitrary to terminate this education at the end of the engagement period. Understanding one another really begins on the wedding day. Thereafter marital education becomes even more intensive. This book can serve as a useful guide to every husband and wife seeking to enrich their lives, as well as the lives of their children, with the values and insights that Judaism brings to marriage.

JACK D. SPIRO

Preface

IT IS NO CASUAL SEQUENCE THAT THE WRITING AND PUBLISHing of *Consecrated Unto Me* preceded preparation of the present volume. The time to commence anticipating one's marriage is long before the beginning of courtship. By mid-adolescence much of the intellectual and emotional background for marriage has already been laid. Therefore my first thought was to formulate a book which would introduce high school students to those insights of contemporary science and perennial Judaism which might aid them in understanding and achieving happiness in marriage.

Before *Consecrated Unto Me* had even been finished, Rabbi Alexander M. Schindler—then director of the Commission on Jewish Education—suggested the desirability of a companion volume which might serve couples standing on the threshold of marriage as well as those recently married. *My Beloved Is Mine* addresses itself precisely to that need. Though it is intended most immediately for Jewish couples, I would hope that much of it might prove helpful to those of other faiths too. The bride and groom who have already studied this before their premarital conference with the officiating clergyman can come prepared with questions, anxieties, and problems they are particularly eager to explore.

Not even the writing of many articles, sermons, and books qualifies one to thank adequately those whose generous co-operation is essential to such an undertaking as this. No one person can pretend to be an expert in all the disciplines touching upon the study of marriage. I have been extremely fortunate in receiving guidance and advice from others who read my manuscript devotedly from the perspective of their professional competences: Dr. Sidney Slater Cohen as a gynecologist-obstetrician, Dr. Herbert I. Posin as a psychiatrist, Professor F. Alexander Magoun as a human relations and marriage counselor, Dr. Julius Kravetz as a scholar in rabbinic literature. Uniquely practical suggestions came to me from two couples of married friends, Mr. and Mrs. Jackson Parker and Dr. and Mrs. Peter Braun. All these are responsible for more than a few sharpened insights and improved expressions. I myself lay claim to whatever errors or omissions remain.

My debt to Rabbi Schindler is immeasurable. Quite aside from being godfather to this book, his profound wisdom, creative energy, and delightful humor were at my service literally both night and day. When he was elevated to the vice-presidency of the Union of American Hebrew Congregations, his successor as director of the Commission on Jewish Education, Rabbi Jack D. Spiro, assumed the onerous obligations of publication mid-wife with dispatch and grace. The pleasing format of the volume is due to the meticulous planning and skill of Mr. Ralph Davis.

I am grateful to my associate, Rabbi Harvey J. Fields, for permission to adapt and use several liturgical selections as supplements. My loyal secretary, Miss Bessie R. Berman, surpassed even her own previous high standard in the tireless typing and retyping of manuscripts.

If I have saved my beloved wife for last, this is only because what is difficult vis-à-vis others becomes an absolute impossibility when I attempt to thank her. It is not easy to be a rabbi's wife. It is often very difficult to be a writer's wife. To be the wife of a rabbi-writer requires almost superhuman patience and forbearance. For more than thirty-six years now Ruth has exhibited far more than an average share of these rare commodities. Her influence and help are on almost every page of this book.

If this work can improve the prospect of marital success for the young couples who read it, if it can elevate the marriages of slightly older couples to a higher level of happiness, it will vindicate every ounce of effort that went into it.

ROLAND B. GITTELSOHN

Boston, Massachusetts
January, 1969

Contents

My Beloved Is Mine

דודי לי ואני לו

«««««««« 1 »»»»»»»»

A Many-Splendored Hope

How happy will your marriage be?

No human experience is so filled with sweet, confident hope as when bride and groom stand before their rabbi, awaiting those words of ancient usage which will unite their lives as one. For every couple, their moment of marriage is a culmination of almost unbearable anticipation and a harbinger of inexpressible hope. The future opens out before them like a bursting cornucopia, unable any longer to contain all its abundant goodness. Nothing but ecstatic happiness looms ahead.

Yet more than a few such couples are doomed to dismal disappointment. For some, marriage will end in the divorce court; for others, it will degenerate into dull despair. During a recent period of seventy years, in the United States, while population was increasing threefold and marriages fourfold, the number of divorces rose twentyfold! On the day they were married, nearly all the couples who failed would have staked their lives on success.

How happy will your marriage be?

A ten-year study under the auspices of a major American college discovered that only one couple in twenty is "quite unhappy." But no more than one in six reported themselves to be "extremely happy."[1] The poet Coleridge disclosed more about himself than about marriage when he said: ". . . the most happy marriage I can picture or image to myself would be the union of a deaf man to a blind woman." Professor F. Alexander Magoun was a great deal more realistic when he wrote: "Some marriages are sheer hell. Most marriages are pretty mediocre. A few marriages are positively delicious."[2]

How happy will your marriage be?

The question is not asked cynically, nor is the possibility of trouble introduced to chill your expectations at the start. It is precisely because marriage can be so wonderful, bringing you the most exalted happiness in the world, that it is worth the effort to distinguish those factors which are conducive to success from those which presage failure. Your relationship to your wife or husband will be an entirely new kind of relationship, one which you have never known before, which it is well-nigh impossible to describe to you in advance. No matter how close or loving you have ever felt toward any other person—a parent, a sibling, a teacher, a friend—this new relationship you are about to assume will touch down to a dimension of intimacy you have never felt and cannot imagine. In order to increase the probability of your achieving the best that marriage can produce, it is necessary from the outset to be aware also of its worst.

How happy will your marriage be?

That depends on many things—the kind of persons you and your prospective mate are, the compatibility between you, your understanding of love, how hard you work together for happiness, your emotional maturity, your readiness for a mutually-fulfilling sex life, your knowledge of Jewish tradition concerning love and marriage, your attitudes toward religion.

The mere fact that you feel so strong an attachment and yearning for each other and that the words of the wedding ceremony will be properly intoned in your presence will not automatically assure you the happiness you seek. No more than an automobile, a tankful of fuel, and a desire to drive from Boston to Los Angeles add up to the promise of a successful journey. In order to reach your destination in good health and with joy experienced en route, you must know the nature of your car and of yourself, the rules for responsible operation of the highly powered machine at your disposal, the rights of others on the road, and the route best calculated to carry you from coast to coast with a maximum of pleasure and a minimum of pain. Failure on any of these counts can bring disappointment ranging from minor inconvenience to major catastrophe. As you sit behind the wheel of your car, the ignition key you turn can activate unbounded happiness or tragic pain—for you and for innumerable others.

No less is true of marriage. Here too it is imperative that you know accurately all the factors involved, that you be realistically aware of human nature in general, of your nature and your beloved's in particular. Here too there is an accumulated wisdom of the ages which can be ignored only at great peril. Here too there are rules for responsible relationships, and your happiness will be enhanced in direct proportion to your knowledge of these rules and your willingness to abide by them. Your wedding ceremony guarantees nothing but promises much. It gives you a legal and ethical franchise to pursue—together with the person whom you love more than any other on earth—the highest happiness known to man.

Your chance for success is probably greater than that of any preceding generation. Like them, your resources include a great body of perceptive insight into the meaning of marriage, made available to you through Jewish tradition. But you can draw also upon much modern knowledge which was unknown even to your parents. Many branches of science–biology, anthropology, sociology, psychology above all–combine to suggest the best routes to success. That success will require more than the reading of books. All that can even be attempted in these pages is to gather, in one convenient place, as much as possible of the wisdom provided by Judaism and science.

How happy will your marriage be?

That depends on how much you care. On how hard you try. On how scrupulously–at times perhaps even painfully–you seek the truth about yourselves.

How happy will your marriage be?

Only you can answer that question. You and your spouse. You and time.

«««««««« 2 »»»»»»»»

"This Funny Thing"

PROBABLY THE MOST MISUNDERSTOOD AND ABUSED WORD IN THE English language is *love*. People speak of *loving* their homes, their cars, their food, their dogs, their parents, their friends, their brothers and sisters, their husbands and wives. Obviously, a word that can be given so many meanings is in danger of soon having no meaning at all. Since marriage at its best is a permanent relationship between two people who are in love, it is imperative that we begin by trying to define love.

Many attempts have been made. Some years ago there was a popular song, the lyric of which asked "What is this thing, this funny thing called love?" The song writer's response won't help us much. Neither will the intentionally humorous efforts of those who have suggested that love is "an itchy feeling around the heart that you can't scratch" or "a feeling you feel when you feel you are going to feel a feeling you never felt before."

Alexander Magoun was one of the first university professors in this country to pioneer with courses on marriage. He has devoted many years to an accurate understanding of love. After rejecting the jocose proposals above, he has suggested two serious definitions which deserve our attention:

> Love is a feeling of tenderness and devotion toward someone, so profound that to share that individual's joys, anticipations, sorrows and pain is the very essence of living.
>
> Love is the passionate and abiding desire on the part of two or more people to produce together the conditions under which each can be and spontaneously express his real self; to produce together an intellectual soil and an emotional climate in which each can flourish, far superior to what either could achieve alone.[1]

Several aspects of these statements merit further comment. First, let it be noted that love involves voluntary participation in the pains of another person no less than in his joys.

A chasidic tale expresses this truth eloquently. Two friends were drinking together one day in the corner of an inn. They had imbibed enough to reach the stage of sloppy sentimentality, throwing their arms around each other as they loudly professed their love. Suddenly one said to the other: "Ivan, what hurts me now?" Ivan's response: "How should I know what hurts you now, Peter?" To which Peter immediately demanded: "If you don't know what hurts me, how can you say you love me?" From the loosened lips of drunkards—no less than out of the mouths of babes and sucklings—profound truth often flows.

No life can be filled always with sunshine; heartbreak and tragedy also are inescapable components of our human heritage. A willingness to share only the bright and happy experiences of another, while resenting an equal sharing of his disappointments and doubts, betrays something less than maturity either in general or in readiness for genuine love. Indeed, there is reason to believe that in a solid marriage the crises two individuals share may do even more to unite them than their moments of rejoicing and success.

Jewish tradition has long been aware of this truth. One of the things we shall observe later about our marriage ceremony is that the wine shared by bride and groom symbolizes both the sweetness and bitterness of life, which they taste together.

In a good marriage, however, neither partner persistently takes advantage of the other. It is possible to tyrannize another person through weakness as well as strength. For husband or wife to play the role of chronic dependent, always demanding that the other bear most of their joint burdens, bespeaks a neurotic rather than wholesome relationship.

If husband and wife are compatible, each will be contributing strength to the other. In some situations of stress, one will be for the moment stronger; in the next crisis, the opposite may be true. On one occasion, the husband will support the sagging spirit of the wife; another time it will be she who is able to save him from the slough of despair. There have been many moments in my marriage when I would have been utterly unable to survive a peril or threat had it not been for my wife. I have every good reason to believe that at other times it was my love which sustained her.

Marriage is not a picnic. It does, however, have its experiences of indescribable happiness. And these are enjoyed doubly under the impact of love. My first trip to Europe and Israel was made without my wife. Again and again I was aware of how much more I would have benefited from a given adventure or view if she had been with me. On my second visit she accompanied me. The experiences I had enjoyed most the first time meant immeasurably more to me by very virtue of our sharing them together. The excitement and beauty of life are more than doubled when husband and wife share them in love. The tragedy and tribulation of life become ever so much easier to endure when love makes it possible for one to strengthen the other.

No Dictators

It is equally important to observe, from the second suggested definition, that love involves a mutuality which precludes martyrdom on the part of either mate. Neither should be expected to sacrifice or subsume himself for the sake of the other. This is true not only in marriage, but in all interpersonal relationships. The parent who constantly dominates a growing child, who persists in attempting to fashion that child in his own image, who protests that he imposes his will only out of love is demonstrating many things about himself—but a capacity to love is not one of them. The mother whose theme in life is her willingness to become a martyr to her children is an eloquent exponent of masochism, scarcely of love. The husband or wife who completely absorbs the other, who *possesses* and controls him, has not understood the meaning of love at all.

The essence of love is that two people unite their separate lives inextricably, yet each retains his own individuality while fostering that of his mate. This is a very delicate, subtle relationship, one which demands both maturity and sensitivity. Like the separate sections of a symphony orchestra, each plays according to his own timbre and tone, but in harmony with the others. If the violins try to sound like the horns, or the horns to emulate the woodwinds, the result, while novel, is not good music. By the same token, however, if each plays from a different score—in utter disregard of the others—the consequence is even worse. The more truly each section exploits the maximum potential of its own instrument, in a common undertaking with all other sections, the more richly does it enhance the music for all. So, in a marriage which bespeaks mature love, each partner tries to discover his own highest potential and his mate's, then to create an atmosphere and environment conducive to the maximum development of both.

You may have lifted a curious eyebrow when you noticed, in Professor Magoun's second definition, reference to "desire on the part of *two or more* people." A careful reading of the entire definition will disclose that it could apply not only to the relationship between husband and wife, but also to that among brothers and sisters or between parents and their children. Will one definition do for all these manifestations of love? I think not. True, there is a valid similarity among them. It is doubtful in the extreme whether a person who has never known a truly loving relationship with his parents, with siblings and friends, is capable of experiencing love with a mate.

Yet the uniqueness of the love which binds one woman to one man in marriage must not be lost in that which is admittedly common to the several varieties of love. The sexual aspect of love in marriage is in itself enough to make the difference one of kind, not merely of degree. Later we shall discuss the relationship between sexual attraction and love, as well as the extreme danger of confusing the two. For the time being, let it be said simply that sex is one of the most dominant needs of human beings and that a successful marriage between two normal young persons, without a mutually gratifying sex experience, is highly improbable.

At least in part as a consequence of their sexual bond, the partnership of husband and wife assumes that unique dimension of intimacy described in our opening chapter. The most loving association of two brothers living in the same household, of two sisters, or friends—for all that it shares in many aspects of the partnership between husband and wife—falls so far short that any attempt to encompass both in one definition of love will confuse more than it will clarify. Our concern here is the kind of love which exists in a good marriage.

Still Not Easy

If it is possible to approach even as close to a valid definition of love as we already have, then why do so many couples discover, some months or years after their wedding, that they have in fact been betrayed by self-deception? Their confusion inheres in the fact that there is a vast difference between achieving a reasonably accurate definition of love on paper and being able to identify or measure it within oneself. Often when youngsters ask their parents how they will recognize love, they receive some such answer as: "Don't worry; when you're really in love, you'll know it." As comforting as such certainty may be, it just doesn't happen to be true.

Not only is love, in and of itself, a complicated emotion, but it is also easily confused with infatuation and romance. Infatuation is a purely physical, sexual attraction between man and woman. The dictionary defines *infatuate* as *to inspire with ardent passion so as to deprive of ordinary judgment*. Romance is a warm feeling of comfortable attachment, induced and encouraged by soft music and lowered lights and the stuff of which daydreams are made. According to the dictionary, again, *to romance* means *to indulge in visionary fabrications, tell fanciful stories*. Where love is idealistic, romance is idealized. Love recognizes real virtues in the beloved and seeks to encourage their utmost fruition. Romance purports to see virtues which don't really exist.

A seventeen-year-old girl once wrote in her diary: "Love can blot out reality." She was hopelessly and disastrously wrong. Any person who convinces himself that love can defy reality is experiencing romance, not love. Sooner or later he is doomed to disillusionment. Genuine love is possible only when reality is recognized and accepted.

Both infatuation and romance are notoriously divorced from reality. However pleasant they are as momentary diversion, there is an inevitable moment of awakening. Infatuation and romance are both necessary and valuable emotions for every person to experience; indeed, they may even be essential components of love. But it is disastrous to mistake a small part for the whole.

A cynical woman once said to me at the conclusion of a wedding ceremony: "It was nice . . . very nice . . . but once the wedding is over, romance goes out the window." Her disillusioned comment reflected an all-too-frequent-and-unfortunate truth. Poor indeed is the marriage devoid of strong physical attraction and moments of affectionate flight from reality. That wife is enviable whose husband can say to her on their thirtieth wedding anniversary: "Sweetheart, you're beautiful!" That couple is admirable who can, even as they grow older, occasionally float together on "cloud nine," oblivious to fact. But a beneficial diversion can become fatal if confused with permanent policy. Baked Alaska is delicious as dessert; it is not recommended as a steady source of nutrition.

There is no such thing as love at first sight. Often there is infatuation at first sight, followed at the earliest opportunity by romance. These can, in the course of time, develop into love, though more often they do not. The newborn infant whose vocal emanations sound delightfully musical to his parents may become an opera star, but the objective observer will adopt a cautious policy of *wait and see*. The same procedure is wise in approaching the distinction between infatuation or romance and love. The first imperative, then—for you and your intended—is to ascertain, if you can, whether your attraction for each other is really love.

CRUCIAL DIFFERENCES

The first way is by the test of time. Love has a lasting quality which is lacking in romance and infatuation. The latter are often like a match touched to a pile of combustible brush. The flame catches at once, bursts immediately into frightening fullness which gives the deceptive appearance of lasting forever, then quickly subsides and dies. Love is more likely to be a fire built from small beginnings—first a few pieces of kindling, then larger logs to feed the flame, renewed nourishment whenever needed, glowing coals by which one warms himself.

The diagram below may help to clarify the distinction. Except for the rare instance where infatuation or romance leads to love, it begins more dramatically, develops far more rapidly, and expires while love may still be incubating.

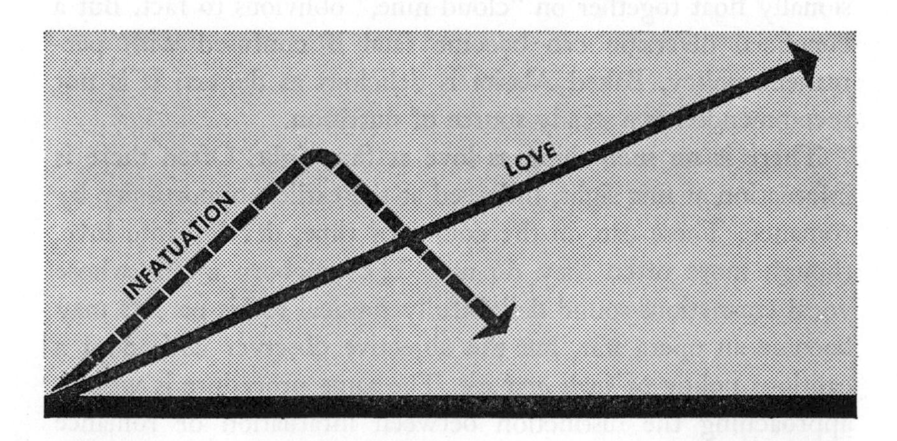

A second criterion for making this most essential distinction is whether the emphasis is on the self or the other person, on getting or on giving. The person who is infatuated is interested primarily in himself; the other person is important only for what she can give him. The frame of reference, whether vocalized or not, is: how-much-pleasure-it-gives-me-to-be-with-you. The person who is truly in love is at least as interested in his partner as in himself; as a matter of fact, he becomes more important in his own eyes, directly in proportion to what he is able to contribute to his partner's happiness. The frame of reference is: how-much-more-adequate-and-secure-each-of-us-feels-because-of-the-other.

A homely analogy may add to our understanding here. A parakeet, unable to tolerate loneliness, can be deceived into thinking it has a companion simply by installing a mirror in its cage. The foolish bird is convinced that it is no longer alone, when in fact it is looking only at itself. In a similar sense, psychologically, the person who is experiencing infatuation is really enjoying the image of himself which he sees reflected in the eyes of the other.

Despite a superficial, preliminary appearance to the contrary, these paragraphs do not contradict what has already been said about martyrdom. Observe, please, that the individual who is involved in a true experience of love was not described as being *more interested* in his mate than in himself, but *at least as interested*. He must begin with a healthy, wholesome, balanced acceptance of and respect for himself. No melodramatic self-sacrifice will do. He must want the same opportunity for self-expression and self-realization that he would eagerly afford to his beloved. And he must strive for those circumstances and conditions which will enable each of them to achieve a degree of self-fulfillment which would be impossible for either of them acting alone.

A world-renowned psychoanalyst, Dr. Erich Fromm, has written eloquently of the capacity to concentrate on giving more than receiving:

What is giving? Simple as the answer to this question seems to be, it is actually full of ambiguities and complexities. The most widespread misunderstanding is that which assumes that giving is "giving up" something, being deprived of, sacrificing. The person whose character has not developed beyond the stage of the receptive, exploitative, or hoarding orientation, experiences the act of giving in this way. The marketing character is willing to give, but only in exchange for receiving; giving without receiving for him is being cheated. . . .

For the productive character, giving has an entirely different meaning. Giving is the highest expression of potency. In the very act of giving, I experience my strength, my wealth, my power. This experience of heightened vitality and potency fills me with joy. I experience myself as overflowing, spending, alive, hence as joyous. Giving is more joyous than receiving, not because it is a deprivation, but because in the act of giving lies the expression of my aliveness.

. . . The most elementary example lies in the sphere of sex. The culmination of the male sexual function lies in the act of giving; the man gives himself, his sexual organ, to the woman. At the moment of orgasm he gives his semen to her. He cannot help giving it if he is potent. If he cannot give, he is impotent. For the woman the process is not different, although somewhat more complex. She gives herself too; she opens the gates to her feminine center; in the act of receiving, she gives. If she is incapable of this act of giving, if she can only receive, she is frigid. With her the act of giving occurs again, not in her function as a lover, but in that as a mother. She gives of herself to the growing child within her, she gives her milk to the infant, she gives her bodily warmth. Not to give would be painful. . . .

> What does one person give to another? He gives of himself, of the most precious he has, he gives of his life. This does not necessarily mean that he sacrifices his life for the other—but that he gives him of that which is alive in him; he gives him of his joy, of his interest, of his understanding, of his knowledge, of his humor, of his sadness—of all expressions and manifestations of that which is alive in him. In thus giving of his life, he enriches the other person, he enhances the other's sense of aliveness by enhancing his own sense of aliveness. He does not give in order to receive; giving is in itself exquisite joy. But in giving he cannot help bringing something to life in the other person, and this which is brought to life reflects back to him; in truly giving, he cannot help receiving that which is given back to him. Giving implies to make the other person a giver also and they both share in the joy of what they have brought to life.[2]

This capacity to *receive-by-giving* is so important an ingredient of love that it deserves further comment. Because of it, the partners in a love relationship are able to discover and develop in each other rich resources of ability and character which may never have been suspected. Each becomes a finer, nobler, more decent human being because of the other. According to Jewish tradition, before Akiba fell in love with his future wife he was only a humble, illiterate shepherd. She agreed to marry him on condition that he would study Torah; obviously, she recognized in him a capacity for intellectual and spiritual achievement of which he had not yet become aware himself. Akiba agreed. After they were secretly married, he left her for two periods of twelve years each, during which he studied assiduously and became the most illustrious rabbinic scholar of his time, the famous Rabbi Akiba.[3] Not every person possesses the potential for great scholarship. Not everyone is a possible genius. But all of us—without exception—have ability and character far beyond that which we have discovered in ourselves. Love—like the warm, beneficent rays of the summer sun—draws this innate energy and goodness to the surface, promoting the growth both of lover and beloved. The famed philosopher, A. N. Whitehead, must have had this in mind when he said: "By myself I am only one more professor, but with Evelyn I am first-rate."[4]

A chasidic story is pertinent at this point. According to the tradition of Chasidism, it is possible to establish communion with the Prophet Elijah through fasting and concentrated study. In order to attain this goal, a nineteenth-century Polish rabbi named Sholem is said to have resolved to fast and remain awake for a thousand successive nights studying Torah. His wife, when she learned of his determination, remained awake each night with him, holding a lighted candle so that he might study without hindrance or interruption.[5]

The stories of both Rabbi Akiba and Rabbi Sholem involve wives who seem to have subsumed their own personalities and ambitions to those of their husbands. In a good marriage this kind of relationship is reciprocal. Each partner discovers the dearest hopes and richest propensities of the other, then derives enormous happiness from helping to actualize what would otherwise have remained only dormant.

Infatuation may be compared to the sound waves projected by a bat as it flies. It emits a squeal, too highly pitched for the human ear, which bounces back from surrounding objects, thus enabling the bat to avoid colliding with them. This is nature's prototype for sonar, the transmission of sound waves through water by a ship, in order to locate submerged submarines. The bat is interested only in itself and its own needs; everything in its environment is "sounded" only in order to guide itself. In like manner, the emotional beams projected by the person who is infatuated are intended to yield benefit only to himself. His objective, whether or not he consciously realizes it, is the pleasure he receives, as it were, from the reflection of himself. Love is like a ship shining the beams of its searchlights out into the dark in order to locate a drifting lifeboat. In this case the primary concern is to find and benefit someone else, though in the very act of finding, the ship's crew themselves feel gratified and fulfilled.

Another analogy, suggested by Alexander Magoun, may help. The person who is infatuated is like a tourist who visits a foreign country for his own edification and enjoyment. The sights he sees, the information he obtains, the new possessions he acquires: these constitute the sum total of his experience. The person who is in love may more accurately be likened to a member of the Peace Corps who spends time abroad to benefit the local population. His primary purpose is to give rather than to receive, yet—paradoxically—he probably ends up seeing more, learning more, and acquiring more than the casual tourist. The very intention to serve others redounds to his own utmost benefit. So it is with love, compared to infatuation.

To Burn or Bless?

A third criterion for distinguishing love from infatuation or romance is actually an extension of the second. Not only is each partner in a true love relationship concerned with the other, the two of them together are very much involved with people beyond themselves. Infatuation and romance are likely to be ingrown kinds of relationship; to the degree that the two people concerned truly share with each other, their vision goes no farther than that. They prefer to spend most of their time alone. Even when they are with others, their interest is primarily centered on themselves. While it is true that those who are in love also enjoy spending some time alone with each other, they seek a wider circle of interest too.

Only a loving person is capable of becoming a lovable person. And the boundary lines of love are broader by far than those of romance and infatuation. There is no such thing as loving only one person in the world, to the exclusion of all others. Romance can be represented by a couple who uses a magnifying glass to focus the sun's rays only on themselves; sooner or later they are likely to be burned. A couple in love tries to direct the rays of the sun so that comfort and warmth may be diffused to others too.

Some of the most beautiful love relationships in history have been between two people whose love prompted them to bring great benefit to others. Elizabeth and Robert Browning wrote exquisite poetry—each with his own pen and in his own style—yet each no doubt stimulated and encouraged by the other. Marie and Pierre Curie together discovered radium, bringing blessing and healing to multitudes. Louise and Stephen Wise established a great synagogue and labored creatively for those less fortunate than themselves. Apparently our ancient rabbis understood this special quality of love. They incorporated the following story in midrashic literature:

> There once lived a pious man who was childless. He prayed for a son, vowing to invite to his wedding-feast every poor person in the city. A son was eventually born to him, and he gave him the name of Mattaniah, namely, a gift from God. The boy grew up and his wedding day approached. The father invited all the students of the Torah and all the poor, who together filled six rooms.
>
> God wished to test the bridegroom, so He sent the Angel of Death, in the guise of a man attired in soiled raiment, to beg for a place at the wedding. The

bridegroom refused on the plea that all who could be accommodated had been invited. Moreover, the man's garments were objectionable.

In the night, the Angel of Death revealed himself, declaring that he was about to take away the bridegroom's soul since he had failed in the test. The bride gave voice to this prayer:

"O Lord of the universe, Thou hast said in Thy Torah that, when a man takes unto himself a wife, he shall bring her cheer for a full year and not leave her. May it be Thy will that my husband live before Thee, and I shall teach him to practice loving-kindness to everyone without discrimination." Her prayer was heard on high, and the Angel of Death was commanded to leave.

What was the nature of this young woman? Her mother was accustomed to draw cool water from a spring for school children. When she became old, her daughter said: "You need not abandon your good deed. I shall lend you the strength of my arm and carry most of the weight so that you may continue to perform the Mitzvah."

It was this consideration for her mother that made her deserving in the eyes of the Lord.[6]

One More Difference

We have seen, then, that love can be distinguished from romance and infatuation by virtue of the facts that (a) it is more enduring, (b) it is characterized by the joy of giving rather than the self-gratification of only receiving, and (c) it stimulates two people to benefit others through their affection. There is one more criterion, however, of immense importance.

Infatuation is purely physical; love is both physical and

spiritual. Perhaps we should pause to clarify the meaning of *spiritual.* We use it here for those aspects of a human being which go beyond the purely physical, for the extraphysical or transphysical characteristics of human experience. My brain is physical; a surgeon can easily identify it and, if necessary, explore parts of it. My mind is spiritual; though it is dependent on my brain, it is not of itself an anatomical entity to which a physician can point. True, when I think, certain electrochemical currents are released in my brain. But these are not my thoughts, they are just the physical manifestations of thought, the way my brain functions while thought is being produced.

The spiritual phases of a man's life are referred to as his soul. They include his capacity to create and/or appreciate truth, beauty, and moral goodness. Just as thought and truth are not physical, so beauty and ethical values are not physical. We often recognize them in physical form, but they are themselves spiritual.

To return, then, to our fourth and final criterion of distinction, infatuation is a purely physical experience; love is physical plus spiritual. The only bond between individuals who are infatuated is their bodies and the physical comforts and pleasures they can obtain from each other. The bonds between lovers include all this, plus an irresistible impulse to create or to appreciate with each other increasing quantities of truth, beauty, and goodness. To say that love is a spiritual as well as a physical experience is to imply that there is something sacred in the love of man and woman for each other. This is exactly what Judaism has always taught.

Dr. Karl Menninger, another renowned psychoanalyst, has written a paragraph which effectively summarizes both this and the preceding criteria for distinguishing infatuation from love. After observing that love is an attraction of whole persons for each other, not just of their genital organs, he continues:

> The world's greatest lovers have not been Don Juans and Casanovas, but Schweitzers, Gandhis, Helen Kellers, and such saints as Francis of Assisi. . . . What psychoanalysis showed was that true love is more concerned about the welfare of the one loved than with its own immediate satisfactions, that it demands nothing, but is patient, kind, and modest; that it is free from jealousy, boastfulness, arrogance, and rudeness; that it can bear all things, hope, and endure.[7]

Back to You

If we have tried at some length to define love, this is because your hope for happiness in marriage depends first of all on the quality of love between you and your future mate. Nothing is more important at the immediate outset than for the two of you to utilize all the wisdom and skill you possess to evaluate your relationship. It will not be easy to do so. The physical attraction which is common to infatuation and romance as well as love is so overpowering that under its impact objectivity becomes extremely difficult. Yet in the interest of your future happiness, you must attempt to achieve it, to see—in the light of the four criteria enumerated in this chapter—whether your feelings toward each other seem to approximate genuine love.

Love is not a static thing; it is a dynamic process. Love either increases or diminishes; it seldom remains the same. Love is largely a matter of right emotional relationship. Perhaps an analogy or two will help us understand it. The parts of a watch must be located and operate in the right relationship in order for one to have a timepiece. If the spring is too large or too small, too strong or too weak in proportion to the other parts, there can be no watch. If all the parts, though they be of proper size, are thrown into an envelope instead of being connected in the right relationship to one another, everything physically necessary for a watch will be in the envelope, yet there will be no watch.

Perhaps an even more apposite analogy is a recipe in cooking. In order for the desired result to be achieved, not only must all the proper ingredients be included, they must be combined in proper proportion and each must be introduced at the recommended moment. Just throwing all the indicated items into a pot, with no regard for blending them into delicate relationship with each other, will produce only a grotesque approximation of the intended delicacy. With reference to both the recipe and the watch, the sum total of the parts in right relationship to each other is more than the sum total of the same parts disorganized. The same is true of love.

Love is a consuming desire to share one's whole life—both physically and spiritually—with a person of the opposite sex; to share that person's sorrows and pains no less than his pleasures and joys. In love, one is at least as anxious to give as to receive. Love is a relationship in which each partner is able to develop his own abilities, to fulfill his own hopes, in far greater measure than either could have achieved alone. Only those who are truly, deeply in love can expect to enjoy a happy marriage.

«««««««« 3 »»»»»»»»

Ready for Marriage?

OUR PRECEDING CHAPTER FAILED IF IT DID NOT CONVINCE YOU that love is a far more complicated emotion than most people suppose it to be. Since marriage demands so much understanding of oneself and one's mate, it is for adults, not for children or half-mature adolescents. We live at a time when better and longer educational preparation is required for every profession or skill. How odd it is that precisely at such a time more and more couples are marrying at a very early age, as if marriage did not call for at least as much preparation and effort as any vocation.

There have been periods in the past when youthful marriages were even more common than today. The Talmud, for example, tells us that "he who reaches the age of twenty and does not marry, spends all his days in the thought of sin." We must bear in mind, however, that the Talmud was compiled in a part of the world where young people mature much faster than in the temperate zones and that life was ever so much less complicated then. For that matter, even our earlier rabbis realized that under certain circumstances marriage must be postponed. Two of their qualifying observations are pertinent at this point:

> A man should build himself a home, plant himself a vineyard and then bring into the home a bride. Fools are they who marry while they have no secure livelihood.
>
> In olden times the pious Sages were willing to go about hungry, to see their wives and children go hungry, and to devote all their attention to Torah and Mitzvot [the performance of religious obligations]. God came to their succor and aided them on their way. In our times, however, there are no such sincere scholars, and they must not rely upon the aid of God if they do nothing for themselves. Nowadays, no one should marry until his livelihood is secure.[1]

In our western civilization, at least until recently, most marriages were deferred considerably beyond the talmudic age of twenty. Yet in the last two decades there has been a reversal of this trend. Statistics published by the United States government in July of 1956 indicated that 49.3 percent of brides marrying for the first time in this country were less than twenty years of age, while 40.2 percent of grooms in that category were no older than twenty-one.[2]

From one point of view, this is good. Authorities recognize that one of our most serious problems of morality grows out of the fact that young people today are biologically ready to wed long before their social and financial circumstances make marriage possible. The earlier marriage occurs, then, the less insistent will be the pressure toward premarital sexual intercourse.

Unfortunately, this is but half the story. The record of success in youthful marriage is anything but encouraging. One authority estimates the divorce rate where both spouses were under twenty-one at the time of their wedding to be six times the rate where both were over thirty-one![3]

Two other experts have summarized their conclusions on this point as follows:

> It is our conviction that many persons marry when they are too young, not necessarily in years but in maturity, in experience, and in the ability to meet the many responsibilities of family living. Such marriages are "bad" marriages, not perhaps because the couple is unsuited to each other, not because of any deficiencies in the persons concerned other than those which time can erase, but because they have assumed life's major responsibility before they were ready to do so. It injures a young horse to do heavy work too soon, the best automobile should not be overtaxed when it is new, a plank breaks when it is overloaded. . . . Marriage means much more than the legality of sharing a common bed.[4]

Then Why So Many?

If the risk is so much greater when couples marry at younger ages, how can we account for the fact that the trend has been in that direction? The first and most obvious answer will be that people acting at the instigation of strong impulses and emotions seldom take time to reason or to examine the experience of others. Even beyond this obvious truth, however, there are psychological and sociological factors which can help explain the dramatic increase in youthful marriages. They include the following:

Boys and girls today begin to date at a much earlier age than they did a generation ago. When I compare the social sophistication of the high school sophomores whom I teach each year in my Confirmation classes to the naiveté and inexperience characteristic of my friends and myself at that age, the difference is astounding. Youngsters in America today learn to dance earlier, start to smoke and drink earlier than ever before. Many of them, by the time they reach their upper teens, begin to feel bored with casual social contacts and consider themselves ready for marriage.

Parents sometimes reinforce this feeling on the part of their young sons and daughters, especially their daughters, by pressuring them to develop socially faster than they otherwise would. Girls are taunted or subtly maneuvered into seeking or accepting dates and are often teased about being "old maids" when they have barely crossed the threshold of their twenties.

Until recently very few young men gave serious thought to the possibility of marriage until they were able to provide a living on their own. This is no longer true. Increasing numbers of parents are willing now to subsidize their children, making marriage feasible while they are still students. There has also been an upsurge in the number of wives who help their husbands earn a living in the first years of marriage. Both these phenomena—subsidization by parents and supplementation of the couple's income by a working wife—carry favorable and unfavorable implications for marital success. At a later point we shall consider the pros and cons; for the present, we are interested only in noting that this too is a factor encouraging youthful marriages.

One of the most interesting social changes in recent American life has been the tendency of high school boys and girls to "go steady." Obviously, a boy and girl who have already grown to depend upon each other for regular social contact in their mid-teens are more likely to enter into marriage at an early age than if their social lives had been more diversified.

Closely related to the foregoing is the undeniable fact that sexual standards among adolescents have changed. While the increase may sometimes be exaggerated, the fact remains that greater numbers of both boys and girls indulge in sexual intercourse during their high school and early college years today than in the past. This lowers the average age of marriage in two ways: (a) more single girls are moved to marry because they have become pregnant, and (b) some couples who would probably have broken up in the course of time have gone so far in their sex relations that they would feel intolerably guilty were they not to marry. On the former of these counts, certain studies suggest that a third to a half of all high school girls who marry are pregnant at the time of their weddings, while a half to three-fourths of high school grooms are forced to marry for this reason.

It is too early to tell whether the contraceptive pill will substantially reduce the incidence of premarital pregnancy. My own guess—only a guess—is that in the age group under consideration it will not. Few of the girls indulging at this age have the foresight and maturity to plan such contraception in advance, and many of the "affairs" which take place among such couples occur under the impact of spontaneous passion. While the pill is undoubtedly more dependable than other forms of contraception, it also requires a longer period of anticipation and a regular usage to be effective. In any event, the increase of youthful marriages up to this point can be traced at least in part to unplanned pregnancies.

A sixth and final factor, though less immediate or obvious, must nevertheless be considered. We live at a time of increasing anxiety and tension. The uncertainties attendant upon preparation for a career, the threatening effects of automation, the turbulence involved in the struggle for civil rights, and especially the fearful threat of nuclear war, all conspire to overload young people today with emotional pressure. Often marriage is sought as an antidote to uncertainty and stress. It appears to offer a safe harbor from the ominous storms of life.

Of what practical consequence to you and to the success of your marriage is this excursion into the reasons for so many marriages which involve youthful brides and grooms? For one thing, if you are yourselves still in this younger age group, it is important that you examine your own motivations. Among the six explanations just given, it is not too difficult to distinguish those which are wholesome and realistic from those which are deceptive and quixotic. But even for couples whose chronological age is more advanced, this discussion should provide nourishing food for thought. Readiness for marriage is not just a matter of the number of years one has lived. We have grown accustomed to measuring intelligence by the I.Q. of an individual, his *intelligence quotient*, the ratio of his intellectual to his chronological age. It would be a great boon for happy marriages if there were an exact way of determining one's E.Q., his *emotional quotient*, the ratio of his emotional growth to his age in years.

Unfortunately, no such device has been invented, nor does one appear likely in the near future. We find ourselves caught in a quandary. Nothing is more essential to success in marriage than emotional maturity, yet few things are more difficult to evaluate. The difficulty must not deter us, however, from trying. No matter what your age or that of your loved one, the greatest favor you can do for yourselves is to catalogue the criteria of emotional maturity and then apply them to yourselves.

MEASURING YOUR E. Q.

Even without precise means of measurement, there are valid standards by which to estimate emotional maturity. The emotionally mature individual displays the following traits:

He learns from experience, both from his successes and his failures. Recognizing that he is an imperfect human being—indeed, feeling no need to be perfect—he realizes that he will continue to make mistakes all his life but successfully avoids repeating the same mistakes endlessly.

He willingly assumes responsibility for his own acts. When the outcome is good, he is ready, without becoming egotistical or boastful, to give himself due credit; when the outcome is bad, he accepts as much of the blame as was really his, without feeling threatened by it and without needing a scapegoat.

There is purpose to his life. The routine of daily detail does not stand by itself, isolated from any larger context. He has projected important long-range goals for himself and plans his activities as progressive steps toward the attainment of those goals. Thus he is able to measure his accomplishment day by day and to feel fulfilled through growth.

He learns to live with unhappy situations which he can neither change nor honorably avoid. Understanding that life cannot always be exactly as he would want it, he distinguishes between those circumstances within his power to improve and those to which he must become reconciled. He exemplifies and follows the well-known prayer which has been attributed to a number of famous individuals: "Lord, give me the courage to change what can be changed, the patience to endure what cannot be changed, and the wisdom to distinguish the one from the other."

He accepts himself—his virtues as well as his faults. Since he does not expect to achieve perfection, he need not castigate himself for falling short. He is able to evaluate realistically both his abilities and his deficiencies. He can accept criticism and disappointment because they are balanced by achievement and success. So long as he has done reasonably close to his best, failure does not represent disgrace.

He is able to do what needs doing now, in the present, neither reliving the past with regret nor preliving the future with undue dread. The emotionally immature or unbalanced person often lives each experience three times: once in fearful anticipation, once in fact, once in morbid remembrance. He thus drains off two-thirds of his effective energy from the task at hand. This does not mean that the mature person lives without careful planning or serious inventory; we have already referred to the need for a meaningful context or plan. The emphasis to be remembered here is that, having planned as carefully and wisely as possible, having carried out his plan as efficiently as circumstances and his own ability permitted, having briefly absorbed whatever was to be learned from the experience just concluded, he then proceeds to plan the next step, without wallowing in remorse or becoming obsessed with what he did wrong.

The mature person does not need to dominate or control others. He finds sufficient satisfaction in improving himself, in exercising his own freedom, and exploiting his own capacities, so that he gladly extends the same privileges to others. When he finds himself in a position of authority, he is able to discharge the responsibilities of leadership without becoming arrogant or destroying the integrity of those who work under his direction. When he is himself a subordinate, he is able to follow reasonable instructions without feeling bemeaned.

He is able to defer a pleasure currently available for the sake of a greater fulfillment which cannot come until later and which depends on renouncing the enjoyment immediately at hand. The mature person denies himself the rich dessert he craves if he is already overweight and his health demands lower caloric intake; his immature friend gluts himself, regardless of what his physician has advised. One who is mature can forego satisfaction of many material wants for the sake of professional or vocational education, the benefits of which will not accrue until several years later. One who is immature wants what he wants when he wants it—which is usually at once.

Another category of qualities which distinguish the mature person is rather difficult to label. Perhaps it can best be identified by such terms as spontaneity, openness, and humor. A mature man or woman enjoys a good joke, whether directed joshingly at himself or others. He is neither sadistic in the employment of humor toward others, nor masochistic in interpreting it as a threat when aimed in his direction. His conduct is frequently characterized by a free and even joyous spontaneity. He gives evidence of enjoying life, not of fearing it.

A final attribute of the mature person is his capacity to grow. His personality is not static nor stagnant. Marriage itself can be a most effective instrument for improved maturity. But it can succeed only if bride and groom bring to it the raw materials of at least reasonable maturity at the time of their wedding. This involves an ability to be flexible, to change opinions in the face of new facts, to seek new kinds of experience.

From Theory to Fact

These criteria of maturity will be only of academic value unless they are applied honestly. There are no substitutes for maturity, no easy detours, no clever little self-deceptions which will succeed permanently. If you and your future spouse refuse to evaluate yourselves honestly now, or overrate yourselves unrealistically, there may be an exorbitant price to pay later. It can be both interesting and instructive for each of you to rate yourselves, then to compare your estimates. Using the chart suggested below and without prior consultation, let each give himself and the other *four points* for *superior maturity*, *three points* for *above average, two points* for *average* and *one point* for *below average.* If there should be wide discrepancies between your self-evaluations and the ratings given by the other, this merits deep concern as to how realistic either or both of you may be.

There is another point to be made in connection with these evaluations. At the 1965 annual meeting of the American Association of Marriage Counselors, Dr. Eleanor Braun Luckey of the University of Connecticut reported on her seven-year study of married couples. She had discovered the immense importance of mates agreeing in their estimates, each of himself and of the other. She said: "Couples who agree with each other about the kind of person the other one is, whether I might agree or not, tend to be the most satisfied partners."[5] In addition, therefore, to measuring your respective degrees of maturity on the following scale, it will be instructive to learn whether you agree on the ratings each gives the other.

Where two individuals are attracted to each other by romance rather than love, it is entirely possible for them to agree in their ratings, yet for both to be inaccurate and unrealistic. An effective check against this can be provided by asking one or more intimate but objective friends to rate the couple too, then to compare all the ratings for each person.

In making these evaluations, several additional factors should be kept in mind. First, remember that very few people, if any, are fully mature by all these standards and in every situation. Each of us is a combination of maturity and immaturity. An individual can be mature in one situation or at one time, inconsistently immature in another situation on the following day. One who is admirably mature in the office or managing a household may be childishly immature at home or in rearing children. Yet for most of us there is a discernibly consistent trend; it should be possible to characterize us as tending in general to be at a certain point on the spectrum of maturity.

Incidentally, if there is too wide a variance in the maturity an individual displays from moment to moment or day to day, that in itself may be evidence of emotional imbalance.

It is also desirable to base your ratings of your partner on as wide a variety of circumstances and settings as possible. His conduct should be appraised not only in terms of how he behaves with you, but also with respect to his family, his friends, and the larger social groups to which he belongs. It is possible for one to "put on a good act" toward a person whom he wants very much to impress; the probability of successfully maintaining such a pose over a long period of time and toward a large group of associates is considerably lower.

Comparing Our Maturity

	MY RATINGS		YOUR RATINGS	
	Of Myself	Of You	Of Yourself	Of Me
1. Learns from experience				
2. Assumes responsibility				
3. Has purpose in life				
4. Accepts the inevitable				
5. Accepts, respects himself				
6. Concentrates on the task of the present				
7. No need to dominate				
8. Able to postpone pleasure				
9. Demonstrates spontaneity and humor				
10. Possesses capacity to grow				

Granted that the most desirable match is between two individuals both of whom are at least reasonably mature, suppose you discover that this is not the case with you and your intended? If marriage were limited to mature couples, the number of weddings in the world would be drastically reduced. Which combination augurs better for success: two persons, both of whom are immature? Or one who is perceptibly more mature than the other? No one can pretend to possess a sure or certain answer to this question. It is my own conviction that, while neither alternative promises anything even remotely resembling an ideal marriage, the first is probably more favorable than the second. As we shall see in our next chapter, compatibility is a factor of enormous importance in marriage. The more two persons are alike—in personal characteristics and temperament as well as in values and goals—the greater the probability of achieving happiness together. It seems to me, therefore, that a wide divergence in maturity between husband and wife would be productive of even more tension and frustration than a sharing of immature traits.

Even this, however, is subject to careful qualification. Immature needs are of different kinds. In either of the imperfect situations proposed in the foregoing paragraph, it is possible for the needs of two individuals either to aggravate or to complement each other. For example: if one partner to a marriage has an immature need to dominate, and the other has an equal need to be dependent—provided that their respective needs are not too extreme and that the individuals are reasonably compatible in most other respects—the prospect for success in their marriage may not be irredeemably hopeless. In any event, few responsibilities of an engaged couple are more important, more productive of future happiness, than a careful, honest evaluation by each of the emotional maturity disclosed by both.

PAST . . . PRESENT . . . FUTURE

Maturity is not a set, static goal which can be attained once and for all time, then forgotten. It is a product of the past, a level of achievement in the present, a hope for the future. The wise man or woman strives for increasing maturity throughout his life.

As a person matures, his values and goals change. At a given point in life it is perfectly proper for a marble or toy to be one's most prized possession. Later, in successive stages, top priority goes to a bicycle, a popular record, a souped-up convertible, a college education, a job, a subscription to the symphony, participation in the struggle for civil rights or world peace. If—at the moment of marriage or through subsequent growth on the part of either mate—an individual who is still at the convertible stage is wedded to one who has achieved the symphony stage, trouble is in the offing. Harry Golden has commented humorously on the changing values of individuals as they mature. When a girl is eighteen, he said, she asks: "What does he look like?" When she is twenty-five she wants to know: "What does he do for a living?" At thirty her question has changed to: "Where is he?"

The matter of maturity as a prerequisite for happy marriage, however, goes far beyond whatever truth there may be in this facetious sequence. The gravest danger in undertaking marriage when either, or both, of the partners is manifestly immature is that neither can be sure where his future development will lead. If they mature along parallel lines, the prognosis for their future can be favorable. If, however, their paths of maturation proceed in divergent directions, they may well be even more poorly matched on their fifth anniversary than on their wedding day. Hence the extreme importance of both personalities being rather clearly shaped and the permanent values of both being identifiably charted before their lives are joined. When two sculptors have barely begun to shape their respective masses of clay, it is too early to tell whether their final works of art will go well together. Only after both have proceeded well along the way is it possible to determine to place them side by side in the same room.

The importance of maturing along similar lines persists throughout marriage. If, after their wedding, the interests of husband and wife diverge too drastically, they will come to enjoy less and less in common. It is pathetically sad to see couples in their fifties who have drifted so far apart through the years that they share only their bed and board. Conversely, there is abundant fulfillment for the couples who increasingly enjoy together their recreations, their hobbies, their most serious social and spiritual concerns. To be retained in later years, however, such mutuality must be cultivated from the beginning.

There are stages through which one grows to the maturity essential for marriage. From birth on, the average person grows into and through periods of his life when the principal object of his affection is, respectively: himself; his parents, first mother, then both; his clique or gang, consisting of his own sex; members of the opposite sex in general; one particular member of the opposite sex, on whom he has a "crush," the targets of such "crushes" normally and healthily changing from time to time; then finally, the one person of opposite sex whom he desires and needs as a permanent partner for life.

It is wise, if you can, to trace these steps in your own life and that of your future spouse. Persons who have skipped any of these stages are not likely to have achieved full maturity. By the same token, those who exhibit as adults too many lingering traces of traits which were appropriate only to an earlier level of life are also poor candidates for marriage.

It is in this context that the current practice of "going steady" at an early age is likely to be dangerous. The young person who has enjoyed a wide range of social experience, who has dated many members of the other sex, who has had the opportunity to relate socially to a variety of personalities, is thereby better able to judge the type of individual suited to him as a partner for life.

The relationship of each mate to his own parent of the opposite sex is of special importance. Modern depth psychology has helped us understand scientifically a truth which was intuitively suspected even by the ancients. At one period of his childhood every normal boy experiences a strong sexual attraction toward his mother and every girl toward her father. In most instances, moreover, this feeling is reciprocated: fathers feel an unconscious sexual attraction to their daughters and mothers to their sons. In psychiatric jargon this is known as the Oedipus Complex. There is nothing abnormal or immoral about it, provided it be a stage from which both parent and child emerge.

Sometimes, however, a young woman may still be too strongly attached, on an unconscious level, to her father or a son to his mother. This is frequently the case when a bride is many years younger than her groom or a husband too much younger than his wife. Each is then searching—again unconsciously—for a father-substitute or mother-substitute rather than a mate. It is important, therefore, not only that the age differential between you and your beloved be confronted (more about this in the next chapter), but also that you be aware of the relationship of each partner to his own parent of the opposite sex. It should be added that in this, as in most other matters, neither extreme is good. Just as a woman errs in seeking as a husband a duplicate of her father, so, if she has harbored deep resentment of her father, she makes a possibly fatal mistake in selecting a man as different from her father as she can.

The Oedipal relationship can be no less troublesome when it is the parent who hasn't outgrown too strong an attraction to a son or daughter. A mother who insists that no girl is good enough for her son or who finds fault with every girl in whom he is seriously interested—a father who exhibits the same pattern of behavior toward his daughter—these are in all probability parents who have not emancipated themselves yet from an intensity of relationship which is quite normal at one stage in life but is fraught with explosive possibilities if it persists.

RUNNING AWAY?

There are two additional complications to be considered on the immensely important topic of emotional maturity. It happens not too infrequently that—consciously or unconsciously—the prospect of marriage represents an escape-hatch from a situation or condition which appears to be intolerable. It can be an unhappy home or parental pressure or a frustrating job or indecision in choosing a vocation or almost any other kind of tension. Marriage can serve either as a convenient escape or an effective psychological weapon with which to strike against an offending parent or sibling or boss.

This danger is compounded by the fact that the mechanism for escape or rebellion is an unconscious one. About all you can do is to be aware of the possibility, and to give it special credence if either you or your intended has been generally an unhappy, frustrated individual. One marriage expert has summarized this situation with exceptional eloquence:

> How often is this "love" which some feel the desire to get away from a quarrelsome, bickering family, a dominating mother, or a tight little office in which one feels stifled? It is understandable that people should strive to get away from that which annoys them, although the basic reasons for the annoyance

> may be in themselves. When you marry, you *assume* responsibilities; you do not *escape* them. A good marriage will mean that life will be much richer and more worthwhile, but it will not be easier. Marriage creates as many problems as it solves. The success of your marriage will depend upon what you are getting into, not what you get away from.[6]

An important implication of this statement is that the person who is suffering a serious emotional disability should not undertake marriage as a cure. One who is experiencing difficulty handling himself and his problems while single will nearly always confront even graver trouble when married. Marriage is not therapy. True, it can contribute to the maturity of a person who is reasonably adjusted at the start, and husband and wife can be of enormous help to each other at times of emotional turbulence, but serious personal problems are best resolved before marriage. If, therefore, either you or your future mate is in the midst of psychotherapy, the course of wisdom is to delay your wedding until your therapy is either completed or very nearly so.

We spoke of two complications. The second is the danger of falling into a bad marriage on the rebound. Quite often a person who has just been jilted or has himself recently broken off a romantic relationship will almost immediately take up with a new partner and rush with unseemly haste into a permanent attachment. Though psychologically simple to understand, this is fraught with immeasurable harm. To terminate a relationship on which one has depended for emotional security and status can be painful in the extreme. To seek reinforcement for damaged self-esteem and pride is natural. An emotional vacuum is as difficult to tolerate as a physical vacuum. For that very reason, however, one's objective judgment is, under these circumstances, likely to be less than its best. If either you or your beloved, then, has recently rebounded from disappointment in what had seemed to be love, there is every reason to proceed now with extra caution and delay. Make sure that you are being positively attracted to something wholesome and good, not negatively repelled by a frustration or defeat which is difficult to endure.

A final word on emotional maturity: Parents frequently worry that marriage will seriously interfere with the academic success of a couple still involved in collegiate studies. This need not be so. If the bride and groom are otherwise qualified for marriage—which means to say, if they are both mature and compatible, if their continuing studies and marriage can be adequately financed with a margin for emergencies, if pregnancy is prevented until their college courses are completed, if they possess stamina enough to fulfill the double responsibilities of domestic and academic life—marriage, far from reducing their success at learning, can appreciably increase it. But before any couple concludes that this favorable prognosis is valid for them, they must scrupulously inquire into their honest status on all the conditions just enumerated. A student who is happily married can do ever so much better work than one who is frustrated and tense. This I know from my own personal experience.

Jewish tradition seems to have known it too. Thus we have been told: "A man who marries may be a true servant of God, since he can concentrate his mind upon desires of the spirit rather than of the emotions."[7] It was in part insight such as this which prompted the fathers of Jewish girls in Eastern Europe to encourage the marriage of their daughters to promising scholars, then to support the young couple while the husband continued his studies.

If both husband and wife are still students, this can add a significant strand to the bond which unites them. If the wife must work in order for her husband to complete his professional or graduate studies, complications are possible. She may come to resent the heavy responsibility imposed upon her, while he may develop guilt over the need to accept her financial support. There have also been instances in which a working wife and a studying husband have been appalled to discover after a few years how great an intellectual gap had developed between them. Where conditions are right and these problems can be precluded, the fact that one or both partners are in college need not of itself mitigate against their marriage.

The Question Remains

We have not finally and firmly answered the query with which this chapter commenced. Are you and your beloved ready for marriage? Only the two of you can answer this question. By the same token, the two of you stand to benefit most if your replies are valid, to suffer most if they are not. There is no set age in years and months, no exact point of time, at which everyone is ready to marry. Some persons in their late teens may be better prepared than others whose age is twice as great. Competence for marriage is more a matter of emotional maturity than of chronological age. There are couples who definitely should marry at an early age, others who should avoid marriage as if it were a plague, until one or both have achieved more maturity. The exasperating, often agonizing dilemma of marriage counselors and rabbis is that the couples who need most desperately to wait are frequently the very ones most impulsively determined to proceed in haste.

Are you really ready?

«««««««« 4 »»»»»»»»

Right for Each Other?

CAN WE ASSUME THAT A MAN AND WOMAN WHO KNOW THE meaning of love, who are capable of giving and receiving love, and who are both reasonably mature are automatically assured of happiness in their marriage? Unfortunately, no. While the prognosis for success is obviously better with affirmative than with negative responses to the questions raised in the preceding chapters, we have only begun our inquiry. Even two fine, adult individuals—both ready for a mature love relationship—can fail if they are not properly matched. A marriage can be bad not because of glaring defects in either person, but because they were just not right for each other. The choice of the person who is to be your life-partner, then, is one which must be made with utmost wisdom.

In some civilizations this weighty responsibility rested not on the bride and groom, but on their parents. For many centuries an important functionary in the Jewish community was the שדכן (*shadchan*) or matchmaker, whose professional function it was to negotiate with parents for the matching of their children in marriage. There are other culture groups in which this practice is carried to such an extreme that bride and groom do not even meet until the day of their wedding.

Before dismissing this procedure out of hand, we should recognize that it had some advantages. Parents can sometimes be more objectively sensitive than their children to such factors as similarity of background, parallels of personality, or financial competence and prospects. They are also not likely to permit a daughter to remain unmarried. There can be no question, however, despite vestigial remains of such parental initiative among some immigrant groups, that in our social setting the pendulum has swung to the opposite extreme. From having had everything to say in the choice of a mate for their child, parents are now often excluded from the decision entirely.

Balancing the rights and demands of parents against the rights and needs of their grown children is a subtle, at times an excruciating experience. A medieval rabbi, Judah ben Samuel of Regensburg, knew this. He wrote:

> Parents may not hinder a son's marriage that he may continue to work for them; let him take a wife and remain with them still. If he can find no wife at the place where his parents live, and these be aged and need his care, let him not leave that city; and if, taking a wife, he can no longer care for such helpless father and mother, let him remain unwedded. If he can pay for the support and care of his parents, then he has a right to seek a wife and settle elsewhere, only let him see to it that they [presumably, the support and care] are not such as are repugnant to the parents' feelings. If his choice has fallen on a worthy girl of honorable parentage, but his father or mother wish to force him to take one not worthy, because her relatives offer money, he need by no means yield to his parents' wishes, for their proceeding is blameworthy.[1]

Where the general relationship within a family has been healthy and loving, parents will be invited into the process of selecting a mate; their advice will be welcomed, though not necessarily always followed. The primary responsibility, of course, must rest upon the couple itself.

Jewish tradition has not been unaware of how heavy this responsibility is. The Talmud advises: "Be quick in buying land; be deliberate in taking a wife."[2] Rabbinic literature also contains a not-so-subtle suggestion to parents that theirs is at most a minor role in the selection of mates for their grown children. This is the inescapable inference from the story of how perturbed King Solomon is reputed to have been when it was revealed to him in a dream that his beautiful daughter was destined to marry one of the poorest young men in his kingdom. He disapproved the match and was determined to prevent it. So he built a palace on an inaccessible island and surrounded it with an impregnable stone wall, locking his daughter and her servants in to protect her from her prospective groom.

Some time thereafter the young man Solomon had seen in his dream was wandering one cold night in the forest. Lacking enough clothing to keep from freezing, he came upon the carcass of a bull and climbed into it for warmth. As he slept, a huge bird snatched up the carcass, flew with it many miles, and dropped it on the roof of the island palace. When the princess went to the roof the following morning, she beheld the handsome young man; at once they fell in love. After a time they were married in the presence of her servants.[3] Our rabbis apparently were aware that not even the utmost effort of a strong-minded king could prevent his daughter from marrying whom she would.

Not So Easy

The scholars and spokesmen of Judaism recognized that it is no simple matter to match men and women for marriage.

> A matron once asked Rabbi Jose ben Halafta: "What has your God been doing since He finished making the world?" "He has been matching couples in marriage," was the reply. . . . The matron declared that she could do as much herself; nothing was easier than to couple any number of slaves with as many slave-girls.
>
> "You may think it easy," said Rabbi Jose, "but it is as difficult for God as dividing the Red Sea."
>
> The matron accordingly tried the experiment with a thousand males and as many female slaves, setting them in rows and bidding this man take this woman, etc. The next morning they came to her, one with a broken head, another with gouged-out eyes, a third with a broken leg; one man saying: "I don't want her," and a girl saying: "I don't want him." Thus was the matron constrained to say that the mating of man and woman was a task not unworthy the intelligence of God.[4]

Does this talmudic tale imply that marriages are made in heaven? It would seem so, from the comment made elsewhere: "Forty days before the formation of a child, a Voice proclaims in heaven: 'So-and-so's daughter is to marry so-and-so's son!' "[5] Post-talmudic rabbis, however, emphasized that human cooperation is needed too for divine choice to be effective. This we find especially in the final sentences of the following quotation from the זהר (*Zohar*), great sourcebook of medieval Jewish mysticism:

> Each soul and spirit, prior to its entering into this world, consists of a male and female united into one being. When it descends on this earth the two parts separate and animate two different bodies. At the time of marriage, the Holy One, blessed be He, who knows all souls and spirits, unites them again as they were before, and they again constitute one body and one soul, forming as it were the right and left of one in-

> dividual. . . . *This union, however, is influenced by the deeds of the man and by the way in which he walks. If the man is pure and his conduct is pleasing in the sight of God, he is united with that female part of his soul which was his component part prior to his birth.*[6]

In a later chapter we shall turn our attention to a modern interpretation of the connection between God and love. For the time being, let it simply be noted that our ancestors expressed their conviction that marriage is a noble, sacred enterprise by associating it with God. While recognizing that in a very real sense God enters into every successful love experience between man and woman, we cannot pass the buck to Him in the selection of a mate. We must attempt to discover for ourselves what it takes for two people to be successfully matched for life. And any two individuals who are contemplating marriage owe it to each other and themselves to ask in depth: are we really well matched?

A Difficult Definition

What we have been leading up to in preceding paragraphs, obviously, is the subject of compatibility. Usually this word is assumed to mean sexual compatibility. While a good sexual adjustment is of undeniable importance—and we shall have much more to say on this shortly—to restrict the meaning of compatibility just to this one area is to distort monstrously the nature of love. There are numerous kinds of compatibility; the wise couple will attempt to judge their congeniality with respect to all of them.

There is, for example, *intellectual compatibility*. Marriage is a meeting of minds as well as bodies. Husband and wife presumably intend to live together for many years; if they have nothing in common intellectually, no serious concerns to discuss and share, they face a future of tasteless boredom. For a bright, egotistical man to marry a dull, doting girl may temporarily meet the needs of both, but before long their relationship will grow tired. Our rabbis knew this long centuries ago. Addressing themselves to a man of intelligence, they said:

> A man should sell all he possesses with the object of marrying the daughter of a scholar or giving his daughter in marriage to a scholar. This is like uniting grapes of the vine to grapes of the vine, which is good and acceptable. But let him not marry the daughter of an ignoramus, because that is like uniting grapes of the vine to berries of the bush, which is something ugly and unacceptable.[7]

A fourteen-year-old patient once told her psychiatrist she could always tell which were the married couples in a restaurant. When questioned concerning her method, she replied: "It's easy! They're the ones who have nothing to say to each other during dinner." Two people who share so little intellectually that, as a general rule, they have nothing to say to each other beyond their immediate problems and needs can expect little enduring happiness in their marriage.

The enormous stress which Jewish tradition places on intelligence in the choosing of a mate is reflected in this passage from the שלחן ערוך (*Shulchan Aruch*), sixteenth-century code of law by which Orthodox Jewish life is still governed:

> A man ought always to strive to win in marriage the daughter of a Torah scholar, and to give his daughter in marriage to a Torah scholar. If he cannot find the daughter of a Torah scholar, let him seek to marry the daughter of a renowned communal leader; if he cannot find one of these, let his choice be the daughter of a congregational leader; if not one of these, then

> the trustee of a charitable fund; if not one of these, let him select the daughter of an elementary Hebrew teacher, but let him not marry off his daughter to an ignorant man.[8]

In reading a reference such as this, it must be remembered that the advice is obviously being directed to one who possesses considerable intelligence himself. It recommends, then, not only the value of intelligence as such, but also the need for this level of compatibility.

Cultural compatibility is implied in our emphasis on the importance of being well-matched intellectually. It is important enough to be asserted explicitly. Do you and your prospective mate both like theater? Art? Music? Books? Opera? Are your tastes in these areas similar or quite different? During your engagement have you found yourselves battling over cultural preferences, or ignoring each other's desires, or learning from each other? Cultural differences can become either a weapon with which two people beat each other, or a priceless opportunity for each to expand the horizons and enrich the life of the other. The probable success of your marriage can be in part predicted by the pattern of cultural accommodation you have already established.

This is an important consideration in the creation of culture as well as in appreciating it. It is surely not essential for both husband and wife to be creative in the same field, though this can be an asset if neither feels competitively threatened by the other. What is essential—if either is creative—is that the partner appreciate what is being created and encourage its continuance. A scientist who has no use for art, who is allergic to museums and exhibits, would make a poor husband for a painter whose skill with the canvas is exquisite but to whom a laboratory is first-cousin to a horror chamber.

Insofar as love is concerned, the old adage, "opposites attract," is nonsense. Opposites—in personality, in temperament, in values, in cultural proclivities—may for a time be infatuated with one another. They will never know the meaning of love.

Religion is a part of culture, viewed in its broadest context. The ultimate values and ideals of a man and woman—which means to say, their religious orientation—also call for a high order of consistency if their marriage is to succeed. Our very brief listing of *religious compatibility* at this point is due only to the fact that an entire chapter will be devoted to it later.

Social compatibility is also important. The minute this is mentioned, I expose myself to criticism as a snob. The risk is worth assuming if I can succeed in emphasizing the fact—and it *is* a fact—that, all other things being equal, two individuals who emanate from similar social backgrounds have a higher probability of marital success than two who do not. Cinderella-type matches of rags and riches lead to happiness more often in print or on film than in life. All serious studies of marriage show this to be true. Similarity of social background reduces the likelihood of wide discrepancies in the customs, values, expectations, and ambitions with which husband and wife confront each other and their friends. The point to be made here is not that one social setting or class is superior to another, only that—whatever the class—it is wise for bride and groom to come from the same one.

The Talmud makes a rather curious comment in recognizing this truth. Advising a prospective husband not to take a wife of superior rank, it adds: "Go down a step in choosing a wife."[9] There may have been a certain amount of validity to this condescension in a patriarchal age when man was the measure of most things. Surely in our civilizational setting, however, when successful marriage depends upon a mutual partnership between husband and wife as equals, too great a degree of social disparity in either direction is a liability.

Money Talks—And Tells

Next is *economic compatibility*. What we have in mind here is not the financial resources of bride and groom respectively—that would really be included in social background—but rather their attitudes and ambitions on financial matters. The marriage of an extravagant spender to a compulsive saver does not augur well. Neither does that of a country club devotee to one who would prefer to buy paintings and books. In short, it is important not only that the couple agree generally on saving versus spending, but also that they see alike on the direction their spending is to take. In Chapter VI we shall consider at greater length the role of financial management in marriage. For the present our concern is with consistency between the financial attitudes and needs of husband and wife. This is essential for its own sake, in order to avoid excessive controversy over money. It is even more significant, however, because one's approach to money and its uses tells a great deal about his personality as a whole. Money is a symbol—next to sex, perhaps the most important symbol in many lives. This is especially true in our type of economically oriented culture. The feelings of an individual toward money disclose significant aspects of his total character. The compulsive spender is an altogether different kind of person from the obsessive saver; in marriage, they are likely to clash in many areas quite beyond the domain of the dollar.

Here are good questions to explore with utmost honesty: If we unexpectedly found ourselves with a surplus of a thousand dollars, would we agree on how much of it to spend and how much to save? And having decided that, would we both want to utilize in the same way the part we planned to spend?

The answer to this last question opens up the entire area of values and goals. Unless the prospective partners to a marriage pursue similar purposes in life, their prognosis for happiness is not good. Here it becomes necessary to be as specific as possible and to consider motives as well as objectives. A friend of mine whose first marriage failed tells me, by way of illustration, that both he and his wife wanted a garden. On the face of it, this concurrence of desires might seem to indicate great compatibility. Actually, it disclosed nothing of the sort! He wanted a garden because he loved flowers; she wanted one to impress the neighbors. What may at first glance have given the appearance of compatibility was in fact quite the opposite!

A husband who desires to purchase paintings as an investment is on that score not well matched to a woman who chooses paintings for the beauty of the art itself. In short, it is necessary to compare *reasons* and *motives*, not just superficial symptoms, if one would truly measure compatibility.

Before leaving the subject of financial compatibility, a word should be added on marrying for money. According to an old quip, it is just as easy to fall in love with a rich girl as with a poor one. Yet the matter is not so simple. If the wealth of either bride or groom was an inconsequential or minor consideration in the attraction between them, it need not unduly concern us. But if such wealth was a primary and proximate cause of the attraction, there may be trouble ahead. For one thing, unless both were wealthy, our previous comments about social compatibility would be pertinent here. Aside from that, a whole complex of problems could develop out of a relationship in which one mate feels inferior to or excessively dependent upon the other. This is especially explosive if the husband is dependent upon his wife and her family. The relationship between husband and father-in-law when the former is an employee or junior partner of the latter is fraught with possibilities both good and bad. To act as if it presented no problems at all is to be guilty of irresponsible naiveté. Later we shall address ourselves directly to one's relationships with his in-laws and the wisdom of relying on financial help from one or both sets of parents. For the time being, let it simply be entered upon the record that marrying expressly for the sake of money is more likely to be a negative than a positive factor in the determination of success.

Here again the wisdom of our ancient rabbis was remarkable. The Talmud contains two epigrammatic admonitions on marrying for money:

> He who weds for money will have delinquent offspring.[10]
>
> He who looks for the earnings of his wife sees never a sign of blessing.[11]

Compatibility is also essential in *a wide variety of personality traits*, any one of which may seem by itself to be only of minor consequence, but all of which together build up to major proportions. If one mate, for example, is rigid while the other is permissive and lax—if one is punctual and the other careless of time—if one is neat and the other sloppy—if one is a shy introvert and the other an exuberant extrovert—their future together promises to be rocky. Not only will they constantly quarrel over the direct issues they confront—over the disciplining of their children, the budgeting of their time, the management of their household, the intensity of their social life—these apparently superficial divergences also bespeak deeper differences in personality which will plague them. In the daily commerce of sharing bed and board, little annoyances are symptomatic of bigger problems and soon assume major significance themselves. In his extravagantly amusing play, *The Odd Couple*, Neil Simon portrayed how true this is even for two men sharing an apartment. It is far truer for husband and wife.

Since a primary enterprise of marriage is the rearing of a

family, *similar attitudes toward children* constitute yet another valid dimension of compatibility. To improve your prospect for a happy marriage, you should agree on whether or not to have children, on the number desired and how they should be spaced, on at least the major principles of educating and disciplining them. While it is too much to expect a complete program of child development before you are even married, there are significant and revealing questions that should be asked right now. Do you both like or dislike being with children? Are you attracted to the same kinds of children? Do you agree or disagree on the way your parents reared you, on the way your friends are rearing their offspring? Alert attention to this kind of comparison now can avert considerable tension and heartache later.

STILL MORE

As long as this list has already become, we have by no means finished yet with the kinds of compatibility which are essential in marriage.

Similarities in leisure time interests are too frequently overlooked by couples contemplating marriage. Yet they are extremely important. Our economic system is such that—with the relatively rare exception of the husband and wife who work together in a profession or business—most couples will be destined to spend by far the greater portion of their waking hours apart. The amount of time they manage to spend together evenings and weekends, then, becomes crucial in shaping the success of their marriage. Two of the earliest scientific students of marriage in this country concluded, after extensive investigation, that couples who share and enjoy all their leisure activities together have fifteen times as much chance for marital happiness as do couples who lack such sharing.

There is grave danger that a marriage may degenerate into

nothing but a convenient fiscal arrangement for managing a household and providing sexual satisfaction. Couples who permit this to happen in their relationship are cheating themselves. Only if there are parallel leisure time preferences at the start, and a strong desire by both to spend as much, not as little, time together as possible, can their marriage be realized in full. A good question, then, to face right now is whether, in addition to enjoying each other's company, you also enjoy doing the same things together.

The importance of this factor has been underscored by Dr. Henry A. Bowman, a University of Texas sociologist who specializes in the study of modern marriage. He has emphasized that "leisure pursuits serve as common interests or as points of departure for conflicts." They therefore can either exacerbate or dissipate tension. Trouble is in store for couples who strongly disagree either on the use of their leisure or on how much time they want to spend together.[12]

The immediately preceding paragraphs should not be misconstrued to mean that husband and wife must spend every minute of their leisure time together. Separate hobbies or avocations can certainly be tolerated in marriage—provided they do not dominate most of a couple's spare time and if the proportion of time spent together is agreeable to both.

Compatibility in age has already been mentioned in Chapter III. While no one can project an iron-clad formula, there is no doubt that too great a disparity in age is not good, regardless of whether the husband is much older than the wife or she than he. In addition to what has already been said regarding the dangerous unconscious factors which can be involved in such cases, there are two extremely serious practical problems when the bride is substantially younger than the groom. The first emerges from the fact that the life-expectancy of women in the United States is appreciably greater than that of men. The average wife must therefore anticipate that her husband will probably predecease her, leaving her later in life as a widow. The greater the age-spread between them, the longer her probable period of loneliness. Admittedly, this isn't the pleasantest kind of consideration, especially at a time of such unmitigated happiness as the approach of one's marriage. Yet the wise person will not, for that reason, avoid it. Marriage is meant to be a partnership for life. No sensible person would enter into a long-range business contract without considering the remote as well as the immediate circumstances. No less should be true of marriage.

The second serious practical problem, when a husband is many years older than his wife, has to do with their sexual relationship. A woman of twenty and a man of thirty-five can enjoy a mutually gratifying sex life together. But when she is fifty-five and he seventy, their sexual adjustment may be complicated. This is another area in which it is wise to base your marriage on the long-run, not just the immediate future.

During the very week that this chapter was first being drafted, the impending marriages of two Hollywood stars were announced. One, at the age of sixty-one, was marrying a woman of twenty-seven; the other, forty-nine years old, was matched with a girl of nineteen. It was the third or fourth matrimonial bout for both grooms. Some months later a prominent American jurist of sixty-seven married a girl of twenty-three; it was her first wedding, his fourth. The inconstancy of Hollywood marriages—amounting almost to successive episodes of legalized prostitution—is scarcely a paradigm for emulation. Couples such as these may be able for a time to tantalize and titillate each other; the probability of their achieving an enduring marriage is remote. The extreme disparity in their ages is only one of many objections to their distorted notion of love.

The insight and wisdom of Judaism are manifest here too.

According to the Talmud, "he who weds his daughter to an old man, and he who gives a wife unto his minor son, commits a wrong."[13] The Torah directs that when a man dies without having given his wife a child, his brother is obliged to marry the widow so that a child can be conceived to carry on the dead man's name. This obviously preceded the time when monogamy was introduced into Jewish practice. The book of Deuteronomy tells us that if the brother of the deceased is reluctant to fulfill this obligation, "the elders of his city, shall call him and speak to him." In commenting on this passage, the Talmud says:

> This teaches that they gave him advice suitable for him. If he was young and she old, or vice versa, they would say to him, "What sense is there in your marrying one much younger than yourself?" or "What sense is there in your marrying one much older than yourself? Go, marry one who is about your own age and do not introduce strife into your house."[14]

Evidently the rabbis considered too great a discrepancy in age so significant an obstacle to successful marriage that they were willing, on this account, to defer another biblical custom which they deemed to be important.

Interest in other people is another area in which compatibility is important and may be tested. The kind of people whom one likes usually resemble himself, or at least his own conscious impression of himself. Thus our friends are often reflections of our own personalities and values. A man and woman who like each other's friends, who react similarly to a third person whom they both have met for the first time, are at least in this respect compatible. It is worth observing also that, according to reliable studies of marriage, individuals who have many friends of their own sex seem to make better marriages than those with few friends.

A Perennial Problem

There have probably been more indisposed jokes about in-laws than about any other kind of human relationship. Yet there is nothing funny about a couple whose marriage must scale the rapids of tension with parents. In many years of counseling engaged and married couples, the in-law problem is the one mentioned to me most frequently as an obstacle to happiness. True, in-laws are sometimes just convenient scapegoats, plausible disguises by which husband and wife distract their attention from more fundamental sources of aggravation. But they are also the primary source of difficulty often enough to merit our serious consideration. Hence the urgency of *compatibility with your mate's family.*

There is an almost irresistible temptation to object at this point: "But I'm not marrying a family; I'm marrying an individual!" True, yet at the same time not entirely true. The family of your future husband or wife has already become so vital a part of himself that no one can completely divorce them. If you propose to live in the same community with either or both your families, it will be necessary to work out a harmonious relationship. Even if you intend to live at a remote distance from them, emotional ties are much more persistent and pervasive than geographical bonds. A wife whose husband is at odds with her parents can be torn to pieces by conflicting loyalties and loves. A husband whose wife is at war with his parents is in no less lamentable a position. Many a marriage has been wrecked on the rocks of in-law trouble.

On an even more elementary level than this, you are indeed marrying a family. Some of the characteristics you resent in your future in-laws may well be integral aspects of your beloved's personality, though the blinders of romantic infatuation may prevent you from seeing them. If in fact they are present, the more realistic light of daily intimate encounter will expose them. Both the physical and emotional health of your mate have been affected by and are largely dependent upon his family and his relationship to them. Your children will inherit half their heredity from your mate's family; what an ironic twist of fate it is when one perceives in his own child a trait he abhors in his in-laws!

Our sages can be forgiven their genetic error in supposing that children resemble their maternal uncles; the larger point they were attempting to express is nonetheless valid: "Before taking a wife, investigate her brothers, for most children resemble their mother's brothers."[15]

In General

Any professional who spends considerable quantities of time trying to help unhappy couples salvage something of their marriages is amazed over and over again at how infrequently these people gave serious attention in advance to the levels of compatibility outlined in this chapter. You may feel that we have gone to the opposite extreme, that our discussion makes love and marriage seem like cold, rational, almost mechanical relationships rather than primarily matters of emotion. True, in reacting against one extreme we may have swung suspiciously toward its opposite.

Yet there need be no fear that marriage will cease to be for the most part emotionally motivated. There is greater danger by far that it will be *only* emotional. The role of reason with respect to emotion is rather like that of skillful tacking in sailing a boat. Wind of necessity remains one's motive power. But if wind is permitted to have its way, to carry a small vessel wherever it will, the sailor will never reach his desired destination. So, without deploring or denying the value of the wind, the prudent sailor sets his sails carefully and holds his rudder firmly —the better to utilize the power supplied by wind to go where his mind and will have planned. Normal, average human beings need have no apprehension that emotion will be lacking in their love experience. Their realistic concern should be instead whether they have injected enough reason in their relationship to channel their emotions constructively. One does not walk about with a pencil and chart, rating a candidate scientifically before proposing. Nor can computers replace human instincts and emotions. The wise person, however, when he finds himself growing more than casually or platonically interested in another, will pause to reflect on their compatibility before he permits himself to approach the possibility of marriage.

The Bible offers an instructive passage on this point. When offered any gift he might want of God, King Solomon asked for "an understanding heart." Now, one usually associates understanding with the head rather than the heart. Is it far-fetched to suppose that Solomon had in mind the very issue we have raised here? What he was really requesting was a combination most desirable in life generally, in marriage especially: rich emotion tempered by firm intelligence.

It would be a serious error to suppose that husband and wife can or should be carbon copies of each other. Even if such duplication were possible, it would produce an insufferably dull and boring marriage. Our goal should be not to seek exact facsimiles of ourselves, but to make sure that we and our contemplated mates are reasonably similar in most important respects, that we do not differ too irreconcilably in any, and that our divergences complement rather than aggravate each other.

The man or woman who marries in the expectation that he will then be able to remodel his mate, so to speak, is making a foolish mistake. The personal characteristics and temperament of your intended have been pretty well established for life by the time he or she is old enough to consider marriage. Short of either a traumatic experience or psychotherapy in depth, he will remain basically for life the kind of person he is now. Unless you like that kind of person—could gladly live with that kind of person, with both the virtues and faults you perceive—beware of a permanent entanglement! Two people who live together in a loving marriage can indeed affect each other and learn from each other; it has been said that sometimes husband and wife in the course of time come not only to think alike, to anticipate each other's conversation, but even to resemble one another physically. But this is true only if they began with essential compatibility. A home is not a reform school. Don't marry in the expectation of practicing plastic surgery on your beloved's personality or emotions.

Professor Magoun has put the matter very well:

> The only person one ever has the right to try to change is one's self. Immaturity often manifests itself in an attempt to reform the betrothed. A mature person sees faults, balances them against virtues, and accepts another individual for what he is.[16]

True compatibility means that in addition to loving your mate, you must like him. Actually, this statement begs the question; if you don't like him as a person, you are experiencing infatuation, not love. Quite aside from the romantic, sexual magnetism you both feel, is your beloved the kind of person you respect and admire, with whom you would be anxious to spend much time, from whose friendship and companionship you could learn and grow even if there were no sexual involvement?

Some years ago I visited an elderly man whose wife had just

died. The tears he shed were a tribute to genuine loss, not a symptom of self-pity. Nodding his head sadly from side to side, he repeated over and over again: "Did I lose a friend! I lost the most wonderful friend a man could have!" In his humble, unliterary manner, he came eloquently close to summarizing the truth that if, in addition to everything else which binds them together, a husband and wife can feel that they are solid friends to each other, their marriage is likely to be superb.

The reverse side of the coin is illustrated by a woman who said to me, after twenty years of marriage: "Rabbi, I married a man with whom I don't have a single thing in common!" What a miserable pity it is to enter upon so intimate and sacred a relationship with so little knowledge of one's partner! Enormous amounts of suffering could be averted if prospective brides and grooms would more accurately assess their probable compatibility before accepting the responsibilities and opportunities of marriage!

Others with whom we become emotionally involved can have a variety of effects on us. They can make us feel

inferior, or
superior, flattered, possessing an inflated ego, or
satisfied with ourselves as we are, or
acceptable to ourselves as we are but *eager to improve.*

Neither the first nor the second of these alternatives augurs well for marriage. Both are in the nature of illusions. Time has a cruel way of shattering such façades; when it does, little will be left of the marital bond. I can live a long and reasonably happy life with one who makes me feel satisfied with myself as I am. The only truly creative relationship, however, is one which enables me to see not only what I am today, but also what I have the potential to become, and which proceeds to encourage my growth toward that goal.

How do you and your future spouse, each, make the other feel about himself?

NO CRYSTAL BALL

Did compatibility seem like such a simple thing before you read this chapter? And does it give the appearance now of being almost hopelessly complicated? The momentary confusion will be constructive if it enables you to evaluate more realistically how well you are matched.

There are professional tests to help, if you feel the need. Any serious doubt should prompt you to ask your rabbi or a marriage counselor to administer and interpret such a test. It will not be an oracle, giving you sure and certain answers. It can be in the nature of a thermometer which indicates whether your compatibility-temperature is normal or requires further investigation. For most couples a simple questionnaire of twenty items like the following will suffice. I have adapted it by permission from a volume called *Better Ways of Growing Up*.[17] To be qualified as compatible, a couple should rate *much alike* (4) on at least half the listed items, *somewhat alike* (3) on most of the others, and *very different* (1) on no more than three or four at most.

The chart suggested in Chapter III was filled out by each of you separately, then compared. In this case the ratings should be given by the two of you together. Try to be as objective and honest as possible; self-deception is as dangerous for the future as it is tempting in the present. To be impartial and unbiased about a sexually-colored emotional relationship demands almost superhuman effort. But there is enough involved—either of misery or of joy—to make that effort imperative.

HOW COMPATIBLE ARE WE?

1. Very different
2. Mildly different
3. Somewhat alike
4. Much alike

Traits	*Ratings*
Home and social background	
Personal standards of right and wrong	
Ideals regarding home and family	
Desire for and feelings toward children	
Differential in age	
Educational background and interests	
Intelligence	
Religious interests and preferences	
Vocational ambitions and attitudes	
Desire for money and social standing	
Spending and saving habits	
Relative emphasis on home and outside activities	
Cultural tastes: art, music, drama, books, etc.	
Personal habits: eating, sleeping, smoking, etc.	
Circle of friends	
Recreational and leisure interests	
Temperament and mood	
Punctuality and neatness	
Attitudes toward parents of both	
Tendency to be critical or to praise	

«««««««««5»»»»»»»»»

No Blueprint, But–

A THEME ESTABLISHED ALMOST AT THE OUTSET RECURS. THERE is no guarantee of success in marriage. Marital happiness–like every other kind–must be earned. The promise implicit in the words of a rabbi at your wedding ceremony can be either frustrated or fulfilled; the choice is mostly yours.

Love is so dynamic a relationship that very seldom, if ever, does it remain on one level through the years. Like an airplane, which either maintains a minimum forward motion or falls to the ground, the love of husband and wife either increases rewardingly or diminishes disastrously. When love is reduced below the slowest speed at which it can remain airborne, so to speak, it soon crashes into hate. Though it may seem logically paradoxical, it is psychologically true that love and hate are first-cousins. Hate is not the opposite of love; indifference is. Hate is a distortion of love.

Many competent observers of human behavior are convinced that no one is born with an innate need to hate. At birth every infant possesses an almost insatiable hunger for love. Even while still in the hospital nursery, tiny babies can intuitively sense its absence; careful research has demonstrated that when an unloving nurse is on duty, the amount of crying among the infants increases sharply. When a newborn child's need for love is met, he in turn is able to love. When his need is left unfulfilled, his capacity to love is cruelly transposed into hate. As drastically different as these two emotions are, they spring from the same psychological root.

This has a doubly significant bearing on your marriage. First, the quantity and quality of love received in childhood by each partner in a marital relationship influence to a great degree the amount of love he is able to receive and give as a husband or wife. A person who becomes emotionally conditioned early in life to the dread suspicion that no one loves him because he is unlovable finds it difficult at best to thaw even under the beneficient warmth of a spouse's affection. One who spends the most important and impressionable years of his childhood and youth exclusively in the arctic wastes does not have an easy time adjusting to tropical heat.

The second impact on your marriage of the organic connection between love and hate is that patterns of childhood rejection are often repeated in adult experience. A person who has become overly sensitive because of early emotional starvation may interpret—or misinterpret—the slightest aggravation or affront as more of the same. Without even being aware of the process, the wife who criticizes or complains—however mildly or justifiably—is seen as the mother who failed him in his need. The husband who disappoints his wife's expectations in even the most incidental detail duplicates the image of the father who—in either fantasy or fact—had rejected her. When these complicated emotional transferences grow beyond the ability of an individual or a couple to handle, professional psychiatric help may be needed. For most of us, fortunately, an awareness of the possibilities and an alertness to them will suffice.

The foregoing helps us understand why disappointed marital love seldom leads to its real opposite, indifference, but more often to a distortion of itself, hate. Even where an unhappy husband and wife remain together, living what Thoreau called "lives of quiet desperation," their feelings toward each other are more likely to degenerate into smoldering hate than casual neglect. The bride and groom who are eager for their love to blossom into the most compelling and creative ecstasy in life, rather than be corroded into sordid hostility, must strive to learn and follow those laws of human nature which alone can yield the desired result. It would be wonderful—almost too wonderful and simple—if there were a precise blueprint which could guarantee marital success. Marriage is far too personal and intimate a relationship, and individual human beings are too unique in their natures, to make such a blueprint possible. Yet there are directives culled from the experience of other couples, refined by scientific observation and religious insight, which can be priceless to you. In some measure they have already been considered. Our concern now is to ask—in addition to a realistic comprehension of love and emotional maturity and many-levelled compatibility—what factors will determine the quality of your marriage?

Long Arm of the Past

One is the love relationship each of you has already had occasion to observe in your respective parents. In some ways you can probably remember—in more important ways that have been repressed beneath the surface of consciousness—you have been influenced and affected by that relationship since the moment of your birth, perhaps even since you were conceived. How your parents have felt toward each other has helped shape their feelings toward you. The way they have treated one another has had a more consequential effect than their words in the formulation of your attitudes and expectations of marriage. Needless to say, the same is true of your future spouse.

This is more than just theory. Dr. Paul Popenoe, an outstanding authority in the field of marriage counseling, has studied the effect of their earlier home life on the happiness of 4,000 married couples. Of those who had grown up in happy homes, 67 percent had achieved happiness in their own marriages. Of those who had emerged from unhappy homes, only 43 percent were themselves happy.

Does this mean that if your parents or your future parents-in-law were unhappily married, you are doomed to duplicate their failure? Fortunately, not at all. It does mean that you and your future mate should give careful attention to the reasons for their failure. What is there about the unsuccessful parental couple–about each of them as an individual, about their maturity or lack of it, about their understanding of love, about the extent of their compatibility–which can aid you to understand their disappointment and do better yourselves? In short, a disastrous marital experience for either set of parents can be a liability or an asset to the next generation. By learning from it wisely, you can acquire an advantage over the couple who has never been close to such trauma. If, on the other hand, your parents have been fortunate in their marriage, you have enjoyed a living example which is worth more than many volumes of advice.

Wise Use of the Present

A second determinant of your future happiness is the kind of courtship you have experienced. I refer here not necessarily to a formally announced engagement, but to the period of time the two of you have planned together for marriage, and how you have used that time.

An engagement as we experience it today is unknown in Jewish tradition. Rabbinic law describes three stages in the marriage process. First came שדוכין (*Shidducheen*), consent by both parties or their parents to proceed with formal arrangements. The second step was ארוסין (*Ayruseen*), or betrothal. But this was not just an agreement that could easily be broken. It was actually the first step in marriage. The parties were bound to each other both religiously and legally, though not yet permitted to live together; in fact they were not even allowed to see each other alone. A formal divorce was required by rabbinic law in order for this relationship to be dissolved.

If the prospective bride were a virgin, a year had to pass between ארוסין and the completion of the marriage, known as נשואין (*Nisu-een*). Only then could the match be sexually consummated. When the bride was a widow, a month was deemed sufficient interval between the two ceremonies. Both ארוסין and נשואין were marked by religious ceremonies which included the recitation of appropriate blessings and the drinking of wine.

In the course of time the intervention of an extended period between betrothal and final marriage was deemed to be clumsy. The two parts of the ceremony were therefore combined. The Jewish wedding ritual as it is performed today will be described in a later chapter.

While the foregoing is of great historic interest, it is the engagement period as we know it now which will play a significant role in determining your happiness.

The length of an engagement is important; reliable studies indicate that couples who have been engaged for approximately a year have, on the average, a better prognosis for marital success than those whose engagements are either shorter or too much longer. You will recall our earlier reference to the test of time as an important instrument for distinguishing love from infatuation. One of the most significant functions of the engagement is to provide precisely such a test of time.

I must confess to fearful apprehension whenever two people tell me, in a premarital conference, that they have known each other only a few months. I feel very little relieved when they add that they have spent so many hours together in that period that they really know each other well. Valid and complete knowledge of another person is not that easily or quickly obtained. True, one never fully knows another until he has lived together with him under the same roof. But reasonably accurate knowledge is possible, provided enough time and effort go into the search for it. A hundred hours spent together over a period of several months can provide a far more accurate index than the same number compressed into a few weeks.

It disturbs me also to hear a prospective bride and groom confess that they have never faced a serious disagreement, that as a consequence neither really knows how the other would react to controversy or handle dissension. Or to listen, as I did on one memorable occasion, to the voice of an intended groom saying: "I know that Jane is able to give in when I become stubborn; she has done so many times. But I have no idea whether or not I would be capable of compromise on an issue too important for concession on her part. We just never have faced such a situation!" Let no one be so foolish as to suppose that abrasive situations will not occur in marriage—in *every* marriage. The time to test the capacity of two individuals to confront and resolve them is not after, but before the wedding!

To serve its proper function, then, an engagement must afford each couple an opportunity to evaluate their probable compatibility on as many levels as possible. This they can hope to achieve only by seeing each other in a maximum variety of circumstances—when they are angry and sullen as well as when contented and joyous, when frustrated as well as fulfilled, in dirty jeans as well as when dressed formally. I often ask a prospective groom in the presence of his beloved: "Have you seen her with her hair in curlers? Do you know how she behaves when her emotions are in curlers?" Similar questions are equally pertinent in reverse.

What all this adds up to is the importance of evaluating each other realistically, of knowing your future mate's defects as well as his virtues. For be sure of one thing: both defects and virtues are there! If you are unable to identify the former with some degree of exactitude, they will become evident soon enough after the wedding. It is far better to know in advance the kind of caprice or quirk to which you will have to adjust than to be shocked by it later. In a good marriage neither partner expects perfection from the other, because neither is so presumptuous as to pretend perfection for himself.

Your engagement is the most priceless opportunity each of you will have, short of marriage itself, to learn the truth about the other. But a special effort in this direction may be needed. Too many of us have been reared since earliest childhood to disguise our emotions, to construct a social façade for ourselves, to project an image rather than reveal what we really are. This becomes especially pernicious during our dating years when, understandably enough, each of us strives to create the best possible impression of himself. The fine art of camouflage, which no doubt serves a legitimate purpose in casual dating, can be calamitous if carried through an engagement and into marriage.

A marriage undertaken with less than true knowledge is precarious in the extreme. Alexander Magoun has written wisely on this point too:

> The only thing in the world as strong as love is truth, and there are reasons to believe that as far as marriage is concerned they are different aspects of the same thing. A deep and abiding love is the emotional response to an intellectual recognition of the truth about another person.[1]

It will help you toward the attainment of such truth if you observe carefully how your intended behaves not only toward you, but also toward his family and friends. And for reasons which should not now require lengthy elaboration, it is important also to note the relationship between his or her parents, and to discuss them openly if they give rise to apprehension.

Engagement should also be a time to plan for the future. While details pertaining to the wedding ceremony and honeymoon should, of course, be included, they are the least of the matters to be carefully explored together. There should be conversations in depth also on such topics as your first year's budget, the amount of income to be expected, how much is to be spent and how much saved, what proportion is to be set aside for investment and insurance, where you are to live, in rented quarters or your own home, how many children you hope to have and approximately when, whether the wife is to work, the nature and intensity of your religious identification, and many other matters no less significant. Two people who cannot amicably, intelligently, lovingly, make such plans during their engagement had better hesitate cautiously before marrying.

The wise candidate for marriage will be alert during his courtship to the manner in which his intended mate reacts to a variety of disappointments: to a flat tire when both are dressed formally, to the unavoidable cancellation of a long-anticipated party due to the sudden intrusion of a business responsibility, to interference of illness on an important social evening. He will also initiate such joint ventures as shopping together and preparing a dinner for friends in order to estimate how well the two of them can work together. He will explore the opinions of his sweetheart on important world events, on politics and religion, thus to ascertain how much they really have in common.

Some years ago, near the end of a premarital conference, I was startled when the prospective bride burst into tears. They were turbulent tears, not gentle ones. When they had subsided enough to make coherent speech possible, she said: "Rabbi, I want to get married, but I'm also desperately afraid of it. I don't know whether I'll be able to meet my responsibilities, sexually or otherwise." Such fears are, in reasonable measure, not too uncommon. Many a bride finds her eager and hopeful anticipation at least partially shaded by fear. The period of engagement, if it is used wisely, should help to alleviate such fear. If it fails to, if either bride or groom approaches *the day* with a heavy burden of dread or doubt, the ceremony should be postponed until they have had a chance—by themselves or with professional help—to resolve their foreboding. Undue apprehension is a fragile auspice under which to enter marriage. If more than normal doubt persists, better a cancelled engagement than gambling future happiness against inordinate odds.

LIGHT AND SHADOW

A third contingency on which happiness in marriages hinges is the kindness and consideration each partner shows the other. How pitiable and pathetic it is to see the contrast between the sweetness with which some couples wooed one another and the sullen indifference or hostility which marks their later marital relationship. Some of us never speak with such nastiness to a stranger as we do to those whom we presumably love. Near the beginning of this volume we compared love to a slow, steady flame and infatuation to a spectacular but speedily spent brush-fire. Let it not be overlooked that a flame must be continually fed. Kindness and tenderness are the fuels needed to keep the flame of love burning. A great painting, abandoned in a dump to be covered with grit and grime, is indistinguishable after a while from the refuse surrounding it. A Stradivarius violin, carelessly discarded to accumulate dirt and dust, soon loses its purity of tone. The more precious a possession, the greater the continuing care which it deserves and needs. No possession on earth is more priceless than the love of a husband and wife. It therefore requires the most diligent care.

I recall an emotionally undemonstrative man in his seventies yielding to profuse tears a few hours after his wife had died. He said: "I don't think I ever realized how much she meant to me or how deeply I loved her until I learned she had cancer!" What happened to all the potentially rich years of affection—experienced and expressed—prior to the onset of this woman's fatal illness?

Gilbert Chesterton once said that the way truly to appreciate anything is to remember that one day it may be lost. Carried to its most morbid extreme, this thought can blight love. Understood in proper perspective, it can prevent us from neglecting or ignoring that which will certainly be lost if we take it for granted.

Jewish tradition clearly understood the importance of constant kindness between mates. Thus the Zohar tells us:

> A wife who receives love gives love in return; if she receives anger, she returns anger in equal measure.

An earlier *midrash* is more explicit on the same point:

> A wise woman said to her daughter, who was about to become a bride: "My daughter, if you will respect your husband like a king, he will treat you like a

> queen. If you will serve him like a slave-girl, he will serve you like a slave. But if you will be too proud to serve him, he will assert his mastership by force and will treat you like a maid-servant. If your husband is about to visit his friends, persuade him to bathe and wear fine raiment. If his friends come to his house, welcome them heartily and set before them more than they can eat, so that they will respect your husband. Watch well your home and all of your husband's possessions. He will be delighted with you, and you will be the crown of his head."[2]

We must not interpret too literally this mother's suggestion that her daughter serve her husband as if she were his slave, and the admonition to supervise his bathing and dress could easily lead to nagging. But the spirit expressed in this quotation, a spirit of deliberate effort to demonstrate and express unending affection, is valid advice to both husband and wife.

No one can be expected, over the long run, to give evidence of kindness which he does not honestly feel. But it can be safely assumed—can it not?—that at least at the beginning of their life together the partners to a marriage do feel genuine kindness and compassion toward each other. Why do their tender emotions sometimes deteriorate into something less laudable? In attempting to answer this question, we come upon a paradoxical psychological truth. We know that our actions normally emerge from our feelings. We behave in a given manner toward other persons because we feel about them in certain ways. What is less commonly known, unfortunately, is that the opposite is also true of the relationship between emotion and action. Which means to say: the way we feel about a particular situation or individual is also influenced by our behavior.

During the Second World War, I served as Jewish chaplain with the Fifth Marine Division on Iwo Jima. Because I was more desperately and almost uncontrollably afraid than ever before or since in my life, I wanted more than anything else to run away. My emotion of fear dictated a clear-cut course of action. But I could not run away. Quite aside from the fact that my conscience would have troubled me if I had, there simply was no place to run. More than 75,000 marines and unnumbered Japanese combatants were crowded into an area of eight square miles, surrounded by the menacing sea. My conduct, then, was forcibly shaped more by outer circumstances than by my strong internal feelings. Thus did I learn from my own visceral experience what I had previously known only from books—that my conduct could have perhaps as much effect on my emotions as my emotions undeniably exercised over my conduct. Forced to act as if I were unafraid, I in fact found myself growing less afraid!

This diversion from marriage to combat is not meant to be cynical. The dynamic of behavior so evident in the one situation is no less applicable to the other. We begin marriage with the kindest, most compassionate feelings for each other. If we express those feelings by appropriate action, they become strengthened and reinforced. If we take them for granted, if we assume it is unnecessary continually to communicate them, if our daily conduct is incongruous with our emotions—soon we begin to cease feeling as warm and loving as we once did. There is, in short, a mutual, two-way connection between what we do and how we feel. They constantly interact on each other for either evil or good.

No Angels

This must not be misinterpreted to mean, however, that any one of us can be never-failing in kindness. There is room for anger in human relations too, room and need. One who cannot honestly handle his hostility and express it openly will also be incapable of expressing love. The success of your marriage will depend also on your ability—while endeavoring to maintain a pervasive atmosphere of kindness—to articulate on occasion your resentment of each other and to criticize each other constructively.

Even the kindest person, enjoying the most wonderful of marriages, will not always—at every moment of every day—feel well-disposed toward his spouse. There are circumstances and times when we must learn to suspend or delay the expression of our negative feelings. But to suppress them as a matter of general policy would be catastrophic. Any strong emotion which is regularly muted or denied becomes a burning acid which destroys both its opposite feeling and the person who hosts both of them. Professor Magoun's advice is worth remembering:

> The wise man does not try to avoid anger; he determines what, for him, is worth being angry about, then is angry at the right person, in the right way, at the right time. *He expresses the anger in a constructive way*, and he gets over being angry as soon as this is accomplished.[3]

Criticism and anger can be expressed either constructively or destructively. The difference is crucial, though sometimes subtle. A wife, disturbed over the way her husband flared up at her mother, can react in either of the following ways:

The minute they are alone, she can explode with: "You had your nerve talking to my mother that way! After all the things she has done for us, you were positively insulting. You just wait until the next time your parents are here; I'll show them as much love as you did to my mother!"

Waiting for a more propitious moment after the emotional

temperature of both has subsided, she can say: "Sweetheart, you're usually thoughtful of mother and I'm sure you didn't realize quite how you sounded this afternoon in arguing with her. I can't really blame you for getting excited; I do it myself. But I don't think she meant to offend you any more than you really wanted to hurt her. Next time, if you can tell me your criticism and let me carry the ball for you when I'm alone with her, perhaps that would make things easier for all of us."

In both cases the wife has made her point, in the second more effectively and with less emotional abrasion to either her husband or herself.

There will be outbursts and flares of temper between almost any two people living in the intimacy of marriage. What we must do is strive to keep them to a minimum, to have over with them as speedily as we can, to avoid as far as possible saying things we don't really mean, and to apologize when we have been wrong. A good check point for every married person, preferably two seconds before the lightning strikes, is to ask himself: "Which is more important in the end–this thing about which we're quarreling, or our love?" Properly handled, even the arguments in marriage can cement a closer relationship between mates.

You will recall our earlier suggestion that this is another of the crucial areas to be explored during your engagement. How have you handled your disagreements, especially on matters which at the time seemed vital to either or both of you? How long does it take for the quarrel to be resolved? Is it usually the same one who gives in, or is there a pretty even balance in this respect? How deep have the scars been and how enduring the pain? Your honest answers to questions like these can be most revealing as you anticipate the handling of stresses and strains in your marriage.

A rabbinic directive is relevant here: "Love without admonition is not love."[4] This certainly is not meant to recommend regular indulgence in carping criticism. Love should by-pass minor imperfections and eschew nagging. But if it fails to yield constructive admonition, it cannot realize one of its most essential values, helping the loved one to fulfill more of his richest potential.

An Invaluable Key

It will help inestimably to maintain the difficult combination of overall kindness and honest expression of hostility if husband and wife can accept each other as unique human personalities, each with a temperament and set of problems peculiarly his own. Basic to such acceptance is a recognition of the fact that men and women differ in their essential natures and needs. It made for enjoyable entertainment in *My Fair Lady* when Henry Higgins plaintively wailed his impatience with Eliza Doolittle through the song, *Why Can't a Woman Be More like a Man?* But the fact of the matter is that women are, in some important respects, not at all like men, nor are men like women. If, moreover, the two sexes were to become emotionally and intellectually identical, far more would be lost than gained.

The altogether proper clamor for equal rights on behalf of women becomes hopelessly distorted if it presupposes no essential differences between them and men. Such differences, as a matter of fact, show themselves at a very early stage in the development of children. Dr. Evelyn Goodenough of the Gesell Institute for Child Development has conducted some fascinating experiments to disclose this. Children between the ages of two and four were ushered into a room where they found a box of brightly colored plastic blocks which they had not seen before. An observer and a tape recorder were also in the room. The reactions of the boys were nearly always focused on practical interests dealing with the arrangement and structure of the blocks. They asked such questions as: "How many blocks are there? How strong are they? How do you think I can stack them?" There was little deviation from this line during the ten-minute period of observation.

Little girls, exposed to the same stimulus, reacted quite differently. Their interest in the blocks themselves was sustained for no more than about three minutes. By the end of that time, if not sooner, they would look up from the blocks and ask the observer some such query as: "Did you know I'm going to a party tomorrow and my mother bought me a new dress?" Or, "Do you know that my grandpa has a new car?" They were also inclined to flit from topic to topic, having little or no connection to the blocks at hand.

When the mothers and fathers of these children were interviewed, most of them felt that by and large male thinking was apt to be direct, analytical, and resourceful; female thinking impressed them as illogical, indirect, and excessively sentimental.[5] If differences as substantial as these are apparent in children no older than four, it would be naive to deny them in adults. With no attempt at disparagement or odious comparison, it can be said with accuracy and fairness that in its approach to practical problems the male mind tends toward the rational, works more slowly and thoroughly than a woman's, and is usually less emotional than hers. The female mind is, on the average, more emotional, more sensitive, and more intuitive. It is dangerous to generalize too extravagantly, and of course there are exceptions to all such sweeping descriptions, yet on the whole they are true.

What does this have to do with your marriage? Just as neither you nor your mate has any right to mold the other into an image of himself, so neither of you is wise to expect men and women to react precisely the same. There are situations in which male propensities can be most helpful, others in which typically feminine traits will avail better, and many more in which the approach best calculated to succeed is a combination of both. A good marriage becomes more probable in the proportion that husband and wife accept each other's individual and sexual uniquenesses, trying to benefit from them, not to beat each other down. It almost goes without saying that the more understanding of this sort an individual gives, the more he will receive.

TOO BUSY

Another factor of immense consequence is the amount of time husband and wife spend together. We have already mentioned, in connection with compatibility, the importance of agreement in their leisure time activities. But such agreement is of little value unless it be implemented. In an earlier and simpler economy most people had no choice. There were enough responsibilities revolving around the household to keep not only father and mother but also their growing children occupied in a variety of joint ventures. Today—with smaller quarters, frozen foods, electronic gadgets for cleaning, more voracious vocational demands keeping men away from home, the increasingly strident distractions of the entertainment industries abroad and television at home—corrosive inroads threaten both the structure and integrity of our families. Even when husbands and wives are together for their leisure hours, too often they share only a passive spectatorship as they watch an expert display his prowess. Far from truly and deeply sharing in meaningful activity, too many mates today seem scarcely to know each other. A study made in California even before the wholesale advent of television showed that 76.4 percent of total leisure time activity was being spent watching others perform, rather than actively participating oneself. With television as ubiquitous and popular as it is now, the figure would unquestionably be even higher.

I recall an occasion when I sat with a stunned and shocked husband whose wife had died a few hours before. They had been married over thirty years; while their marriage had not been one of preeminent success, it wasn't too different from many others. In an attempt to encourage the ventilation of his inmost thoughts and feelings, I asked the man what his wife's interests had been outside her family and who her closest friends were. After a moment or two of troubled silence, he responded: "Rabbi, I'm afraid I can't answer that question . . . I just don't know." Each of them had possessed his own circle of interests and friends; the two circles had almost never converged.

We must be realistic. Unless husband and wife are engaged in a joint profession or business, their opportunities to spend meaningful time together during most of the week will of brutal necessity be limited. All the more reason, then, not to shun each other completely on the weekend. It is understandable that a man should want to fish or play cards or compete in golf with other men. But if he makes these his primary weekend pursuits, leaving only a grudging remnant of time and concern for his wife, he cannot expect much in the way of marriage. The members of a family who use their home as a motel, a convenient place to sleep, change clothes and eat—occasionally but not necessarily doing some of these things together—cannot hope to experience love at its best. Dr. James A. Peterson has expressed this very well:

> Hard physical effort such as scaling a mountain or hiking a great distance or lugging a canoe over a portage or playing a hard-fought set of tennis—all of these enable us to release some of the aggressions built up within us. We invest ourselves in these acti-

> vities and when they are finished there has taken place a kind of catharsis that has value.
>
> There is a type of psychological help for children called play therapy which is based on the definite recognition that creative play enables the child to release feelings hitherto inhibited. In the same way the play of husband and wife releases pent-up feelings and clears the way for more positive feelings.
>
> Recreational events are the sunshine among shadows, the highlights of sometimes gray marital experiences. But every experience in the family influences all other experiences. When a couple solves their difficulties in a game they are provided with a new pattern for resolving difficulties in other areas. After several such recreational experiences the budget-planning session will be conducted in a little different atmosphere with more gaiety and good humor.[6]

A final word of caution is in order before moving on to other considerations. The amount of time two people will find it possible to spend together will vary from couple to couple. It will depend not only on how much they really have in common, but also how much each is personally able to give and to share. This means that compatibility is essential not only in the substantive terms of what two people share by way of content, but also between their personalities. One who is extravagantly outgoing and another who finds it difficult to express himself and to share are not likely to make a good match.

Loud and Clear

Another component of happy marriages is too important to be assumed, yet too obvious to allow for elaboration at length. Husbands and wives must at all times strive to keep their lines of communication open. Nothing is more conducive to contamination in the marital relationship than a person who retreats into sullen silence at the first sign of disagreement. Better by far an explosive moment—if no better choice seems possible—than refusal to communicate at all!

One couple who came to me for aid in repairing a badly damaged marriage had reached the point where their only means of verbal exchange—living in the same house!—was to write each other letters which were duly deposited in locations where they would surely be noticed. Needless to say, it was by then too late for my help to avail. Whatever bothers either mate about the other, or about their relationship, should be articulated. Not, hopefully, in a key of carping criticism and complaint, but in an honest desire to come through to each other "loud and clear." Moody withdrawal and obstructed channels of communication are twin blights which will shrivel even the most promising blossoms of marriage.

SECOND CHANCE

Though the vast majority of my readers will no doubt be anticipating their first marriage, a few words should be addressed to those who—either because of divorce or death—are contemplating a second.

No one can posit an exact period of time which should intervene between the death of one's mate and a second marriage. Much will obviously depend on thc individuals involved, on their needs and their children's, on the quality of their first marriages, on how long and how well they have known each other, and on any understanding which a husband and wife may have reached while both were alive. Certainly enough time should elapse to demonstrate a decent respect for the deceased and to allow for wholesome recovery from grief. The number of months or years necessary to accomplish these twin tasks will vary from person to person. What will apply universally is that only after the recreative work of bereavement has been accomplished can any person accept a second marriage without the risk of intolerable guilt.

Jewish tradition was alert to the fact that each situation involving remarriage must be judged according to its own circumstances. Rabbinic law, therefore, permitted a second marriage with less than the usual delay where a widower had no one to care for his young children or if he had not yet fulfilled the biblical injunction to produce progeny.

Reliable studies indicate that a man or woman whose first marriage was happy is likely to remarry more quickly than one whose first marital venture was unsuccessful. There will, of course, be exceptions to any such generalization, but the rule as such is valid.

Our earlier warning against rushing into marriage too hastily "on the rebound" applies also to those who are so lonely after divorce or death that they disregard all the normal cautions of intelligence and discretion. A second marriage, no less than a first, can be either insufferable or ecstatic. The rules calculated to yield success are the same.

Special care is necessary for the person whose first attempt has ended in divorce. It is imperative for him to inquire into the causes of his previous failure—particularly those which can fairly be attributed to himself—and to guard against a repetition of disaster. Many persons exhibit a repetitive pattern of failure; after one unfortunate choice of mate, they will appear to be making the very same kind of fatal selection again. Perhaps this is why the divorce rate is higher for second marriages than for first, higher yet for those who have taken their marriage vows a third time. Approximately one-third of the marriages of individuals previously divorced end again in divorce.[7] The frequency of divorce in this country has led some foreign observers to comment that many Americans view the choice of a mate much as they do the borrowing of a library book. One reads the first few chapters; if they fail to excite the reader's interest, the book is returned and another is tried. Fortunately the picture is not one of unrelieved gloom. In 1948 there was 1 divorce in the United States for every 2.5 marriages. By 1960 the ratio had been reduced to 1 for 3.9 marriages.[8]

Our immediate concern, however, is with the prognosis for success when a divorced person enters upon a second marriage. Much depends on whether the first venture is treated as a learning experience, with every possible effort expended to correct mistakes and refine flaws. Failures need not be repeated. A second marriage can be supremely happy.

Not Forgotten

Two additional factors of enormous significance in determining the prospects for your marriage have been eliminated from this part of our discussion, not because of neglect but because entire chapters will be devoted to them later. They are the influence on marriage, respectively, of sex and religion. Suffice it to say for the present that both are indispensable ingredients in any recipe for marital happiness and success. Before turning to them, however, we devote a short chapter to certain financial problems which play a significant role in determining the outcome of every marriage.

«««««««« 6 »»»»»»»»

Of Matters Mundane

THE IMPORTANCE OF FINANCIAL COMPATIBILITY AS A BAROMETER of personality adjustment has already been covered. Money enters into marriage in a more direct manner too. While it is true that financial difficulties are likely to reflect more fundamental causes of dissension, the management of money is itself an immediate problem of marriage which the wise bride and groom will include in their planning. Either too little or too much money can frustrate all hope for happiness. That insufficient means for comfortable living can impose a severe strain on a marriage needs no argument. That the opposite is no less true may not be quite so apparent.

I once counseled an attractive young couple at whose wedding I had officiated a year or two earlier. They were troubled with considerable tension. Near the end of our time together I said: "Part of your trouble is financial." "Oh no," was the immediate and joint response, "you're wrong; we don't have any financial problems at all. We both have quite a bit of money as well as stocks left to us by our grandparents." And they proceeded, without any prodding, to tell me the extent of their liquid assets. But neither one of them had comprehended what I had said. Their trouble *was* in part financial;

they suffered from too much downright luxury, handed to them on their wedding day with no effort on their part at all. True, they may have experienced trouble even without such easy affluence, but whether as symptom or cause, financial abundance was an integral part of their problem. In terms of socio-economic background they were compatible; but their values were distorted and they had no economic goals for which to strive together.

It is naive in the extreme to suppose that those with a great deal of money are automatically assured a happier marriage than those with very little. One marriage counselor has reported an interesting study he made in the area of Los Angeles. In an exclusive suburb he came upon a family whose income was $100,000 a year, but whose home was filled with ugly conflict. In a trailer court he met a crippled man who lived with his arthritic wife and adolescent daughter. They were remarkably happy on the very small income he managed to earn as a part-time watchman. These two couples scored lowest and highest respectively on a marriage adjustment test given to a large number of families in Los Angeles county.[1]

This does not mean that poverty is conducive to happiness; rather that wealth is by no means a guarantee of success. Much depends, as we have already had occasion to say, on the expectations and values of a given couple. Economic security in reasonable measure is essential. There are some, however, who feel less secure on $1,000 a week than others on $100.

Whatever their income, married couples must learn to manage their resources together. For either one to be the business manager for both is not advisable. The family budget should be planned together; in fact, as soon as children are old enough, they should be involved in the process too. Decisions as to how much to lay aside for insurance, for investment, for a nest egg, for deferred spending on large items—all these should be made together. If you and your future spouse are already accustomed, each of you, to project and administer a budget for one person, you have a head start toward carrying on the same kind of enterprise now for two. If either of you is entering upon marriage with a backlog of debt or of extraordinary financial commitment, this should be made known to the other and should be included in your budget.

The rabbis whose sermonic excerpts are recorded in the Midrash were aware of the fact that financial cooperation between the partners is an essential component of successful marriage. They used the following parable:

> Once a man engaged in robbery by night, keeping his family in luxury as a consequence. The wife of a neighbor complained to her husband: "What ill-luck is mine that I am married to you. The man across the way keeps his family in every comfort." The husband replied: "But rumor has it that he is a thief. Do you wish me to become like him?"
>
> The wife answered: "I care not what your occupation is, provided you give me the luxuries I crave."
>
> Being enamored of his wife, the husband begged his neighbor to allow him to participate in his next enterprise. The police were informed and laid a trap for him. The experienced robber succeeded in escaping the snare but the novice was captured and hanged.[2]

In our day no less than theirs it is essential that husband and wife want the same material things, plan together on how to obtain them, and keep each other fully informed on their joint financial status. A wife whose economic ambitions outstrip her husband's legitimate acquisitive abilities can easily ruin him, their marriage, or both.

Is it wise, in this connection, for two people to marry when they know that at least temporarily they will be dependent upon financial help from their parents? No categorical answer can be given this question; much depends on the kind of people they and their parents are. Ideally, parents should be happy to provide such assistance and young couples should be able to accept it without reactions of either resentment or guilt. Yet there are psychological booby traps in such arrangements; no couple should make this decision without at the very least being aware of them. There is an almost irresistible temptation for parents who are supplying all or part of a young couple's income to interfere in how it is spent. More subtle but no less contaminating is the tendency of the recipients to feel guilty over their dependency on parents and, as a consequence, to resent the very hand that feeds them.

It is my own strong conviction that, especially at a time when the gap between psychological readiness for marriage and its practical possibility is growing wider, parents who can afford to should make it possible for well-matched, mature couples to marry before they are financially independent. But such help should not be proffered unless the giver is prepared to exercise no control over how it is spent and the recipients are able to accept it without any loss of self-esteem. In some circumstances it may be the wisest course for parental help to be extended, at least ostensibly, in the form of a loan; this may aid in the preservation of integrity. To wipe such a loan off the books at a later date may be less threatening than an immediate and outright gift.

Those who are inclined to suspect that this is only a post-modern problem will be interested in the comment of a chasidic rabbi:

> A passenger on a ship patiently awaited the day when it would reach port. When the ship was nearing the harbor, a storm drove it back to sea, much to the chagrin of the traveler. Likewise a man is afflicted

> with anxiety for his sons and daughters until he succeeds in rearing them to maturity. Then he hopes to be freed from worry regarding their lot. But his oldest son comes with his troubles, seeking paternal counsel and the father's retirement is delayed. The daughter also comes with her problems, and once more his hope of a quiet life is postponed. Few of us are ever entirely free from worry and the necessity of continuous labor in this world.[3]

WORKING WIVES

The same pressures which have increased the number of young couples accepting financial aid from their parents have also multiplied the proportion of wives who work. This too is hardly a novel phenomenon. My wife and I were married in the fall of 1932, in the depth of an economic depression and at a time when I still faced four years of additional graduate study before receiving my rabbinic ordination. During those four years we both worked at a multiplicity of part-time jobs, even while continuing our respective academic studies. I could not honestly have reported which of us brought in the larger share of income during a given month. We do not in the least regret our early financial struggle, or the inability of our parents to assist at that difficult time. We are convinced that our marriage was enriched by it in a way we could never have otherwise known. What we have now—or will have for the rest of our lives—rests on a foundation built by both of us.

Yet it would be naive just to extrapolate from our experience and to endorse our example without qualification. Here too there are psychological complexities which each couple must confront and surmount. To some husbands, a working wife poses a serious threat to their own masculinity. To others, a wife who follows her own career becomes an intolerable hazard to male prestige. Some women, who have looked forward for many years to the time when their daily labors would no longer be needed, may bitterly resent what appears to them to be an unjustified imposition. All such reservations and doubts should be fully explored by each couple during the engagement period. If they cannot be resolved, marriage should at the very least be postponed until such time as the husband can carry the full financial burden alone.

For those, however, to whom this is not a problem of serious proportion, there are two reasons—over and above that adduced from my own experience—which recommend that young wives continue to work. In another context we have already mentioned the many electric and electronic gadgets which make it unnecessary for most wives to spend more than a very few hours a day chained to the household chores which imprisoned their mothers. What are they to do with the major part of their days? To resort to an endless round of bridge games or golf will surely not add to their stature as self-respecting human beings. Nor will it enable them to keep intellectual pace with their husbands. The woman who, by work, stimulates herself to become a vigorous, creative person will be a better wife to her husband and one day a far superior mother to her children than one who permits herself to become a martyr either to her home or her family. This is one reason for the recommendation that young wives involve themselves in interesting work, even if there is no financial need for it. Similar values can accrue from work which is voluntary, provided it be something which the woman herself believes to be significant and which involves a sense of commitment and responsibility on her part. Most women who commence their years of marriage this way will also want to return to gratifying work of some sort—at least on a part-time basis—when their children are of an age which no longer demands their whole time.

The second reality which recommends such work is one of anticipation. It is commonly known that for some women the onset of menopause, more commonly known as change-of-life, is accompanied by serious emotional disturbances. Part of this is unquestionably a consequence of glandular changes which take place in their bodies when the process of menstruation ceases. But more menopausal turbulence than is popularly supposed may be due to another factor. The husband of such a woman is usually at the very peak of his career. Her children, if they are not already married themselves, are away at college. Suddenly she discovers—or may even just uncomfortably suspect—that no one on earth really needs her between the hours of 8 a.m. and 6 p.m.

This is an almost intolerably devastating conclusion for any person of integrity. All of us need to feel useful and needed. Of course a woman of fifty or fifty-five is still needed by her husband, the more so if their marriage has been a good one. But for a person of intelligence and responsibility, that isn't enough. It will be remembered, hopefully, that one of the distinctions previously assigned to love is its capacity to stimulate the lovers toward committed interest in the welfare of others. The wife who knows, even after her child-bearing-and-rearing years are ended, that others beyond her immediate family still need her, and depend upon her for work which is significant, will be better equipped to cope with the complications of menopause than her neighbor whose horizons have never expanded beyond husband and children.

The preceding paragraphs touch upon one of the mainsprings of mental and emotional health. Every normal human being possesses a reservoir of productive capacity, an area in which he can contribute something of significance to others. From a moral point of view, we have no right to deny this potential to our fellowmen. In terms of acquiring and maintaining healthy personalities, we owe no less to ourselves. A physically healthy person who remained perpetually in bed, never exercising his muscles, would soon degenerate into illness. An emotionally balanced individual who permitted his productive capacity to become stultified would reap no less calamitous consequences. Dr. Erich Fromm has expressed this truth with exemplary eloquence:

> Happiness is an achievement brought about by man's inner productiveness and not a gift of the gods. . . . Happiness is the indication that man has found the answer to the problem of human existence: the productive realization of his potentialities and thus, simultaneously, being one with the world and preserving the integrity of his self.[4]

In short, the woman who discovers and exploits her creative potential thereby becomes a better wife.

A word of caution, however, is required. Work, assumed as a supplement to the responsibilities of home, can be productive and healthful. Work, resorted to as a desperate escape from the commitments of wife and mother, can be utterly destructive. Maintaining a home and rearing children lovingly is also a career, one of the noblest and most necessary careers in the world. It is the one career which only a woman can completely fulfill. It demands the very best of her nature, the keenest of her intelligence, the deepest of her love. No success achieved outside her home can compensate for failure here. True, there are many moments of tedium attendant upon the management of a home and the instruction of children. But there are also times of insufferable boredom in the most brilliant profession outside the home. No task confronting us is more crucial for the survival of mankind than rearing children capable of love. And, whether we choose it so or not, biology and economy conspire to make this primarily the responsibility and precious opportunity of women. Everything a wife undertakes by way of outside career, then, must be placed within the context of this priority.

There need not be irreconcilable conflict between the two. Certain studies undertaken at Columbia University show conclusively that working wives may actually spend more meaningful time with their children than wives who do not work.[5] More important than the number of minutes or hours per day a mother spends with her children is what she does with that time.

In the last analysis, the decision on "career" or "no career" for a wife must depend upon her own individual make-up and her husband's. If the intelligence, disposition, and talents of a woman are such that she cannot comfortably discharge the dual obligation, her home should be her career. If her own personality and that of her husband and the relationship between them makes it possible for her to do both, in most cases she will be a more richly fulfilled person as a result.[6] Even where the decision is to concentrate exclusively on the domestic scene while their children are young, most wives would be well advised to resume their interrupted education or career after household and maternal responsibilities no longer demand all their attention.

The Talmud seems to have anticipated this problem too: "It is not seemly for a woman to sit in idleness."[7] This does not mean that ancient rabbinic authorities would in every respect approve contemporary practice. They would certainly not countenance a married woman's working for a man other than her husband. But they did recognize the need for every wife to keep busy.

Butcher, Baker, Candlestick Maker

We have not yet quite exhausted the relevance of finance to marriage. Most brides know in advance the probable occupation of their grooms. Yet all too few take this into serious consideration in contemplating the probable success of their marriages. No factor so significant to a man as his profession or business can fail to have an important impact on his marriage. We know, for example, that certain vocations seem to carry with them a higher probability of marital happiness than others. These include the work of professors, chemical engineers, and clergymen. Those tending to show a lower score are laborers, mechanics, and traveling salesmen. This correlation must neither be pushed too far nor altogether ignored. It can easily be understood in terms of the personality traits which might direct a man toward one or another occupation, also as the result of environmental circumstances peculiar to particular pursuits. It is mentioned here, not because it should be a priority consideration in any woman's selection of a mate, but because her husband's way of earning his living will certainly impinge on their life together.

Jewish tradition was acutely aware of this. The rabbis therefore stipulated that the wife of a tanner could, if she wished, ask a rabbinic court to pressure her husband for a divorce. Apparently in ancient times animal dung was used in curing hides. Especially before the institution of the daily bath, a man who spent most of his day at this inelegant business could scarcely have smelled very attractive at dinner. If his wife found the odor too offensive, she could ask that their marriage be dissolved.

The tanner today poses no exceptional problems for his wife;

other occupations do. The wife of a traveling salesman, for example, must certainly be prepared for periods of lonely separation from her mate. The wife of one whose work must be done at night will have to accommodate to a topsy-turvy kind of personal and social schedule. A wife whose husband's vocation brings him into daily, perhaps even intimate contact with other women must learn to curb whatever inclination she possesses toward jealousy.

Two professions in particular are vulnerable to extraordinary marital pressures: medicine and the clergy. The fact that I am a rabbi and the son of a physician enables me to perceive that in some respects the problems are similar. In both instances, for example, the practitioner's wife must settle for the enforced absence of her husband, sometimes at the very moment she wants or needs him most. The young intern or resident faces regular night duty in the hospital. After he has commenced his private practice he is constantly subject to emergency calls. His family must grow accustomed to the possibility that, just as they are ready for a dinner appointment, a picnic or party, a theater engagement, the shrill intrusion of the telephone bell rudely interrupts their plans.

The trespasses on the life of a rabbi and his wife can be equally annoying. The serious illness or death of a congregant commandeers him too. Endless meetings, conferences, and pastoral visitations expropriate the evenings he would prefer to spend with his family. The tensions and frustrations frequently forced upon him by insensitive members of the congregation and board are sometimes unjustly ventilated against his wife and children. His family often bitterly resents the time and attention he seems to give so generously to everyone but them.

A role performed by both doctors and rabbis is that of father-substitute. Especially the women among their patients and congregants respectively are apt to develop strong emotional attachments to them. On occasion such attachments and emotional dependencies seem to reflect the search more for a surrogate-husband than for a father. All this both the doctor or rabbi and his wife must understand and accept. There can be no doubt that it increases the tension with which their love must cope. If they are mature individuals and their love is strong enough, they will carry these extra stresses not only adequately but even with blessed touches of humor.

Have we given the impression that in a professional marriage all the understanding and acceptance are the obligations of the wife? Then let a stringent corrective be applied at once. It is so easy for the ambitious young physician to exaggerate the amount of time he really needs to spend away from his wife, so tempting for the neophyte rabbi to assume that no building can be dedicated, no banquet digested, without his personal benediction. The conscientious man who is determined to give his profession everything it demands, with no more than meager leftovers for his wife, will soon have no marriage left worth cherishing. A balance must be established from the start, with major priority granted to both objectives, with a recognition by husband and wife that sometimes their marriage will temporarily be subordinated to pressing professional demands, but at other times the preference should be reversed. A doctor- or rabbi-husband owes as much deliberate budgeting of time to his marriage as he does to his profession.

If the wives of physicians and rabbis must realistically anticipate greater problems than others, they are also the potential beneficiaries of more substantial satisfactions. There are probably no occupations in which husband and wife can share a profession more abundantly. Surely there are none in which loving mates are in more urgent need of each other's understanding and cooperation. Except for professional confidences, they can confront the anxieties and perplexities of their life as a team. Both the risks and the rewards of marriage are greater for them than for most others. But the gap between them and other couples is one of degree, not of kind. They simply highlight, in magnified proportion, the vocational problems and possibilities to be confronted by every married couple. True, each man marries a woman and each woman marries a man. But a career is both an extension of its participant's personality and an influence in the further development of that personality. For that reason above all, it must of necessity be included in the calculus of marriage.

Since the impact of vocational or professional stress is likely to press upon marriage more insistently from the wife's point of view, an additional word may be directed toward her. Often women tend to identify only the disadvantages of their husbands' occupations, paying scant attention or none to the advantages. True, the physician's or rabbi's wife will see less of her husband than she might wish from day to day. But she may also have greater than average opportunity to share his career, to travel with him, to spend periods of time with him in a country retreat. A balanced perspective will help alleviate pressure, enhance advantages.

In several ways, then, financial factors enter into the marriage. Earlier we saw that love is realistic while romance is illusory. To contemplate marriage as if there were no financial complications to be confronted is to be patently guilty of a purely romantic approach.

No one—in a chapter, a book, a whole set of books—could successfully encompass all the behavioral conditions on which a good marriage depends. I have tried here and in the preceding chapter to suggest only the most important: the love relationship of your parents, the quality of your courtship, the continuing kindness and consideration you extend to each other, the honesty and maturity with which you are able to handle hostility, your ability to accept each other as unique individuals and to welcome the differences in temperament and emotion between women and men, the amount of time you spend together and what you do with that time, your success in the joint management of family finances, your agreement on the desirability of wives working, the wisdom with which you anticipate the special circumstances to be imposed on your marriage by vocational or professional demands, your attitudes toward religion and sex.

It is to the last of these that we now turn our attention.

«««««««« 7 »»»»»»»»

God or the Gutter?

WE HAVE COMPLETED SIX CHAPTERS WITHOUT MENTIONING, except for an occasional casual comment, the subject of sex. A generation ago that would have been impossible. The very best books on marriage available thirty years ago dealt chiefly, if not entirely, with sex. It was believed then even by experts that if newlyweds were furnished with accurate, reliable information that would help them achieve a good sexual adjustment, everything else they desired would follow. The basic premise underlying this view was that sexual satisfaction was either synonymous with love or was its precondition and cause.

Today we know better. Not that we place a lesser value on the role of sex in marriage than did our immediate predecessors, but we recognize the relationship as being reversed. Sexual satisfaction is a consequence rather than a cause of love. Intercourse gives two persons who already love each other an ecstatic way to express and at the same time enrich their love. To pretend that sexual adjustment produces love makes as much sense as to claim that one's body temperature produces disease; it amounts to confusing symptoms with causes.

No one has understood this more perceptively or expressed it more eloquently than Dr. Erich Fromm. He has epitomized the older view as follows:

> The underlying idea was that love is the child of sexual pleasure, and that if two people learn to satisfy each other sexually, they will love each other.

He proceeds to summarize a newer and more accurate approach in these words:

> Love is not the result of adequate sexual satisfaction, but sexual happiness—even the knowledge of the so-called sexual technique—is the result of love. . . . Fear of or hatred for the other sex are at the bottom of those difficulties which prevent a person from giving himself completely, from acting spontaneously, from trusting the sexual partner in the immediacy and directness of physical closeness. If a sexually inhibited person can emerge from fear or hate, and hence become capable of loving, his or her sexual problems are solved. If not, no amount of knowledge about sexual techniques will help.[1]

A good marriage between two young, normal, healthy partners, without a mutually gratifying sexual relationship, is virtually impossible. But the place to begin is with love, not sex. Hence our deferment of sex to this point.

Why should it be necessary to describe the elementary anatomy and physiology of sex to readers of an age to be married? It shouldn't be, but unfortunately—and sometimes tragically—it is. For the average child or youth, accurate, honest information about sex is just about the most difficult commodity in the world to obtain. Recent research among college freshmen disclosed that no more than about 40 percent had received their sex education from their parents. And not all of that by any means was accurate or authentic. Two-thirds of the boys and two-fifths of the girls reported that friends their own age had been their primary sources of information.[2] Too often what this amounted to was only the blind leading the blind. Much of the information—or misinformation—conveyed was of the gutter variety, turning what should have been the most creatively beautiful reality in human experience into something shabby, something irredeemably sordid and cheap. Even where a conscientious effort was made to communicate truth, frequently the curriculum included only the facts of reproduction, not the incomparably glorious and delectable role of sex in the love relationship of marriage. Three decades of premarital counseling have brought me repeated astonishment at how little is known about sex, even by some who are otherwise knowledgeable and sophisticated.

For some fortunate readers, parts of this chapter will be no more than review. Even they, however, may be able to garner a fact here, an insight there, which may be decisive in determining their future happiness.

There should be no more reticence about discussing sex than about describing digestion, no more reluctance to recount the facts regarding menstruation than those concerning a nosebleed. All are manifestations of incredible purpose and plan within the human body. There are many kinds of evidence in nature—in its orderliness and beauty; in the pervasiveness of one chemistry and law from the submicroscopic atom to the outermost reaches of space; in the emergence of life, consciousness, and morality from dead, inert matter—showing that it could not be the result of mere happenstance or chance. Our ability to learn enough about the laws of the universe and to depend upon them sufficiently to send three men off to orbit the moon, a quarter of a million miles from earth, and to have them splash down six days later at the exact anticipated moment, less than four miles from the ship awaiting them, is indicative for most of us that some kind of Intelligence or Power is responsible for the whole of existence. We may disagree as to the nature of that Power and the exact manner in which it operates, but there is widespread consensus that it exists and that its name is God.

None of the evidence in outer space or on our own earth is more wonderfully convincing than that of our human bodies. The most highly skilled engineer, using the most ingenious and complicated of computers, could not possibly have planned bodies and minds that function as efficiently and purposefully as ours. Regardless of the temperature surrounding us, the internal heat of our bodies in good health remains within a fraction of a degree of the norm; no matter how much or how little liquid we consume, the balance of water within us is maintained at a constant level; when we ascend to higher altitudes, where less oxygen is available for each red corpuscle to transmit to our lungs, the number of these miniscule conveyers is immediately and automatically multiplied; the instant infection strikes us, our white corpuscles spontaneously mobilize for defense—these and innumerable additional functions of the human body impress us with the Creative Intelligence which undergirds the entire universe.[3]

Nowhere is this evidence more compellingly beautiful than in the sexual structure and functioning of human beings. In nature's prehuman economy it is not necessary that extreme pleasure, joyous sharing, and rapturous bliss attend the survival of the species. Soon we shall see how mundane the process of propagation is on subhuman levels. But with us, millions of minute details have been so designed that it becomes possible for men and women *through a single act* to create new life, to attain the ultimate in physical and spiritual delight, to articulate and simultaneously enrich their love, and to establish the foundation for families. A recital of how all this is possible far exceeds any ordinary recitation of biological facts. It enables us to share with God one of His most exquisite secrets.

THE SEXUAL EQUIPMENT OF MEN

A diagram of the male sexual organs appears on our next page. It shows, first of all, the penis, which serves the dual purpose of conveying from inside to outside the body both urine from the bladder and semen during sexual excitation. At once we come upon one of the astounding feats of engineering adumbrated above. The two functions of the penis are actually incompatible. Urine contains an abundance of acid; spermatozoa—the infinitesimal seeds which impregnate a woman—cannot live in the presence of acid. To prevent the destruction of spermatozoa by the acid in urine, two things take place when a man becomes sexually aroused. First, a muscle closes off the bladder, making it impossible to urinate. Secondly, the prostate gland and seminal vesicles secrete an alkaline fluid which counteracts the effect of any acid which may have remained in the urethra from previous urination. The urethra, incidentally, is the tube which extends inside the penis.

The size of the penis, like that of all bodily organs, varies from one individual to the next. When a man is not sexually excited, it is in the limp position shown in the diagram and is about 3½ to 4 inches long. When sexually aroused, it extends itself diagonally upward from the body, usually reaching a length of 5 to 6½ inches. The angle of erection assumed by the penis exactly matches that of the female vagina, making entrance and intercourse painless. There is no relationship between the size of a man's penis and the intensity of his sexual capacities, any more than the size of his hand determines whether or not he is to be a writer.

At birth the tip of the penis is covered with a flap called the foreskin. The process of circumcision removes this flap, entirely exposing the tip. We shall comment in a later chapter on the religious significance of this ceremony in Judaism. Let it be noted for the present only that circumcision has been shown to be so healthy for the male that it is practiced in this country today as a strictly surgical procedure for most Christian male babies too. It also seems to reduce the incidence of cancer in women who have had intercourse.

THE MALE SEX ORGANS

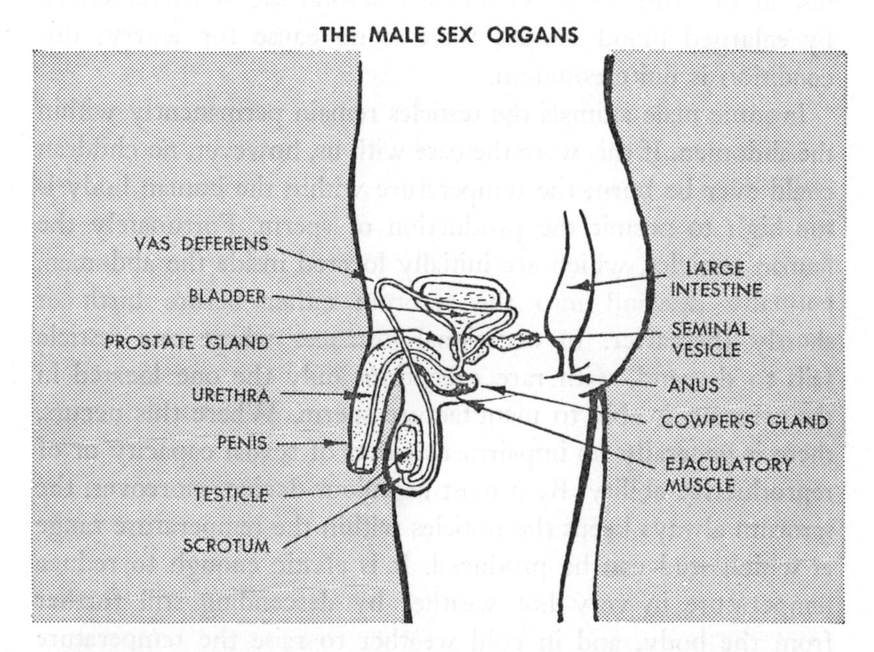

The sack or bag beneath the penis is called the scrotum; it holds the testicles, two small, oval-shaped balls which manufacture spermatozoa. These, by the way, are also called sperm; the singular is spermatozoon. Each testicle—about the size of a small walnut—contains a series of fine tubules which, if stretched out, would extend a quarter of a mile. Again we discover magnificent planning. If his testicles were exactly the same size and hung evenly side by side, a man would suffer excruciating pain whenever they were crushed together. As it is, when an athlete, for example, is struck on a testicle, the pain is intense and can be injurious. For the most part, however, such discomfort and danger are averted by the fact that the left testicle is normally larger than the right and hangs slightly lower. As a consequence of this convenient arrangement, when a man's thighs are compressed one testicle slides by the other instead of crushing it. Where the scrotal sac is characterized by enlarged blood vessels, there is no cause for worry; this condition is quite common.

In some male animals the testicles remain permanently within the abdomen. If this were the case with us, however, no children could ever be born; the temperature within the human body is too high to permit the production of sperm. Fortunately the human testicles, which are initially located inside the abdomen, normally descend into the scrotum either before birth or shortly thereafter. In occasional instances where one testicle fails to descend, with rare exceptions only the one located in the scrotum is able to manufacture sperm. Where this occurs, there is generally no impairment either of sexual capacity or of reproductive ability. By a most ingenious device, moreover, the scrotum always keeps the testicles within the temperature range at which seed can be produced. It is elastic enough to reduce temperature in very hot weather by descending still further from the body, and in cold weather to raise the temperature by contracting and coming up closer to the body. The most complicated thermostat contrived by human intelligence is neither more wondrous nor more dependable than this!

The testicles begin to manufacture sperm when a boy reaches puberty, usually between the ages of ten and sixteen. At the same time they commence to cause the external physical symptoms of manhood: a lowering of the voice, hair under the arms, on the chest, and surrounding the scrotum. Once produced, the sperm are stored in the testicles as well as the seminal vesicles. When the supply exceeds the storage space, and there is no discharge through intercourse or masturbation, the surplus is automatically released in the form of nocturnal emissions, more commonly called wet dreams. The sexual physiology of adolescents is so steeped in unforgivable superstition that some young men fear their wet dreams are a symptom of abnormality or of incapacity to experience a gratifying sex life in marriage. Nothing could be farther from the truth. For sperm to be spontaneously released through the penis during sleep is no more abnormal than for water to overflow a bottle which is full.

Each vas deferens has attached to it a seminal vesicle, the function of which is to supply a yellowish substance which thickens the semen, making it more efficient as a carrier and preserver of sperm. Ordinarily these seminal vesicles are kept closed by muscles in the prostate gland; during sexual excitation they open, permitting their secretion to pass into the urethra and become a component of the semen.

Cowper's gland—named after the doctor who discovered it—secretes a slippery fluid which performs the same purpose in sexual intercourse that lubricating oil does in the engine of a car. The upward-downward motion of pistons in their cylinders would cause friction which would burn them out if an effective lubricant were not provided. Similarly, the inward-outward motion of the male penis in the female vagina could cause considerable discomfort were it not for the lubricant supplied by Cowper's gland in men and two analogous pairs of glands in women.

The Sexual Equipment of Women

The sexual anatomy of women is no less ingenious than that of men. Already partially anticipated in the foregoing description, it is shown in the next diagram. The vagina is a passage or canal through which sperm enter a woman's body and, if she becomes pregnant, a fully developed child emerges at the end of nine months. Like the male penis, the vagina varies in size, not only from one person to the next, but also between moments of sexual relaxation and excitement. The vagina expands much more slowly than the penis, a phenomenon to be remembered for later comment; otherwise the increase in size between these two organs is quite similar. It is possible—but quite rare—for a husband's penis to be too large for his wife's vagina to accommodate with comfort. Even where this occurs, a competent physician can advise on how the vagina opening may be dilated and which positions and techniques for intercourse are most advisable for that particular couple.

No other part of the body in either sex possesses the automatic elasticity of the female reproductive apparatus. In a virgin the opened vagina is about three-fourths of an inch in diameter; after some months of intercourse it stretches to about an inch and a quarter; during childbirth it expands to five or six inches, then gradually resumes its normal size. What a shame that such anatomical efficiency is so often just taken for granted instead of being recognized as the near-miracle it is.

From birth the entrance to the vagina is usually covered by a membrane called the hymen, the thickness and toughness of which vary greatly from person to person. This can pose a problem the first time intercourse is attempted, although in many virgins the hymen is broken or stretched to the point where it causes no pain. Ancient peoples believed that if the hymen was no longer intact on her wedding night, this was certain evidence the bride was not a virgin. In some cultures a white sheet was placed in the marriage bed and witnesses had to attest the next morning that it had been stained by blood. While no one in our civilization is quite that crude, there are

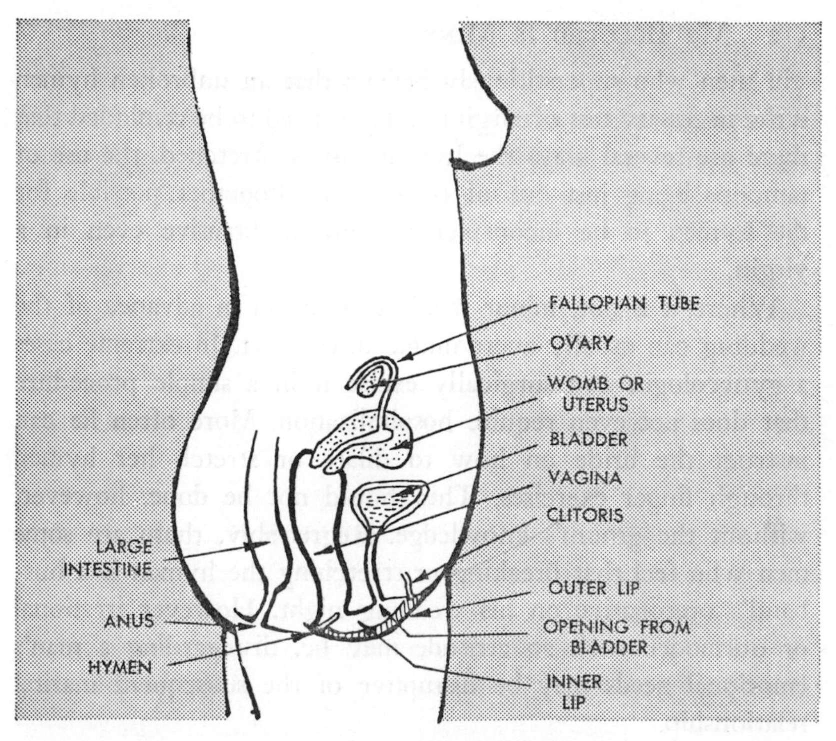
FALLOPIAN TUBE
OVARY
WOMB OR UTERUS
BLADDER
VAGINA
CLITORIS
LARGE INTESTINE
OUTER LIP
ANUS
OPENING FROM BLADDER
HYMEN
INNER LIP

THE FEMALE SEX ORGANS

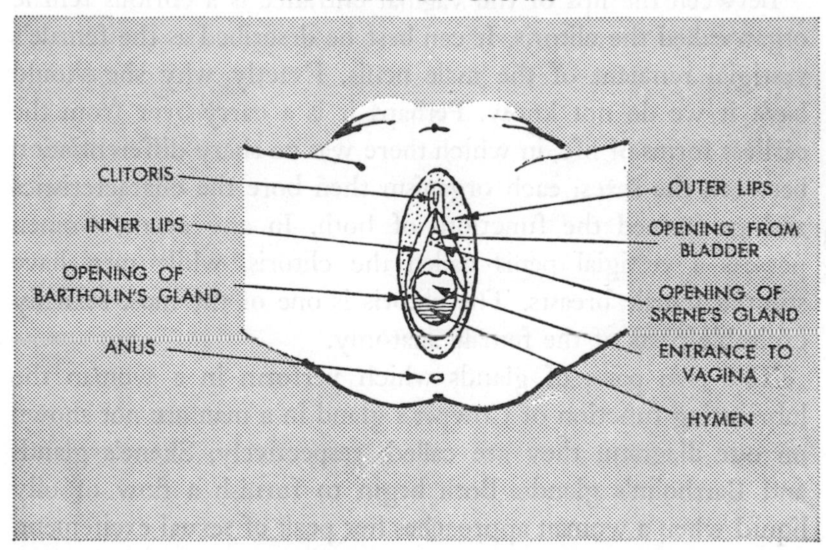
CLITORIS
OUTER LIPS
INNER LIPS
OPENING FROM BLADDER
OPENING OF BARTHOLIN'S GLAND
OPENING OF SKENE'S GLAND
ANUS
ENTRANCE TO VAGINA
HYMEN

still men who superstitiously believe that an unbroken hymen is the necessary test of virginity. They need to be reminded that there are several ways the hymen can be stretched, the use of tampons being just one of them. It is altogether possible for the hymen to be inconspicuous and unobtrusive even in a virgin.

Where it is not, minor medical attention in advance of the wedding can usually avert undue discomfort. In extreme cases a gynecologist can surgically excise it in a simple procedure that does not even require hospitalization. More often he can instruct the bride on how to dilate or stretch her hymen through finger exercises. This should not be done, however, without the groom's knowledge. Regrettably, there are some men who feel that breaking or stretching the hymen is a husband's prerogative on his wedding night. However irrational or outmoded such an attitude may be, disregarding a man's emotional needs may be disruptive of the subsequent marital relationship.

Between the lips of the vaginal entrance is a curious female organ called the clitoris. It can best be described as the female's vestigial remnant of the male penis. Exactly why she should have it we do not know. Perhaps it is a carry-over from the earliest forms of life, in which there was no sharp differentiation between the sexes; each organism then bore the characteristics and performed the functions of both. In any event, women possess a vestigial penis called the clitoris, while men have stunted female breasts. The clitoris is one of the most sexually excitable parts of the female anatomy.

The two pairs of glands which perform in a woman the lubricating function of Cowper's gland in a man are not shown on our diagram; they are called, respectively, Skene's glands and Bartholin's glands. Both begin to furnish a flow of oily liquid when a woman approaches her peak of sexual excitement.

Even before they commence secreting, however, her vaginal walls begin what can best be described as a "sweating" process, preparing the way for intercourse. Often this phenomenon does not occur for several weeks after childbirth. Where such is the case or where there is insufficient natural lubrication, discomfort can be avoided by using an artificial lubricant.

The ovaries are storehouses for a woman's ova or eggs, all of which are present in her body at birth. It has been estimated that a normal human female possesses between 300,000 and 400,000 ova. In the male, sperm are manufactured commencing with puberty. In the female, ova are present from birth, but commencing with puberty one egg usually ripens each month, alternating between the two ovaries. All of which adds up to the distinction that the testicles are a factory, while the ova are warehouses.

Ovulation is the name given to the monthly ripening of an ovum. Only in rare instances does it occur during menstruation. Ovulation causes a ripened egg to move into the Fallopian tubes, which extend from the ovaries to the uterus or womb. The narrow neck of the uterus is called the cervix. If sperm from a male is in a woman's vagina at the time such an egg is in the Fallopian tubes, it is attracted to the egg, penetrates it, and conception has begun. As soon as a spermatozoon has thus penetrated an egg, no other spermatozoon can do so. It is normally possible for a woman to be impregnated only for a period of twenty-four to seventy-two hours during each menstrual cycle. This fertile period varies so greatly, however, even within a given woman's pattern, that attempts to regulate pregnancy purely through such calculations are extremely hazardous.

It was once erroneously believed that identical twins are caused by two spermatozoa penetrating an ovum simultaneously. We now know this is impossible. Identical twins, like single babies, are produced by one sperm and one egg; because of an unusual and unpredictable arrangement of chromosomes, however, the initial cell divides into two organisms instead of remaining one. Fraternal or nonidentical twins appear in the very rare instances when both ovaries yield eggs or one releases two eggs in the same month, each being fertilized by a separate sperm. Some of the hormones prescribed by physicians in an attempt to induce conception are capable of stimulating the release of several eggs in the same month, resulting eventually in the birth of as many as five or six children at one time. Seldom, however, do all the progeny thus produced live. An egg which is not penetrated and fertilized passes on down through the vagina or into the abdominal cavity, where it disintegrates.

Unlike the male urethra, there is no one passage in a woman which transports both her urine and her sex secretions. It is only near the mouth of the vagina that the bladder outlet and reproductive channels meet.

One Plus One Equals One

The inexpressible wonder of new life is emphasized by the fact that ten thousand sperm in a single line would extend less than an inch, while three million ova would be required to fill a thimble! Out of such miniscule origins does a whole human being develop. The tiny cell which results from the amalgamation of sperm and egg harbors from its inception everything a man or woman will eventually become—stature, shape, strength, color of eyes and hair, tone of emotional disposition. To be sure, there are wide latitudes of possibility within which environmental factors will exercise their crucial choice. But the inner and outer limits of potentiality are established from the instant of conception.

A fertilized egg normally moves down into the womb, which is to be its home for the ensuing nine months. In the womb a fertilized egg slowly develops into a human infant, obtaining all its nourishment from the mother's body. It was once superstitiously supposed that either sperm or egg at the outset had the appearance of a miniature person, requiring only growth in size during the period of pregnancy. We now know that the initial cell of life does not resemble a completed person at all, that it contains a host of chromosomes and genes which carry the traits the infant is destined to inherit from both parents. As it grows from one cell to an infant ready for birth, the fetus retraces some of the major steps through which life generally evolved on this planet. At one early stage it resembles a fish; later it has somewhat the appearance of an amphibian, then of an ape, finally a human being. Thus is the biological history of Man duplicated in the personal development of each man.

In its first eight weeks a fertilized egg grows 275,000 times heavier than its weight at conception. By the moment of birth its initial weight has increased 851,250,000 times. At the end of its first month the fetus has reached a length of about a quarter of an inch; in the second month its length is increased to approximately an inch, in the third month to three inches, and in the sixth month to a foot. At birth the average fetus is nineteen inches long, though of course in the womb it is curled up compactly.[4]

The uterus is the most gracious hostess possible. Each month it prepares for a possible guest. Prior to and following ovulation, its walls thicken with extra blood supply, enough to nourish a fertilized egg if one arrives. If no egg is fertilized that month, this extra nourishment sloughs off the walls of the womb, passing out through the vagina. This, of course, is the process of menstruation. Unless a woman is pregnant, she menstruates once every twenty-eight days. Some women are so regular they can predict with amazing accuracy the exact day menstruation will commence. Others are erratic, making it difficult to anticipate the precise beginning of their periods. There are wide variations also in how women react to menstruation: some go about their regular routine with no physical inconvenience other than the wearing of a sanitary napkin or tampon; others may suffer severe headaches or cramps and sometimes emotional sensitivities too.

Severe physical pain or emotional turbulence preceding or during a woman's menstrual period may be due to faulty sex education in her earlier years. If her mother or older sister made much negative ado about menstruation—perhaps even referring to it by some such ominous term as "the curse"—her attitude toward it could have become one of foreboding and fear even prior to her own initiation. The same consequence could be caused if she had been reared in such a manner as to resent being a woman, feeling femininity and motherhood to be heavy burdens rather than priceless privileges. A physically and emotionally healthy woman, especially if she realizes the remarkable role of menstruation in the preparation of her body for one of its most glorious functions, should be able to take her monthly period in stride. If she finds it to be a harrowing experience, bringing her too severe a strain, she should seek medical assistance.

A considerate husband will soon discover whether or not his wife requires special tenderness during her menstrual flow and immediately preceding it. If she prefers not to be approached sexually at that time, or is easily angered or hurt, he will make every reasonable effort to meet her needs. Despite the fact that the Bible forbids intercourse during menstruation, if neither mate objects, there is no valid reason to avoid it; this is a matter of personal preference. Intercourse during menstruation should not be attempted, however, if it is distasteful or uncomfortable to either partner. A wife who is unusually sensitive at this time of month is entitled to extra tenderness from her husband; she has no right, however, to misuse her menstrual difficulty as an excuse to keep him at bay an undue number of days.

Menstruation continues to the time of menopause or change-of-life, which occurs in most women between the ages of forty-five and fifty-five. Thereafter it is impossible for a woman to become pregnant. It sometimes happens, however, that a woman who believes herself to have passed beyond the possibility of pregnancy hasn't quite reached that stage yet. A child unexpectedly conceived under this circumstance is often called—with feelings that range from gentle humor to grim desperation—a "change-of-life baby." A woman's capacity to desire and enjoy intercourse extends beyond her menopause; indeed, in some cases a couple's sex life becomes more exciting at this stage of their marriage than it has been before.

In menstruation we find another of the marvelous provisions of nature to which your attention has already been called. This is the only circumstance in which blood flowing from an opening in the human body does not normally clot! Were this not so, the vaginal passage would soon be blocked, the conception and birth of children would be impossible, and before long severe infection would cause death.

People once believed that something unlucky or unclean attended a menstruating woman, making it dangerous to have any close contact with her. This may even be in part the origin of separating the sexes during worship in an Orthodox synagogue. After all, one could never tell which women might be menstruating at a given time. Even so enlightened and intelligent a rabbi as the thirteenth-century Nachmanides wrote:

> It appears to me that in days of yore menstruating women were totally sundered from society. They were not allowed to come near anyone, or to speak

> to anyone, for the ancients knew that their very breath is harmful. It seems that they were kept separate in a tent which was out of bounds to everyone else. There is a saying in the talmudic tractate *Niddah* (the Hebrew word meaning a menstruating woman): "One may not touch a niddah . . ." R. Yochanan says: "It is forbidden to walk behind her, or to tread on the ground where she has trodden. It is likewise forbidden to make use of her labor."

Today we recognize this to be sheer superstition. A menstruating woman is living through a perfectly normal phase of her life. She should be treated and should treat herself as such.

THE TWAIN SHALL MEET

The incomparable experience of sexual intercourse or coitus in human life can be properly appreciated only against a background of how conception takes place among subhuman animals. With some—especially certain fish—after the female has laid eggs outside her body the male—without even seeing her—fertilizes them by depositing on them a substance from his body. In others—chickens, for example—the male sprays a fertilizing fluid onto the female while the egg is still forming within her and before the shell has appeared. The egg thus contains its fertilizing agent within itself. In a number of species the male is almost incidental. There are some male fish who attach themselves permanently like leeches to the body of the female, living out their lives that way for the one and only purpose of being available when fertilization of eggs is needed. Among some insects, once the male has fertilized the female's eggs, he becomes superfluous; either he quietly goes off to die by himself or is immediately devoured by his mate. So far as we know, in none of these procedures is there any sensation of pleasure for the participants; their conduct is purely instinctual, serving only the purpose of propagation.

Among mammals—with the exception of whales—sexual intercourse is physically similar to what we experience in human life, yet there are profound differences. Before describing differences, it is worth noting that certain animals have evolved closer to the human pattern than others. The bald eagle and wild goose, for example, mate for life with only one member of the opposite sex. The wolf—ironically enough in view of our using his name to designate a particularly predatory type of human male—mates with only one female during her life span and will take a second partner only upon the death of the first. A poignant experience was reported in *The New York Times* of July 19, 1965:

> Cairo Baboon Mourns, Dies
>
> CAIRO, July 17—A baboon named Berbesh died Friday of devotion to his mate at the Cairo zoo after 10 days of mourning. The *Egyptian Gazette* reported Saturday that, after the death of Samboo on July 6, Berbesh refused to eat. The zoo said he died of "shock and starvation."

While these instances are fascinating adumbrations of human sexual behavior and emotion, we must not make too much of them. They are still a far cry from the full role of sex in our lives.

Among most mammals, including men, fertilization takes place through intercourse. The penis, enlarged and stiffened by passion, is inserted into the vagina, which also becomes expanded when sexually stimulated. It is then moved back and forth with increasing excitement until the male reaches his climax, known as an orgasm. Ecstatic waves of physical delight pulsate through his genital organs as he ejaculates sperm-bearing semen in excited spurts. Each ejaculation—about a teaspoonful in volume—contains between 200,000,000 and 500,000,000 sperm. There is reason to doubt whether females below the human level are capable of experiencing an orgasm. The friction between the human penis and vagina can produce an orgasm in women, with much the same pleasurable physical sensation as in the case of men, but without any ejaculation. Thus are sperm propelled toward the place where one of them may fertilize a ripened ovum, if one is available. Sperm deposited near the lips of the vagina, without actual penetration by the penis, are capable of swimming toward the Fallopian tubes and there making rendezvous with a waiting egg. It is also possible for sperm which reach the cervix to remain alive there for as long as two days, thus perhaps to fertilize any ovum which arrives during the interlude.

Primitive peoples—though of course they experienced intercourse and their women became pregnant—failed to perceive the connection between the two phenomena. They concocted a variety of fanciful explanations for pregnancy. A tribe in Eastern Australia still holds that girl babies are formed by the moon, boy babies by the wood lizard. In Queensland it is commonly supposed that the thunder-god fashions babies from swamp mud, then places them in a woman's womb. Elsewhere among primitives it is believed that a woman becomes pregnant by sitting over a fire on which a certain kind of fish has been cooked or because she has successfully hunted for a specified species of frog. Judged by geological time, our recognition that it is coitus which causes pregnancy is relatively recent.

We have already referred to the differences between animal and human intercourse, even where the physical procedure is much the same. These differences include the following:

Only among humans do the male and female generally face and see each other during coitus.

Only among humans does intercourse serve purposes other

than propagation of the race. In the animal kingdom it occurs only when the female is ovulating and can be impregnated. At all other times she will resist—if need be, with violence—any attempt by the male to mount her. Intercourse between human mates takes place whenever husband and wife wish to express and at the same time enrich their love. It is not limited either to the time of ovulation or the purpose of propagation.

Only among humans is coitus a spiritual as well as a physical experience. When an impassioned male dog meets a female in heat—which means to say, ovulating and therefore ready for copulation—he goes about his business, experiences an orgasm, injects her with semen, and casually departs. There is no love, no permanent relationship, no anticipation of a family—nothing but gratification or pleasure for him and probably just instinctual fulfillment for her. The next time either of them experiences intercourse it will almost certainly be with a different partner and with no more permanent consequence than before.

Nowhere is the meaning of intercourse as a purely physical experience among animals more vividly illustrated than in the observation of Julian Huxley, eminent British biologist:

> . . . many birds will attempt to mate with a stuffed dead female as readily as with a real live one—provided that it is set up in a certain pose; and the sperm for artificial insemination in cattle and horses can be obtained because the mating urge of bulls and stallions is aroused by suitable dummies as well as by live cows or mares.[5]

There are, to be sure, men and women for whom intercourse means little more than that, but it is questionable whether their sex life can in that event be called truly human. With us, if we wish, intercourse can be an expression not only of physical desire but of emotional tenderness, yearning, compassion, and love. It can leave husband and wife not merely satisfied and spent physically, but more closely bound to one another in their pursuit of the true, the beautiful, and the good. Later we shall expand more fully on this relationship between sex and love in human experience. For the time being, let it simply be noted as the most important of all differences between human and animal coitus.

All three of the foregoing distinctions mark human sex life as superior to that of animals. There is one respect, however, in which it can be more degrading and depraved. We seem to be the only species in which it is possible for the male to overpower the female, forcing himself upon her sexually against her will. In short, only among human beings do we find the contemptible practice of rape. Our sex life can be either incomparably more glorified or unconscionably more debased than that of any other creature on earth. The choice is our own to make.

FOR THE NEWLY-WED

There are a number of additional facts about intercourse which should be known to the bride and groom. For one thing, a variety of positions can be used. The more common ones are: (a) face to face, with the husband lying on top of his wife, supporting his weight on his elbows and knees; (b) the reverse: face to face, with the wife in the prone position; (c) face to face, with the two lying on their sides; (d) the husband approaching his wife from the rear, either as they lie on their sides or with her in a semi-kneeling posture—a position which some couples may prefer despite the fact that it prevents them from seeing each other; (e) the husband sitting on a low, armless chair or stool, his wife astride him.[6]

There is no reason why a married couple should not experiment with more than one position if both of them wish to. Most couples will probably discover one posture which suits them best. It has already been mentioned that occasionally a disparity of size in the male and female genital organs may make a particular position more advisable. It is also desirable, if the woman is very much smaller than her husband or is in the latter months of pregnancy, to utilize a position which minimizes the discomfort to her. An obstetrician should be consulted on when intercourse should be stopped during pregnancy and how soon after childbirth it may safely be resumed. Under normal circumstances abstention is recommended only during the final four weeks of pregnancy and for a month after its termination. Indeed, some obstetricians impose no restrictions on intercourse for the pregnant or recently delivered wife. Each woman would be well advised in this respect to follow the advice of her own physician.

The newly-weds who discover from the very beginning that intercourse is a mutually pleasurable consummation are clearly an exception, not the rule. Like every other aspect of marital happiness, a good sex adjustment comes as the result of correct procedure plus patient trial and error, not as a gift. It takes the average couple weeks, sometimes months, not infrequently as long as a year to achieve the positions, the techniques, the timing which are best calculated to stimulate and satisfy both. There is, however, no one formula of sexual success which will suit everyone. This most intimate of relationships must be worked out for each couple on their own.

Essential to success is an understanding of the differences in sexual nature and need between men and women. Men are both more easily aroused and more simply satisfied. The diagram below will indicate that, while women achieve every bit as high a degree of both desire and pleasure, they are aroused to a readiness for orgasm more slowly. This places the primary responsibility for patience and tenderness at the beginning of their relationship on the husband. If he is concerned only with himself, his own passion and its fulfillment, there can be no sexual mutuality in the marriage.

SEXUAL AROUSAL IN MEN AND WOMEN

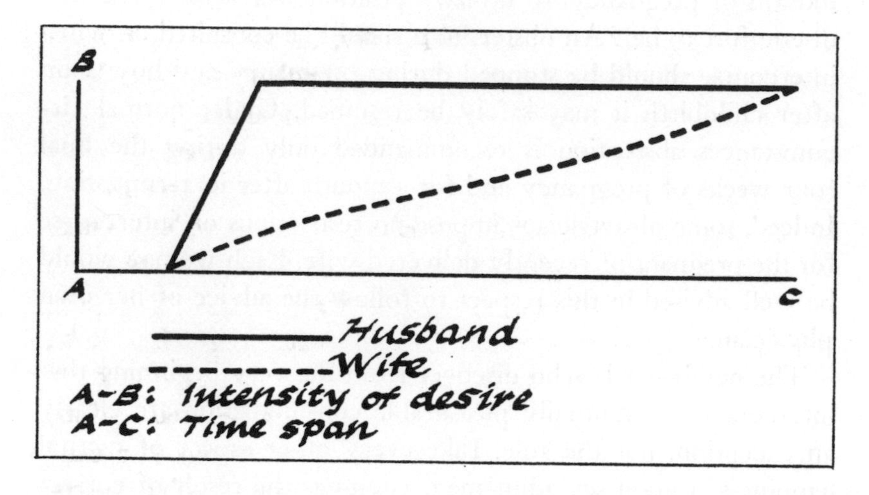

Hence the extreme importance of a husband's restraining himself patiently and indulging in enough loving foreplay to prepare his wife for penetration and orgasm. One of the major misfortunes of our sex mores is that so much petting occurs before marriage and so little afterward. Petting is nature's way of insuring a readiness for intercourse on the part of both male and female; its most appropriate place is the marriage bed. The whispering of sweet endearments, the gentle fondling and kissing of her breasts, manipulation of her clitoris—these are a husband's way of bringing his wife to that pitch of desire and need which will make an orgasm probable for her too. They also afford time for her vagina to expand sufficiently at its slower rate so that it may receive his penis without discomfort or pain. When the size of her vagina has expanded and its outer lips are bathed in liquid secretions from Skene's and Bartholin's glands, she is ready for penetration. No kind of sexual foreplay which is enjoyed by both participants and is obnoxious to neither is reprehensible. The two of them are the only persons in the world with the right to judge what is acceptable sexual procedure for themselves.

Mention should be made, incidentally, of the fact that while most women like to have their breasts fondled as a prelude to intercourse, finding the sensation sexually stimulating, there are occasional exceptions. A loving husband will always quickly discover his wife's preferences and conform to them. In this connection, two gross superstitions should be dispelled. There is no correlation between the size of a woman's breasts and her sexual excitability, any more than there is between the size of a man's penis and the intensity of his sexual urges. Secondly, it is not true that fondling a woman's breasts can cause cancer. No man who approaches his wife lovingly rather than sadistically will ever intentionally be so rough as to give her pain. But cancer is not a by-product of gently fondling the breasts.

The fact that, by his very nature, the initial obligation for patience and tenderness devolves upon the husband does not mean that his wife is devoid of sexual responsibility. Once their trial and error have yielded the best pattern of sexual conduct for them, she should be equally active with him as a participant in their sex life. The ideal situation is one in which both desire intercourse simultaneously. Frequently one will feel the urge first and will be able, without undue effort, to encourage and entice the other. There will be times, obviously, when one mate will have legitimate reason to decline the other's initiative—hopefully, with kindness and tact. In a wholesome, mature marriage, such occasions will be infrequent. A wife should be more than a passive partner in coitus. The initiative can be hers as well as her husband's, and the foreplay which precedes intercourse as well as the act itself should be pursued by both.

Seldom does a man have difficulty in achieving an orgasm. It requires more subtlety and skill for a woman. The ideal objective is for both husband and wife to enjoy orgasms each time they experience intercourse. It is sometimes asserted—even by physicians, who should know better—that a woman is capable of enjoying only emotional satisfaction from intercourse. This is unforgivably false. Both sexes can and should achieve orgasm through intercourse. For both men and women the ecstasy experienced should be physical no less than spiritual. Some couples are able to reach their climaxes simultaneously. It helps if the husband has prepared the way with proper foreplay and if, after penetrating his wife's vagina, he lets her take the initiative, trying to hold back his own climax until she is ready for hers. Even where this proves to be impossible, however, it is important that she be stimulated to the point of orgasm too. It is emotionally unfair and biologically explosive for a man to have his orgasm, then to leave his sexually aroused wife short of fulfilling her needs. If the wife does not reach her climax as a result of contact of the penis with her vagina, it can be induced by sensitive manual manipulation of her clitoris. Most women have their way of "signalling" the imminence of an orgasm. A wise husband learns to recognize such signs and to act accordingly.

One gynecologist with extensive experience in premarital and marital counseling has estimated that on only two out of five occasions of intercourse does the wife achieve an orgasm. He adds that in his judgment 60 percent of the wives he has examined would not care if they never had intercourse after the first six months of marriage. What a shameful waste of the exquisite delight nature has made possible for both sexes! Sometimes this deficiency is due to inadequate techniques of either husband or wife as lovers, sometimes to a generally anemic relationship between them, sometimes to the failure of the wife to accept joyously her God-given potential for ecstasy in love.

As they approach each other sexually, both spouses are wise to be as attractive and alluring as possible. A sandpaper beard or bad breath or offensive body odor is not calculated to enhance the sexual relationship. At one time physicians recommended that women employ a douche after intercourse, for the purpose either of contraception or feminine hygiene. Most authorities today believe that douching is ineffective as birth control and unnecessary as hygiene. Insofar as it connotes that there is something dirty about coitus, something that needs to be washed away, it may even be psychologically damaging. A thorough washing of her external genitals is all a woman really needs to keep clean.[7]

New Knowledge

A further complication in the sexual satisfaction of women centers on the mysterious role of the clitoris in orgasm. Before marriage it is sexually the most excitable of all female organs, the focal point of orgasm. Some women feel that after marriage a gradual shift occurs, with an increasing degree of excitement located in the vagina instead. Authorities disagree on the relative merits of clitoral or vaginal orgasm.

Recent medical research casts doubts on whether there is actually any such thing as orgasm in the vagina. It has been established that the uterus does in fact contract vigorously during sexual climax, but there is grave doubt whether the vagina does. It may well be that some women have been misled by the spasmodic action of the uterus and by the involvement of their whole bodies in marital orgasm to conclude that the vagina has become their chief center of delight. In all probability the clitoris retains its crucial role permanently.

Even here, however, some of our former impressions have been modified by later studies. It was once supposed that in order for a wife to achieve orgasm her husband must maintain constant contact between his penis and her clitoris. This is a difficult thing to accomplish. We now have reason to doubt whether it is either necessary or desirable. The clitoris can be overly stimulated too. It appears that once a woman has been aroused by either manual or penial manipulation of her clitoris, further contact with the general vaginal area, only indirectly or occasionally with the clitoris itself, may be the most effective means of bringing her to climax. This is one of the things each married couple must ascertain by experimentation for themselves.[8]

Whatever disagreement or doubt may persist regarding the relative value of clitoral or vaginal orgasm, there is unanimous accord that the sexual demands of marriage can be met only if—in whatever way they find personally best for themselves—both husband and wife achieve orgasm in each other's arms.

The afterplay is no less significant than the foreplay. Coitus itself is not an isolated act, but rather the climax of an entire syndrome. What precedes and follows determines the quality of the climax. The husband who—directly after orgasm has been attained—turns over at once to fall asleep or jumps out of bed to raid the refrigerator is, in effect, telling his wife that physical release of tension was really his only aim. Though many men may be unaware of it, their need for a continued expression and demonstration of love after coitus itself has been completed is almost as imperative as that of their wives.

How often do most married couples experience intercourse? No question on so preciously intimate a dimension of personal experience can be answered by generalization. The frequency of intercourse will, of course, depend on the physique, the strength, and the sexual potency of the individuals involved. Naturally, coitus will occur more often in the earliest months and years of marriage—perhaps, on the average, two to four times a week—than later. The absolute number of times per week or month is less important than the need for both marriage partners to desire each other and for both to enjoy intercourse whenever they have it.

A final comment is in order before we close this chapter. Our emphasis in Chapter V on the importance of open and honest lines of communication between husband and wife is especially pertinent in their sexual relationship. There is unfortunately reason to believe this is not always the case. Several studies of marriage indicate that the average husband believes his wife reaches orgasm more often than she actually does. They disclose also that most wives estimate the frequency of intercourse at an appreciably higher rate than do their husbands. Whatever this shows about the relative enjoyment of coitus by the respective partners in marriage, it certainly bespeaks an inexcusable clouding of communication between them.

Husbands and wives should not play games of pretense with each other. If she is not achieving orgasm, if either or both are failing to feel fulfillment in their sex relations, it is essential that they convey the truth to each other. Only thus can they lovingly experiment together toward better results. The one who pretends to a satisfaction he doesn't really experience is doing no favor either to his partner or himself. Both are entitled to the fulfillment of their love in mutual sexual satisfaction. By the proper kind of knowledge and effort, they can achieve it.

««««««« 8 »»»»»»»

Sex and Love

OUR PREVIOUS COMMENTS ABOUT THE DIFFERENCE BETWEEN sex and love, as well as the correct causal relationship between them, require expansion. No other kind of confusion is more destructive of a gratifying and creative marriage. Sex is no more synonymous with love than is the heart with the human body. In each case the part, while essential to the whole, is itself far less than the whole. We must be careful neither to minimize nor to exaggerate the role of sex in love. Above all, we must scrupulously avoid assuming the two to be identical.

Harlan Ellison titled his recent short story collection *Love Ain't Nothing But Sex Misspelled.*[1] As a device for capturing attention, this may be successful. As a statement of fact, it is both misleading and harmful. Though inseparably related in marriage, love and sex are by no means the same.

We have already referred to the fact that in human life intercourse is potentially an experience far superior to what it is on the animal level. This potential, however, is not realized by all who call themselves human. Coitus is not the only expression of love between husband and wife; nor is every instance of coitus an evidence of love. One of the serious mistakes of the Kinsey reports is their reduction of all sex experience to sheer quantity. Sexual fulfillment is measured entirely by the number of so-called *outlets* experienced, as if each orgasm is qualitatively similar to every other. The word *love* does not appear even once in forty-eight pages of index to the basic Kinsey volumes!

A man who is masturbating experiences an orgasm but not love. A fiend who rapes a child also achieves an orgasm; it manifests anything but love. A man who reaches an orgasm with his wife may be as self-centered as the masturbator, as sadistic as the raper, or superbly loving. No one has understood the qualitative dimension of coitus better than the distinguished psychiatrist, Dr. Karl Menninger:

> The orgasm of a terrified soldier in battle, that of a loving husband in the arms of his wife, that of a desperate homosexual trying to improve his masculinity, and that of a violent and sadistic brute raping a child are not the same phenomena. The muscles and nerves and secretions may be the same but the orgasms are not the same, and the sexuality is not the same.[2]

Sexual satisfaction, in short—outside or within marriage—can be good or bad, desirable or degrading, wholesome or diseased.

The tendency to equate sex with love is deplorable. It is a gross distortion to call intercourse "making love." A popular magazine hit painfully close to much of our current confusion when it published a cartoon in which an ardent young man says to the rumpled and disarrayed girl he is passionately embracing: "Why speak of love at a time like this?"

Our society too often promotes sex on its lowest and cheapest level. Lurid ads, revealing dress, erotic entertainment—all conspire to impress upon us the purely sensual aspects of sex, rupturing it brutally from everything that makes it human rather than bestial. No less corrosive is the influence of those who would convince us that sex is only a physiological urge, comparable to hunger or an itch and as easily satisfied. They overlook the fact that civilized people accept certain restraints even in the way they eat or scratch themselves. This evaluation of sex, moreover, settles for a stage of evolutionary development reached a million or more years ago.

We are sometimes told that the exercise of control in the satisfaction of our sexual urges can be harmful to mental health. No psychologically literate person would deny man's enormous need for sexual release or the value of wholesome sex fulfillment in his striving for mental as well as physical well-being. But man has other needs too, on which the sometimes delicate balance between illness and good health hinges. Among them is his need to be truly human, to match with his attitudes and behavior the level of evolution he has already attained. A rock is fulfilled just by being; nothing more is required in order for it to satisfy its *rockness*. A dog, rooted to one spot of earth, restricted to the immobility of the rock, would not have fulfilled its *dogness*. Grass justifies itself simply by sprouting a green blade; no more is expected of it. A rose bush restricted to the level appropriate for grass, limited only to the production of green stems, would have failed to achieve its *roseness*. All of which means that each product of evolution must be itself, must actualize its potential, must realize its margin of superiority over the stages of development which preceded it. A man cannot achieve emotional health if he settles for being less than a man. In addition to following all the environmental prescriptions recommended by Freudian psychoanalysis, to be a healthy *man* he must find out who he is and strive to be more than an animal.

The most perceptive of our psychoanalysts themselves are aware of this. Thus Erich Fromm has written:

> The complete satisfaction of all instinctual needs is not only not a basis for happiness; it does not even guarantee sanity.[3]

Dr. Povl W. Toussieng, a Danish psychiatrist at the Menninger Clinic, has expressed a similar conviction:

> The history of mankind is man's struggle against his impulses. He has never completely won that struggle and there are many defeats, but we cease to be human if we merely give in to our impulses.[4]

All of which adds up conclusively to the fact that not every orgasm is conducive to mental or emotional health. Only those which are expressive of man at his best, which emerge out of truly human love, can contribute to our long-range welfare.

Judaism has excelled in understanding the subtle but immensely important relationship between sex and love. It is more than a linguistic coincidence that the Hebrew Bible uses the word ידע (*yada*)—meaning *knew*—for intercourse. Thus we read, in Genesis: "Now the man knew his wife Eve and she conceived and bore Cain. . . ." Our ancestors knew that coitus on the human level was meant by God and nature to be something more than just physical contact and release. It involves two individuals *knowing* each other—respecting and caring for each other deeply in both physical and spiritual dimensions—loving each other maturely enough to desire a permanent sharing of their lives and partnership in the creation of new life.

The eminent Jewish philosopher, Martin Buber, is responsible for articulating the distinction in human relations between "I-It" and "I-Thou." "I-It" means treating another person as if he were only a thing. If I move a chair aside because it stands in my way, there is an "I-It" relationship between the chair and myself. It makes no difference to the chair where it is placed or how often it is moved. But if I rudely bump you because you happen to be in my way, it does make a difference to you. You are a "Thou," not an "It"; you are a human being, with feelings, fears, hopes, and needs very much like my own. I have no right to manipulate or use you for my own purposes if they do not coincide with yours. I must relate myself to you on an "I-Thou" basis. To fail this is to act as if only I were created in God's image, not you. And in the last analysis, to treat you as if you were only an impersonal means for the satisfaction of my needs degrades myself too.

In no sphere of interpersonal relationships is this truer or more imporant than in sex. Within or outside marriage, when one person exploits another only for the gratification of his own sensual desires or the inflation of his own ego, he has violated one of the most precious principles of Judaism and of sound human relations.

What does all this mean to the bride and groom? That their sexual relationship must at all times express and enrich their love. That coitus is something they do *with* each other, not *to* each other. That they cannot hope to achieve a good sex relationship if either approaches it from the perspective of: what's in it for *me?* . . . how can I meet *my* needs? . . . how can *my* desires be satisfied? The sex life of husband and wife must be a paradigm of their entire love relationship. Consistently we have asserted that love is distinguished from infatuation by its emphasis on receiving through giving. It follows that the person truly in love must be as desirous of giving an orgasm to his mate as to experience one himself—not just because it affords him a sensation of manipulative power, but because he cannot be happy in his own orgasm unless he is also extending the same kind of joy to the one he loves.

Intercourse between mates must be consistent with every other aspect of their relationship. They cannot expect to neglect or ignore each other generally, to indulge in selfishness or abuse at all other times, yet to enjoy a good sex life in bed. That kind of coitus may be normative for animals, surely not for men and women. This is one of several areas where women are generally more sensitive and subtler than men. Often a husband will desire intercourse directly after a marital quarrel—either to appease his guilt or to ritualize the reconciliation. At this point his wife is likely to want no part of his proposal. For her even more than him, each act of intercourse is inextricably related to the totality of their relationship, especially to the incidents and mood of the immediately preceding moments.

The intercourse-quotient of a couple will be no higher than the general quality of their interpersonal relationship. Sex cannot be the only level on which they possess intimate contact. Their mutual ecstasy through coitus will be precious precisely in the proportion that it supplements their many other avenues of intimacy. Thus do they enhance their sex life in the present, while at the same time establishing firm foundations for an abiding love which will bless them long beyond their years of intercourse.

Only Theory?

Intellectual understanding and emotional acceptance of the proper relationship between sex and love is indispensable for the making of a happy marriage. But this is more than just a matter of theory. Such understanding is a link in a chain, both preceded and followed by other behavioral links. Which means to say that your evaluation of sex as you approach your marriage is colored by your handling of sex in the past and must influence, in turn, your sexual behavior in the future. No one of us can completely divorce himself from his past. Unless we make a deliberate, substantial effort to the contrary, we carry our premarital patterns of sex conduct with us into marriage. It is essential, therefore, that we try to understand the past in order to confront the future intelligently and wisely.

The ineluctable implication of all that has been said about

the relationship between sex and love in human life is that intercourse should be reserved for one's marriage partner. No useful purpose can be served by indulging here in a long argument favoring premarital chastity. You stand now on the threshold of marriage. You and your future mate have either been chaste or not; the clock cannot be stopped, nor the calendar turned back. The few words we devote to this subject, then, are written not in a spirit of recrimination or reproach, but to offer encouragement to those whose previous behavior has been consistent with human sex experience at its best, and to open the way to correction and growth for others.

Too much of the case for chastity in the past has been centered on the negative reasons for it: the twin dangers of pregnancy and of venereal disease. It has been facetiously summarized in quasi-poetry as follows:

> There was a young lady named Wilde,
> Who kept herself quite undefiled
> By thinking of Jesus
> And social diseases
> And the fear of having a child.

While it would be irresponsibly naive to discount these negative reasons altogether, to deny that despite many scientific advances they still trap more than a few young people in unmitigated tragedy, there are much sounder grounds for favoring premarital chastity by both sexes.

It is extremely difficult to indulge in sexual activity on a lower level for several years before marriage, then suddenly to transform the same physical experience to a different and higher level. The young person who yields to the temptation of experimenting sexually with a variety of partners is becoming acquainted with coitus only in a physical, animal way. He or she is destructively divesting sex of its spiritual association with love. His early fumblings, moreover, are almost certain to occur in the worst possible circumstances: furtively, hastily, fearfully, with pervasive overtones of guilt. Because of these distractions, even the purely physical pleasure of intercourse is likely to be impaired. His earliest impressions of coitus will probably be inadequate and incomplete, perhaps even disillusioning and grim. Far from having an advantage as he approaches the marriage bed, he may have a good deal of erasing and correcting to do.[5]

There is good reason to look askance at the popular assumption that premarital sexual experience makes one a better husband or wife. The logic here is no more valid than to say that the more one reads cheap, vulgar literature in his teens, the more likely will he be to appreciate and enjoy the best of books later. The kind of sex experience one gains from premarital indulgence is precisely the opposite of what coitus ought to mean in marriage. Sexual adjustment, in any event, is so intensely intimate that, even physically, accommodation to one woman is no guarantee of similar success with another; it may even make such success more difficult. Dr. Aaron Rutledge has written wise words:

> To a marked degree, sexual adjustment is something that happens between two particular people, not to people in general.[6]

There is, moreover, reason to doubt the oft-repeated assertion that premarital intercourse makes for a better sexual adjustment in marriage. This may well be true in the initial stages of marriage—due either to the effect of previous experience or to the fact that the individuals involved are more highly sexed than others. But studies both in this country and England suggest that in their sexual adjustment those who are virgins on their wedding days eventually surpass those who are not.[7]

Sober research by competent social scientists tends to confirm the theoretical premise that premarital chastity is an asset in the search for marital happiness. A few of the many authentic experts whose extensive studies have led them in this direction have expressed their conclusions in these words:

> . . . husbands and wives with no experience of premarital intercourse have the higher probability of marital success, whereas couples in which husband or wife had premarital relations with spouse and others have the lower probability.[8]
>
> (Dr. Ernest W. Burgess and Dr. Paul Wallin)

> One's chances of marital happiness are at present favored by the selection of a mate who has not had intercourse with any other person.[9]
>
> (Dr. Lewis M. Terman)

> Investigations of happiness in marriage indicate that those who were virgins at the time of marriage or who had had intercourse only with the person they eventually married were happier on the average than those who did not fall in either of these two categories.[10]
>
> (Dr. Clarence Leuba)

If, then, you and your future mate have both remained chaste, all other things being equal, you have the advantage. Your opportunity to experiment and learn together, to taste of a wondrously new excitement for the first time, to associate coitus from the beginning only with love, to grow toward fulfillment by sharing both successes and failures—all this gives you a priceless margin over others.

AND IF NOT?

But suppose either of you has already had intercourse. Does that doom your marriage from the start? Not at all. It simply means that awareness of your disadvantage must induce you to special effort toward overcoming it. Among the characteristics of maturity we catalogued several chapters back was a capacity to learn from mistakes. Nowhere is this more necessary than in the correction now of any faulty patterns of sexual conduct which you may already have acquired. If you have practiced intercourse only as release from physical tension, separate and apart from feelings of tenderness and lasting love, you must attempt from the very outset of your marriage to elevate your sexual conduct to a higher and nobler level. If, in the past, intercourse has represented for you only an instrument of power to reinforce your masculinity or a magnet for the attraction and possession of male affection, now you and your mate must together attempt to give it a different meaning. If you have sought sexual satisfaction previously in several directions, now you must concentrate every bit of your effort, zeal, diligence, and love toward one and only one partner—your husband or wife. Your responsibility now is not to wallow in self-pity or remorse, but to convert yesterday's errors into tomorrow's hopes. It may take prodigious effort, but it can be done.

A special word of warning is in order on this point. The earlier comment that we tend to carry into marriage our premarital attitudes and behavior patterns applies with urgent emphasis to the relationship between premarital indulgence and adultery. Contrary to a good deal of popular superstition, the man or woman who has not remained chaste is more likely—we repeat, *more* likely—to engage in adultery than the one who has been willing to wait. Extensive research by Dr. Ira L. Reiss conclusively demonstrates this to be true. After presenting the evidence, Dr. Reiss explains it as follows:

> These men separated sexual behavior and affection in their premarital coitus; it is therefore not difficult for

> them to engage in extramarital coitus purely for pleasure. . . . This sort of training may well be conducive to double-standard extramarital intercourse in later years.[11]

Other researchers have arrived at similar conclusions. Thus Dr. Lewis M. Terman, one of the earliest pioneers in the scientific study of marriage, inquired into the percentage of husbands who often felt a desire for extramarital intercourse. Among men who had remained chaste before marriage, he found less than 10 percent in this category; among those who came to marriage as noncelibates, the proportion was 21.7 percent.[12] More or less lost in a multitude of more spectacular conclusions announced by the famous Dr. Kinsey is data disclosing the same pattern to prevail among women. Only 13 percent of those who were virgins at the time of their weddings had experienced one or more extramarital adventures by the age of forty. Of those who were not virgins when married, the comparable figure was 29 percent!

Whether one interprets these data in terms of a causal relationship or believes the type of person who yields to sexual experimentation before marriage is likely also to feel the same compulsion after marriage, the fact remains that a positive correlation does exist between premarital intercourse and adultery.

This correlation should be permitted to speak for itself, without either exaggeration or denial. It points obviously to the need for exceptional caution, precisely by those who have already experienced intercourse prior to their weddings. The golfer who has already acquired a faulty swing faces a far more difficult task in correcting it than one who learns the proper swing from the beginning. In like manner—though far more consequentially—the bride or groom who approaches marriage with the wrong kind of sexual experience or attitude must expend greater corrective effort than one who commences with a clean slate. The first prerequisite for such effort is an honest confrontation of the facts.

Closer to Home

Let us assume that neither you nor your future mate has experienced intercourse. You are in love and engaged. It may be a matter of months, or weeks, or only of days before your scheduled wedding. It would be naive to pretend that you have not already experienced some degree of physical intimacy. Is it still necessary or advisable that you draw the line this side of intercourse? In his implicit recommendation of premarital chastity, Dr. Leuba credited an advantage to those who are virgins or "who had intercourse only with the person they eventually married." This might seem to flash a green light for those who are engaged. Does it?

No one can honestly deny that such a situation is significantly different from promiscuity. There is merit in the assertion that the formality of a few words spoken by a rabbi exerts no magic in the living and loving relationship between man and woman. Yet sober reflection will reveal that even the element of truth thus expressed is an oversimplification. The entire wedding ceremony—not just the formulae pronounced by the rabbi—symbolizes a total and permanent commitment of husband and wife to each other. Intercourse assumes its proper and proportionate place in such a commitment. During the period of engagement, the sex relationship is likely to remain out of context.

Hence I would recommend chastity even for the engaged couple. Jewish tradition agrees. Referring to the fact that if a cup of wine has already been tasted, it is too late to pronounce a blessing over it, the Talmud states: "A woman is like the cup of blessing: if one has tasted it, it becomes faulty."[13] I rest my case, however, on more than a quotation from the past.

The danger of intercourse resulting in either pregnancy or a venereal disease is no less with an engaged than with an unengaged couple. Most states require blood tests before a marriage license can be issued; there is no such protection for the couple who "jumps the gun." The association of one's earliest experiences of intercourse with furtiveness and guilt and the improbability of a successful and mutually gratifying sexual adjustment under these circumstances are scarcely less for the engaged couple than for others. And there is always the very real, sometimes corrosive and destructive suspicion: *if with me, with how many others before?* An easy intellectual dismissal of such doubt now is no guarantee that it may not erupt as a gnawing, nagging obsession later. Many husbands and wives have discovered in dismay that they were not so "emancipated" as they had thought.

To these facts should be added the frequency with which engagements are broken. One estimate has it that half the engagements in the United States are terminated short of marriage. It is a rare year in which I myself do not have at least one wedding ceremony cancelled after all arrangements have been made and the invitations issued. In one instance the cancellation came just forty-eight hours before the scheduled ceremony. Where the couple has already indulged in intercourse, albeit only with each other, their relationship may be complicated in any of three ways. First, it is possible for an oppressive burden of guilt to be carried into the marriage, with permanently contaminating effect. Second, the very fact that a couple has indulged in intercourse can increase the probability of their engagement being broken. We have already referred to the sensitive, delicate relationship between love and hate. Guilt or lack of respect is often the precipitating agent in upsetting the balance. There is an example of this in the biblical book of Samuel II, where we are told that King David's son, Amnon, felt so passionate a desire for his half-sister, Tamar, that he conspired to be with her alone and begged her to submit to him. When she refused, he raped her. No sooner had he achieved his desire than we read: "Then Amnon hated her with exceeding great hatred; for the hatred wherewith he hated her was greater than the love wherewith he had loved her." The writer of that tale possessed profound psychological insight. He knew that under such circumstances a person often projects his own guilt upon his partner, as a result of which deep love turns into even deeper hate. The third possibility poses a paradox. While some engagements may indeed be terminated because of premature participation in coitus, others which should in fact have been ended are prolonged for the same reason. This is likely to occur when two people who have reason to doubt their suitability as permanent partners blind themselves to their very cogent apprehensions because, consciously or unconsciously, they feel they have already gone too far to contemplate a change of course.

All in all, then, the wisest choice would appear to favor chastity for the engaged couple too. The studies of Burgess and Wallin substantiate this view. Using a scale of their own invention, by which to measure the success of engagements, they have concluded that "the engagement success score of persons who had intercourse tend to be lower than the scores of those who were continent."[14]

Dr. Max Levin confirms this conclusion from a psychiatric point of view:

> There are sincere and high-minded young people who . . . see no reason to wait for the wedding night,

> and they wonder why they can't start their relations now—a kind of buy now, pay later program. But this, too, is a mistake.
>
> There are cases where intercourse before the wedding leads to trouble. The bridegroom, sometimes as early as the honeymoon, begins to feel a certain contempt for his bride. He thinks of the golden days when he courted her, and recalls with a feeling of shock that he didn't find it too hard to induce her to go to bed with him. The bride, too, is filled with contempt—contempt for herself. She gave in too easily to her lover's demands. She begins to hate him, feeling that he had taken unfair advantage of her ardent nature and her love for him. These destructive emotions grow, like a blister on the toe that turns to sepsis, and the once happy couple, now embittered, begin to wonder how they ever got the idea that they were meant for each other.
>
> The safest course for an engaged couple is to wait until they are married. A young man who respects his fiance will not pressure her to go to bed with him. And she in turn will understand that his self-restraint is a sign of his respect and devotion, and she will love him all the more.[15]

One important question remains regarding intercourse during the period of engagement. Isn't it wise for a couple to test their sexual compatibility before marriage rather than to discover afterward that they have made a mistake? Let it be said first in response that not even a successful premarital adjustment can obviate the very real possibilities of subsequent suspicion and guilt, to which reference has previously been made. The fact is, however, that seldom will such premature experimentation actually test what it is intended to disclose. We have already alluded to the fact that the circumstances usually surrounding premarital intercourse are scarcely propitious. A couple experiencing coitus in marriage has everything going for them. A couple impatiently anticipating marriage has nearly everything going against them. They may seem to have failed when in fact and with patience they might have achieved satisfying success. They have made the gross mistake of treating sex as if it were isolated from an entire syndrome of associations with which it must be identified in a truly human love relationship.

To Tell or Not to Tell

Should bride and groom be honest with each other regarding any intercourse they may have experienced with others? Wise men differ in their responses to this sometimes excruciating question. The one thing on which most of them will agree is that the answer must in each case be attuned to the individuals involved. Certainly a difference must be recognized between a case of promiscuity and a single "slip" which never recurred.

Some will be generally disposed not to look for trouble. They may even suspect that the truth-teller is either masochistically seeking to punish himself or sadistically striving to force the other to share his burden of guilt. They may add that a match which might otherwise have yielded a good marriage may be broken off if a proposed mate is emotionally unable to cope with such heavy truth.

Others—without denying an aspect of validity in this reasoning—will advise nonetheless that full truth be told. They will ask whether the partner who chooses to suppress past experience will be able permanently to surmount all resultant guilt, whether subsequent suffering or tragedy may not be attributed to the secret indiscretions, what the consequence will be of previous experience being inadvertently discovered at a later date.

It would be foolish—and probably futile—to disguise my own preference for the second of these alternatives. If marriage is to come even reasonably close to the ideal portrayed in these pages, to a total sharing of life, does it not follow that its basic premise must be truth? Would anyone doubt that if either partner knew himself to be sterile or incurably diseased or uninsurable, he would confront an inescapable moral obligation to disclose this information prior to his wedding? The only basis on which secrecy can be upheld regarding previous sexual experience would be the claim that this is less important to a couple's marital welfare than their health in general. Those who opt for full disclosure about previous sexual experience in general would, of course, feel even more emphatic about any past incidence of pregnancy, abortion, or venereal disease.

Granted that some matches may be terminated by the exercise of truth. The inescapable question then remains: How good would these marriages have been in any event? The time for truth, however, is not just before a scheduled wedding. If told at a much earlier juncture in the relationship, preferably when it has first begun to be serious, it will either minimize the pain of parting or bind the individuals into an even firmer union.

THOU SHALT NOT—

Our only substantive reference thus far to the subject of adultery has been the evidence that premarital irresponsibility increases the probability of similar behavior after the wedding vows have been pronounced. There is need, however, to face adultery more directly, to acknowledge that its incidence has probably increased, and to recognize that its effect on any marriage is likely to be disastrous. The Seventh Commandment is not the only prohibition of adultery in Jewish tradition. Among the objects of covetousness against which the Tenth Commandment warns us is our neighbor's wife. The writer of Proverbs, referring to "the evil woman" and "a harlot," warns his readers not to lust after them:

> Can a man take fire in his bosom,
> And his clothes not be burned?
> Or can one walk upon hot coals,
> And his feet not be scorched?
> So he that goeth in to his neighbor's wife;
> Whosoever toucheth her shall not go unpunished.

Similarly, the Prophet Hosea makes it clear that the law against adultery applies to men no less than women. He cautions his listeners that they cannot expect their women to be punished for such offences while they themselves are equally guilty:

> I will not punish your daughters when they commit harlotry,
> Nor your daughters-in-law when they commit adultery;
> For you yourselves consort with lewd women,
> And you sacrifice with harlots.

The Talmud too underscores the importance of sexual faithfulness between husband and wife: "In marriage a person reserves his partner for himself as a sacred object."[16] It may well be that originally this restriction applied only to wives. In our day of sexual equality, however, it is valid for both marriage partners.

In the earliest stages of Jewish legal development adultery was a crime for which only women were indicted; men were apparently free to indulge in extramarital adventures. The fifth chapter of Numbers prescribes a grim, humiliating public test to be imposed on any married woman suspected of having cohabited with a man other than her husband. The Talmud, obviously perceiving the unfairness, mitigated the severity of the biblical procedure. It decreed that a wife could not be convicted of adultery unless it were proven that she had been warned in the presence of two witnesses not to have any communication with the man in question, yet had afterward met him secretly under circumstances conducive to the crime.[17]

Rabbinic law also made it clear that men were not immune from the charge of adultery. Thus, one who was suspected of having experienced coitus with another man's wife was not permitted to marry her if she were subsequently widowed or divorced![18] It was decreed, moreover, with reference to the biblical test of bitter waters intended to expose a woman's infidelity:

> Only when the man is himself free from guilt, will the waters be an effective test of his wife's guilt or innocence, but if he has been guilty of illicit intercourse, the waters will have no effect.[19]

This excursion into ancient Jewish tradition would be incomplete without acknowledging that legally a husband could be convicted of adultery only if his sexual exploit had been with a married woman. Extramarital intercourse with a partner neither married nor betrothed was frowned upon, but not considered a crime. This was one of many kinds of evidence attesting to a double standard of sexual ethics.

Our modern knowledge and insight can tolerate no such dichotomy. A man must be no less sensitive to the damage he inflicts on his wife and himself, or on the future marriage of a single girl, than to the harm he does to another man.

The most elementary argument against adultery is, of course, that it threatens the stability of the family and makes it impossible for children to be sure of their male parentage. An even more persuasive approach emerges from a proper understanding of the meaning of love and its relationship to sex. This is why we introduce the subject here, only after exploring the true significance of sex and love on the highest human level. Surely if intercourse climaxes a total physical-plus-intellectual-plus-emotional-plus-spiritual partnership, rather than merely a transitory physical liaison, it must be limited to one's husband or wife. Any exception to that rule will be destructive both of the individuals involved and of their love.

The crude insensitivity which often accompanies adultery is grimly illustrated by the comment of a husband whose wife had come to me for counseling. To her remonstrances against his confessed infidelity, he responded: "You have no cause to complain! I'm not depriving you of a thing: you still get the same allowance. . . . I never even leave the house to be with my mistress until you're asleep." The callousness of other unfaithful husbands and wives may not be quite so gross, but the difference is likely to be one only of degree.

Among contemporary writers Dr. George N. Shuster has put this aspect of the problem very well:

> . . . we are coming slowly to recognize that the psychological impact of infidelity—on the man and the woman involved, on the injured partners and particularly on the children of the married couple—is far greater than we had previously thought. Anyone who thinks that adultery, gone into however lightly and however gracefully, cannot completely shatter the life of the injured partner is terribly mistaken.[20]

To assume that monogamy is just one of many convenient but arbitrary arrangements—not much better or worse than others—imposed upon the individual by an authoritarian society is miserably to misunderstand the meaning of love and marriage. A faithful one-to-one relationship between husband and wife has been found by millennia of experimentation to be the very best plan possible for the preservation of love and the achievement of happiness. It is arbitrary only in the sense that it conforms to human nature at its best and cannot be violated, therefore, with impunity. The dismal shadow of even one indiscretion can blight a marriage for years.

I myself have been approached by the "illegitimate" daughter of a prominent and respected community leader, in the hope that I would intercede for her with her father. She had already attempted several times through the years to see him personally but without success. So far as I am aware, no one else in the city knew of this episode out of the man's past; but he knew it himself. What must that knowledge have done to his marriage? To his emotional balance? To his conscience? To his relationship with his wife and children? Many odd aspects of that man's behavior, inexplicable and mysterious to the community at large, are understandable, at the very least, to me and to himself. More than once I have wondered what he would give to erase this episode from the record of his memory.

Incidentally, the word *illegitimate* was placed in quotation marks above to indicate that in fact there is no such thing as an illegitimate child. Every child is legitimate and innocent. It did not ask to be born. It obviously had no control over the circumstances of either its conception or its birth. There are illegitimate parents, not children.

Dr. Frank Caprio, a practicing psychiatrist, has made an extensive study of marital infidelity. He concludes that it is nearly always a manifestation of illness:

> *Infidelity, like alcoholism or drug addiction, is an expression of a deep, basic disorder of character.* It is often a symptom of a depression or unhappiness unresolved since childhood. It has its roots in the insecurity of the individual childhood. Infidelity is more likely to occur among the neurotic than the so-called normal.

After thus tracing the probable origin of adulterous conduct, Dr. Caprio writes effectively also of its consequences:

> Men and women given to infidelity often become victims of chronic insomnia or indigestion or a host of other psychosomatic symptoms of repressed guilt.[21]

Fantasy and Fact

Even a man or woman who is partner to a perfectly wonderful marriage can be tempted on occasion to indulge in intercourse with someone other than his mate. Much depends on environmental circumstances as well as the nature of the individuals concerned and of their marriage. In this respect there is a vast difference between the teachings of Judaism and those of Christianity or, at least, of Jesus. In the New Testament (Matthew 5:28) he is reported to have said that a man who even thinks about having intercourse with someone other than his wife is guilty of adultery. Judaism does not confuse thought with action. It recognizes realistically that a temptation which is resisted is quite different from one to which we yield. True, there would probably be something psychopathic in a person who was continually being tempted to have an extramarital affair. It must also be recognized that a sequential connection exists between thought and action. Our rabbis cautioned against evil thoughts by day on the ground that they can lead to evil deeds at night. And among the sins for which we request forgiveness on Yom Kippur are those we may have committed בהרהור הלב (*b'har-hur ha-lave*)—"through the evil meditations of the heart." Notwithstanding this, however, Judaism does realistically recognize that there is a difference between fantasy and action. In a later chapter we shall consider other differences between the attitudes of Judaism and Christianity toward marriage and sex.

In a good marriage—as in life generally—the wise person tries to establish prudent lines of policy in advance of specific crises. Husbands and wives will talk about such matters freely and will reach joint decisions on the basis of what they both want out of marriage and of the long-range effects of unfaithfulness on their relationship to each other. Both will then remember that free will is a flexible commodity. Each step we take either limits or enlarges our freedom for the next. The husband who invites his secretary out for drinks and dinner, the wife who accepts the luncheon invitation of an old boyfriend, have—both of them—appreciably circumscribed their remaining freedom. The delicate balance between indiscretion and control can become so tenuous as to be imperceptibly tipped by the mildest emotional breeze. Only if each decision is made in line with overall policy, with what we earnestly desire the final outcome to be, can we be reasonably confident of success. In the perceptive words of a physician: "The path from flattery to an affair is a short crosscut."[21] This is another instance of the oft-repeated truth that in every decision we gain something and lose something. We cannot have it both ways. No one can clip the coupons of immediate and unlimited sensual pleasure, yet at the same time build the kind of marriage investment which will in the long run yield maximum happiness to his mate and himself.

A final word about adultery: Suppose a man and a woman—both trapped in unhappy marriages—develop an attachment to each other and have reason to believe they could experience a good love relationship. Are they justified in going all the way sexually? Is it not possible that coitus between two such persons who truly love each other could be more ethical and meaningful than between either of them and a mate who is no longer loved? Even an affirmative answer to the second of these questions does not automatically imply a similar response to the first.

Many complications must be confronted by such a couple. For one thing, whatever hope there may still be for repair of either unhappy marriage will be obliterated by their contemplated conduct. A sexual liaison between them could well be the *coup de grâce* for their existing marriage. Sexual side excursions are not consonant with the concentrated and diligent effort required to shore up a wobbly marriage. But even if all such hope be already gone, even if the two of them are in fact compatible and could conceivably enjoy a good permanent partnership, whatever chance they might have for mutual happiness would be impaired by choosing the premature and irresponsible option now. Their love relationship could be tarnished by ineradicable guilt if initiated under such inauspicious circumstances. They would be accountable for whatever injury might come as a consequence to their mates and children. Their actions in the present will soon enough congeal into the indelible impressions of the past. Out of such a contaminated past, menacing specters can reach out like the arms of an octopus to choke whatever chance they might otherwise have had for eventual happiness.

So long as human beings remain fallible, mistakes will be made in marriage as in all areas of conduct. When such a mistake has in fact occurred, when the most conscientious corrective effort has failed, when all hope for a reasonably happy future has been dissipated, the marriage should be dissolved in the most honorable way possible, with the least incidence of injury to all parties concerned. Only the individual who has successfully executed all these steps has earned a moral right to enter upon a new love relationship with someone else. A decent respect for his own integrity and ultimate happiness, even more than for the opinions of others, should compel this course of action.

A mature appreciation of the relationship between sex and love bears many ineluctable implications for our conduct: premarital chastity, improvement of earlier behavior patterns where they have been faulty, sexual restraint during one's courtship and engagement, fidelity to one's mate in marriage itself. Still other implications remain. To these we turn our continuing attention in the next chapter.

«««««««« 9 »»»»»»»»

Both Sides of the Threshold

FOR THE WISE COUPLE, A LONG PERIOD OF PREPARATION PRECEDES marriage. Indirectly this preparation commenced when you were born. From the first moment you rested as an infant in the arms of your mother, you began to learn the difference between acceptance and rejection. During the earliest weeks of life outside the womb, you commenced to experience the happiness which comes from close physical contact with a person who loves you. By their reactions to your first curiosity about your own genital organs, your parents started to teach you something about either the goodness or the evil of sex. And we have already seen that the quality of love you witnessed in your childhood home has had an indelible effect on your own capacity to love. All this is really part of your preparation for marriage.

In a more immediate and direct sense, your period of courtship and engagement has constituted a conscious anticipation of marriage. All this should culminate now—preferably two or three months prior to the wedding—in premarital conferences with both your rabbi and a competent physician who specializes in this field.

Your preliminary meeting with the officiating rabbi should not deal primarily with procedure at the ceremony; these details can easily be communicated in a mimeographed document. It is of far more urgent importance for the rabbi to discuss with you the kind of question we have raised in these pages. The completion of this book will probably leave you with any number of unanswered queries which should be addressed to the rabbi during your conference with him. And the general conclusions you will derive from this volume—concerning the prerequisites for a happy marriage, the spiritual components of love, the contribution of religion to marital success—can be applied personally to you and your intended.

The value of your rabbinic premarital conference will hinge on complete honesty among the participants. Any questions, anxieties, or doubts should be voiced openly. The rabbi should speak to you frankly, even if this means hurting your feelings or blunting your hopes. Whatever serious problems he exposes can be ignored only at your own peril. Of course, the content of your conference should be held in strictest confidence by all. If either you or the rabbi feel that additional conferences are required, as many as may be needed should be scheduled—either with bride and groom together, or with one alone, should that be your preference.

Suppose—after all arrangements have been made with the rabbi, the caterer, the florist—and perhaps even after the invitations have been mailed—your rabbinic premarital conference leaves a residue of doubt concerning the advisability of your marriage? Any embarrassment caused by postponement of your plans will be as nothing compared to the anguish that can come from proceeding without resolving your reservations. The pain of a broken engagement—and I do not for an instant minimize it—is a small price for avoidance of a marriage which is not right. The inconvenience of postponement can yield abundant dividends if the additional time is used for further preparation.

A premarital medical conference is no less valuable than one with your rabbi. Preferably it should be with a gynecologist who will examine the bride, refer the groom to his family physician or a genito-urinary specialist for examination, then meet with bride and groom together. It is wise for the two physicians to consult each other on their findings before the final medical conference occurs. In the rare instances where there are anatomical obstacles to a normal sexual adjustment, a careful examination of both male and female genital systems will reveal them. It will also reveal whether the penis and vagina are compatible in size; if not, the gynecologist can either stretch the vaginal opening or recommend positions for intercourse which are best calculated to succeed. Should the bride possess an unusually tough hymen, this can be either dilated or, in extreme cases, surgically excised with little difficulty or pain. If the bride gives evidence of suffering from pelvic muscle spasms which might prevent successful intercourse, this problem too can be alleviated in advance.

If the physician examining the groom discovers an undescended testicle or a history of glandular infection, he may recommend a sperm analysis. Some circumstances may warrant special attention to the prostate and prostatic fluid. The penis, testicles, and scrotum will, of course, be carefully inspected.

Another factor to which physicians will be alert during their premarital examinations is the blood type of both parties to the contemplated marriage. Without going into technical detail, if the father's blood is RH^{+} and the mother's RH^{-}, the possibility of danger to the baby or its mother is considerably increased. This kind of complication, while relatively rare, should be discovered, where it exists, before marriage.

The importance of premarital medical examinations is evidenced by the fact that thirty-seven states now require them, over and above a blood test. Unfortunately—sometimes tragically!—these laws are implemented with less than admirable diligence. A study of 2500 recently married individuals in Michigan revealed that although 90 percent voiced approval of the law, only thirty-five percent had observed it. In some instances negligent physicians signed the necessary forms without performing an examination; in other cases the signature was forged or false documents were provided by commercial laboratories.[1] In the long run couples who evade this kind of protection are cheating primarily themselves. And perhaps their children.

A medical examination of both partners before marriage is likely to be even more important in the future than it is now. Early in March of 1967, Dr. Charles A. Janeway, physician-in-chief at the Children's Hospital Medical Center in Boston, predicted that gene tests would one day be possible.[2] Such tests could disclose the statistical probability of a particular couple's producing a child that might suffer from a recessive disease which had skipped his parents' generation but remained part of his heredity.

Finally, the physician is the proper person to recommend methods for birth control. Since all birth control techniques require careful instruction to be effective, this is one of the doctor's most essential premarital functions. As in the case of the rabbi, here too there is imperative need for utter honesty during the conference and for additional sessions with the physician if problems remain unresolved.

Both premarital conferences should be utilized not only to fill in gaps in your knowledge but also to talk out openly and frankly any anxieties, fears, or doubts you may harbor—about sex or any other aspect of marriage.

Planned Families

Most authorities are agreed that a bride should not immediately become pregnant. She and her husband owe each other a reasonable length of time to make the necessary adjustments between two complicated personalities before a third is introduced into the picture. Every child has an inalienable right to be born into a happy home. Couples who are having a rough time of it and who contemplate conceiving a child in the hope that this will help solve their existent problems assume a frightful risk. Just as the emotional difficulties of the individual bride and groom should be reasonably resolved before they marry, so their maladjustments together should be brought under control before they conceive a child. Far from diminishing the problems faced by husband and wife, children increase them. Born to parents who are basically unhappy together, babies become the most pitiable victims. They deserve better.

My experience suggests that all couples should wait at least a year—most, perhaps twice that time—before attempting a pregnancy. And after the birth of their first child, others should be spaced according to their financial, emotional, and spiritual capacity to provide adequate nourishment. This means that accurate knowledge of birth control techniques is essential. Added to such knowledge, there must be diligent practice. A very large proportion of unplanned children result, not from the failure of a particular method, but from the fact that it was not used properly. Quite aside from the problems posed by an unwanted child, a fear of possible pregnancy with each attempt at intercourse can prevent bride and groom from achieving the mutual delight to which they are entitled in their sex life.

Contraception can be accomplished in several ways, by no means of equal reliability or value. The methods most commonly used today are: (a) the wearing of a thin sheath called a condom on the penis to prevent entrance of sperm into the vagina; (b) insertion by the female of a diaphragm which covers the opening between vagina and uterus, preventing sperm from moving into the Fallopian tubes; (c) use of a medicinal jelly by the female, as an added precaution along with the diaphragm, in order to kill sperm; (d) ingestion by the female of a pill which prevents ovulation, thus making fertilization impossible; (e) injection of a contraceptive, sperm-killing foam into the vagina prior to intercourse; (f) insertion into the womb surgically of a small plastic or metal ring which, for some reason not yet fully understood, prevents pregnancy.

There have been reports of research on a pill to be consumed by women after intercourse for the purpose of preventing pregnancy. In view of the fact that such medication, if proven effective and safe, would actually prevent not conception, but normal development of the fertilized ovum after conception had actually occurred, the question must be raised whether this would not in fact be a form of abortion rather than contraception. In any event, the efficacy of this procedure remains to be established.

Tiny, microscopic holes in either the condom or diaphragm can permit sperm to reach an egg, thus causing pregnancy despite the use of these contraceptives. There can be overflow seepage of semen from the condom even where no holes exist. A condom can also interfere with the pleasurable sensations attending coitus for both the female and the male. The method used most widely in recent years has been the diaphragm, together with either a contraceptive jelly or foam. The diaphragm must be accurately fitted to each individual woman; she must be instructed to use it properly and to retain it in position at least eight hours after intercourse. Many young brides insert their diaphragms each night before retiring, so that any amorous enterprise which follows need not be interrupted. A properly fitted and accurately infixed diaphragm should cause no discomfort. Increasing numbers of physicians are now recommending the pill, though some doctors feel further research is needed on both the side effects and the long-range results in later life. Where used, the pill must be taken for twenty days of each menstrual cycle, as directed by a competent medical man. Skipping even a single day or commencing to take the pills one day late in the cycle can allow conception to occur.[3]

Because they are woefully unreliable, two so-called birth control methods employed by some couples have not even been listed. One is withdrawal, which means commencing coitus but not completing it; as soon as the male feels his orgasm coming, he quickly withdraws his penis in an attempt to prevent sperm from entering the vagina. There are several dangers to this procedure. First, few men can exercise the necessary degree of self-control under the impact of immediate passion. Second, it is destructive of the pleasure attendant upon intercourse and also unhealthy to interrupt the act at the very moment it reaches normal climax. Third, some sperm frequently begin to issue from the penis even before the onset of orgasm; when this occurs, pregnancy can result despite withdrawal prior to the climax itself. It should be remembered, moreover, that even when sperm are ejaculated outside a woman's body but in the direction of her vagina, they can swim toward the Fallopian tubes, causing conception.

Withdrawal is severely condemned in a biblical passage sometimes mistakenly construed to refer to masturbation. In accordance with existing religious law, Onan was ordered to cohabit with his brother's childless widow in order that she might conceive. "But Onan, knowing that the seed would not count as his, let it go to waste (or: spoil on the ground) whenever he joined with his brother's wife. . . . What he did was displeasing to the Lord, and He took his life. . . ." (Gen. 38:9f.) Whether such dire punishment was meted out because Onan had practiced withdrawal as such, or because he thereby refused to follow the prevailing practice of producing a child to bear his dead brother's name, is open to interpretation. Post-biblical Jewish religious authorities leave no doubt, however, that this passage condemns withdrawal under all circumstances.

The other undependable method is that of rhythm, the one contraceptive procedure sanctioned by the Catholic Church. We have already observed that the only time a woman can become pregnant is during the span of each menstrual cycle when, because ovulation has just occurred, a ripened egg is available. If coitus is limited to the days when no egg is in her Fallopian tubes, it can cause no pregnancy. While this is in theory true, there is so wide a variation in the menstrual cycles of some women that accurate calculation of the safe period becomes extremely hazardous. For that matter, even in women whose menstrual schedule is regular, ovulation can shift back and forth within the cycle, affected by such factors as body temperature, allergies, a cold, or even emotional stress. A further peril emerges from the fact—already mentioned—that it is possible for sperm which reach the cervix when no ripened egg is available to remain alive and potent there for as long as two days. Any ovum which arrives on the scene during that interval may be fertilized.

A mathematical study of the rhythm method, made by Andre J. de Bethune, professor of chemistry at Boston College—a Catholic institution—was published in the December 27, 1963, issue of *Science*. Much of its reasoning and technical methodology are beyond the average nonscientist reader. Its conclusion, however, is both startling and significant. The author has worked out a table of statistical probability which indicates that, even assuming a fertile period as short as only twelve hours out of each menstrual cycle—in fact, only one-half to one-sixth the average length of ovulation—a couple could have intercourse no more frequently than twice each month if they wanted to be reasonably sure, using only the rhythm method, their children would be spaced two years apart. To have four years between children, their coitus would have to be limited to once a month. This means that in addition to its unreliability for the purpose of birth control, the rhythm method also imposes an intolerable strain on the sex life of a married couple by placing "out of bounds" for sexual purposes not only the days of menstrual flow but also those when conception can occur.

Dr. Robert E. Hall, who directs the birth control clinic of Columbia-Presbyterian Medical Center in New York City, has calculated that in order to achieve maximum success in family planning through exclusive use of the rhythm method, a woman whose menstrual periods are regular would have to refrain from intercourse not less than ten days each month. This, in addition to the actual days of her menstrual flow, if she and her husband chose to refrain then. A woman whose cycle is irregular would have to abstain for a longer span each month.[4]

Dangerous Alternatives

A careful implementation of contraceptive advice received from a competent medical authority will provide a very high degree of protection against unplanned pregnancies. Occasionally, however, even with the most diligent procedure a wife will unintentionally conceive. What to do then?

The immature couple will be tempted to vent their disappointment and apprehension by blaming each other. There is obviously no profit in such scapegoating. One of the first wholesome steps should be to discuss the situation with each other and, where possible and desired, with someone whose judgment they trust. This can be a parent, rabbi, physician, or friend. It frequently helps to ventilate one's anxieties in a permissive, objective frame of reference.

A wide variety of drugs may be recommended to the involuntarily pregnant wife. No chemical agent can terminate a pregnancy without risking incalculable damage to fetus, mother, or both. A menstrual period induced by ingesting medication would have occurred anyway. Some drugs, while failing in their intended purpose, may damage the brain of the fetus, eventually causing birth of a retarded child. Rather than resort to any such risk under the impact of panic, the wise couple will realistically evaluate all pertinent medical, emotional, and religious factors involved and try to arrive at the best solution for themselves and the child they have conceived.

The very worst alternative—unless recommended by a conscientious and capable physician—is abortion. This means artificially inducing the fetus to detach itself from the uterus and to pass down through the vagina. Some religions consider this to be a form of murder. Others hold that if a continuation of the pregnancy jeopardizes the mother's life or if there is reason to suspect that a defective or retarded child may be born, abortion is justifiable.

Our tradition views abortion as a difficult and complicated subject. Except for certain dissident sects, only Philo and Josephus among ancient Jewish writers condemned it outright as a capital offense. Though it is quite probable that abortion was practiced by ancient and medieval Jews under carefully stipulated circumstances, the subject is not treated at length in our religious literature until the seventeenth century. The failure of Judaism to reject abortion as categorically as did Christian tradition springs from the fact that our authorities did not regard the unborn fetus as a human being with a soul.

If, therefore, during pregnancy or even the initial phase of childbirth a mother's life is in jeopardy, the unborn child may be sacrificed to insure her survival. Only after the infant's head has emerged—or according to some authorities, the greater part of its body—is its life considered as important and valuable as the mother's. Thereafter, neither life may be sacrificed to save the other. Most modern authorities on Judaism hold, however, that the infant's life may still be sacrificed if necessary to save the mother. Since a newborn child is not considered entirely viable until the thirty-first day following birth, up to that point—especially if both lives are endangered—the mother retains priority.

Under no circumstances did Judaism approve the practice of abortion merely to terminate an unwanted pregnancy. Only for the sake of the mother's health, either physical or emotional, was it condoned.[5]

Every state in our nation considers abortion just for the sake of terminating an unwanted pregnancy to be criminal. Unless a panel of physicians agrees that abortion is medically necessary, it cannot be legally performed. Even when medically and legally allowable, abortion can be executed with reasonable safety only between the fourth and twelfth weeks of pregnancy.

The result of all these complications is that most illegal abortions take place under unhygienic conditions and are often performed by unskilled hands, with a high incidence of injury and death. Under such circumstances the risk of serious infection is very great; a woman who is subjected to such a procedure estimated that as many as one out of five pregnancies in the may also be rendered incapable of having children. It has been

United States—a horrifying total of a million a year!— terminates in criminal abortion. These incidents are responsible for the death of perhaps 10,000 women a year, with an additional 300,000 subsequently admitted to hospitals for treatment of hemorrhage or infection. Eighty percent of these operations are performed on married women, the balance on single girls, many of them teenagers.[6] Not to be discounted by any means is the cost in emotional complications. Even married couples who carelessly conceive, then destroy the fetus they have created, can suffer immeasurable guilt which often corrodes their future sexual relationship. In recent years there has been a notable increase of sentiment favoring the legalization of abortion in instances of rape or when there is reason to fear the birth of a defective child. It is not likely, however, that our society will soon accept abortion merely to terminate an unwanted pregnancy. The best way—the only secure and reasonably certain way—for birth control to be achieved is by the prevention of conception.

We defer to our next chapter a discussion of what Judaism teaches concerning birth control.

AND SO WE BEGIN

The courtship has been accomplished, the engagement is completed, all premarital preparations are concluded, the ceremony is performed, the reception held, the wedding cake cut, and at last the couple is alone. Their honeymoon has commenced. Some marriages are irretrievably ruined during their earliest days; others are so surely set on the right path that success is all but assured. Which will it be for you?

Up to this point everything has been theory. The conduct of bride and groom on their honeymoon indicates whether their understanding of marriage and love is only intellectual or is sufficiently part of their characters actually to function in their new life together.

The most essential function of the honeymoon is to give the newly-weds the best possible opportunity to commence adjusting to each other as husband and wife, not to help them see the world. It is wiser, therefore, to remain in one place than to travel exhaustingly. The ideal locale is one where other honeymooners are present but each couple can salvage its own privacy. There should be interesting things to do together, but not so many as to cause excessive fatigue. I have known married couples who seemed almost afraid to be alone, who sought constant distraction as protection against getting to know one another. The honeymoon is a time when newly-weds should spend just enough time with others to highlight their primary purpose of becoming better acquainted than ever before with each other.

The importance of the first attempt at coitus can scarcely be exaggerated. Should the couple be exhausted from a ceaseless round of festivities, culminating in the wedding ceremony and reception, it may be better and wiser to defer their first intercourse for a night or two. If the bride is particularly timid or fearful, even a longer postponement may be advisable. In the event of pain at the first attempt to penetrate, the groom should try to proceed at a pace which will avoid discomfort for his wife. Whatever he can reasonably do to make their initial encounter not one of aggression or conquest, but rather of loving mutuality, can pay enormous dividends in terms of future happiness.

Yet his tenderness and patience should not be abused. I know a husband whose wife refused him intercourse until they had been married three months; I have been told of another who waited five years. A woman married three decades once admitted to me that she still was unable to appear naked in the presence of her husband! For a newly-wed husband to permit his bride, if she wishes, to undress at first alone, to let her take the lead in pacing the speed of their initial lovemaking, is to demonstrate consideration which any normal wife will remember with gratitude the rest of her life. But for her to torture him sadistically over a prolonged period betrays a psychopathic unwillingness either to face the responsibilities or to enjoy the ecstasies of marriage.

Any failure to achieve mutual gratification and pleasure in the early intercourse of the honeymoon should be accepted by bride and groom as part of the normal trial and error of marriage. If they appear to be making no progress in this respect over many months, professional aid should be sought. To increase the probability of success, it is essential even on the honeymoon to establish the open and honest lines of communication to which we referred in an earlier context.

For understandable reasons, sex is likely to play a larger role during the honeymoon than it will after a few years of married life. But even the honeymoon should be more than just sex. This is a couple's first precious opportunity to nurture a total love relationship—a joyous meeting of bodies and minds, of hearts and souls—to which their sexual union will testify. Sex, in short, should occupy its proper and proportionate place from the start.

On the Fringe

In connection with the practical significance of sex in marriage, it is advisable that we comment on a few peripheral problems which most couples will never face. For the few who do, however, and for those others who may be called upon to understand and help them, brief guidance is in order.

Some couples, while refraining from intercourse prior to marriage, develop the habit during their courtship of giving each other orgasms through manual manipulation during what is commonly referred to as heavy petting. They may then be tempted after the wedding to continue this familiar, easy route to sexual pleasure and release, rather than to embark upon a more difficult course of experimentation which will enable them to reach their orgasms through coitus. It would be foolish to deny that some of the values accruing from sexual fulfillment in love can come to such couples too. But they will not have shared in the deepest dimension of sexual fulfillment; it is therefore worth their while to eschew the enjoyment with which they are already familiar and to work—patiently and persistently, if need be—toward a consummation far more complete than any they have thus far known.

A closely related problem is that of masturbation. Every marriage counselor knows of brides—or more probably, grooms—who have approached the sex experience of marriage consumed either by unrealistic guilt on this account or by unreasoning fear that earlier masturbation may have made a normal sex adjustment impossible. Such apprehensions are the fruit of ignorance which may have been forgivable a generation ago but which cannot be condoned in the light of our knowledge today. We now know that masturbation is the normal, natural experience of most boys and of many girls at one period of their lives. It has been estimated that perhaps as many as 90 percent of males and over half the females in our culture indulge in it during adolescence. I am among those who are convinced that it is preferable to premarital intercourse if sexual tensions become intolerable. The point to be most emphatically made here, however, is that, unless practiced excessively, masturbation is not harmful and does not preclude a good sex adjustment in marriage.

The rare exceptions may be due to guilt and fear induced by ignorance when, in fact, there should be neither guilt nor fear attendant upon this practice. Or to the persistence of masturbation as one's chief source of sexual pleasure, in preference to the effort which is often required before husband and wife together can achieve mutually gratifying orgasms. While masturbation is not harmful, neither is it likely to express or enrich one's love for his mate; at best it is a self-centered procedure, in which an individual concentrates on his own pleasure rather than cooperating with a loved one, to the end that each may receive in the proportion that he gives. Where two people have achieved a good marriage, including a good sexual adjustment, and—because of distance, travel, or illness—one partner is unavailable to the other for an extended time, there can be no harm in resorting to masturbation for temporary release. Surely it is preferable to adultery. But if it becomes a regular substitute pattern, replacing coitus, the probability is high that marriage will be harmed.

Even rarer than either of the preceding problems is that of homosexuality in the male or lesbianism in the female. An outright homosexual, of course, is not likely to enter upon a heterosexual marriage. But some few individuals are bisexual, which means to say, they are capable of achieving at least a limited kind of satisfaction with members either of the opposite sex or their own. I have myself counseled a father of two children who was deeply disturbed over the fact that he also felt a strong sexual attraction to certain males. At the earliest opportunity I channelled him toward psychiatric assistance. All that need be said here is that any person—in or out of marriage—who has reason to suspect that he harbors homosexual tendencies should seek professional help without delay. There is reason to believe that all of us go through a period of intense attraction for individuals of the same sex; we mentioned this in our earlier discussion of the stages through which we normally develop toward maturity. Homosexuality or bisexuality can perhaps be understood best as an arrestment of growth, a failure to emerge fully from an earlier to a later level of development. The overwhelming probability is that a person who has felt enough attraction to the opposite sex to make marriage possible will be susceptible to treatment and cure if his abnormality is submitted to professional treatment soon enough.

A somewhat more common fringe problem is that of frigidity in the female or impotence in the male. Where the underlying cause of such difficulty is physical, it can often be detected during the medical premarital examination and subsequently corrected. If the inability to function sexually with success is a manifestation of emotional disturbance, psychotherapy will be needed to cure it. In that event an enormous investment of patience and understanding will be required during therapy on the part of the patient's mate.

There are instances in which what appears to be frigidity or impotence may be a temporary or marginal difficulty in effecting a solid sexual adjustment. When this is the case, every evidence of loving tenderness and consideration can help thaw out the cold front. A wife who at first experiences difficulty in achieving an orgasm can be helped enormously by an understanding, patient, and persistent husband. A man who has temporary trouble sustaining an erection needs reassurance of his masculinity and virility, not carping criticism or attack. Needless to say, if either type of problem fails to respond to the best efforts of a loving mate, professional attention should be sought. No couple, however, should permit the problem of impotence or frigidity to persist unattended for too long a time. If their own best efforts to understand and accept each other, to establish and encourage a generally loving relationship, of which sexual expression will be an inevitable aspect, do not appear to be progressing, professional help should then be sought.

Though it is not likely to be one of the early problems of marriage, some couples are bitterly disappointed after a time to discover that they are apparently unable to conceive a child. Much new knowledge concerning sterility has come to us in recent years. Many such couples can be helped. Medical experts can usually ascertain whether it is husband or wife who is responsible for the failure; once this has been discovered, quite often the deficiency can be corrected. Inability to conceive may as often be due to emotional as to organic causes. Sometimes after such a couple has adopted a child and is able to relax their effort to conceive, the happy discovery is made that the wife is, after all, pregnant.

Where conception proves to be impossible over a period of a year or more despite the best medical effort, most couples will consider the feasibility of adopting a child. There are risks involved in adoptions, but then there are risks in the natural process of conception and birth too. These can be reduced to a tolerable minimum if the adoption takes place only through an approved agency which conducts an intensive investigation both of the adopting parents and of the child. Let no one foolishly imagine that it is impossible for two people to love an adopted child as if they had biologically conceived it themselves. One of my favorite true stories is of the mother who, when asked which of her two children had been adopted, stopped to think for a moment and replied: "You know, I actually have difficulty remembering!"

So much, then, for the extremely significant role of sex in marriage. Perhaps in some ways it may be compared to the appreciation and care of excellent instruments by the musicians in a great orchestra. Without such instruments, superb musical performances are impossible. Yet at the same time, only sensitivity to the ineffable majesty of good music will impel a musician to purchase and treasure his instrument. So it is with sex. Without a mutually gratifying expression of it, a superb marriage is most improbable. Yet only an awareness of what marriage can mean as a total experience, only an appreciation of intercourse in its relationship to love, will enable any couple to achieve the sexual satisfaction they desire and to which they are entitled.

«««««««« 10 »»»»»»»»

Old Voices–New Truths

THERE HAS BEEN FAR TOO GREAT A TENDENCY IN RECENT YEARS to assume that all religions agree in their ethical values. While it is true that the various strands of Christianity and Judaism share much ethical aspiration in common, there are also significant differences. In no area is this truer than in their respective attitudes toward sex. It would be foolish to pretend that there is only one Christian or one Jewish point of view on sex. Yet a careful examination of what may be called the main-line historical approaches of the two traditions will disclose major divergences. The Jewish bride and groom who are aware of what their faith teaches about sex, love, and marriage, and who attempt to apply these precepts to their marital behavior, possess an asset of inestimable value. Many of the truths emphasized today by modern science were anticipated by our ancestors long centuries ago. We shall be better able to appreciate them if we attend first to the views of Christianity.

It is not our purpose here to invite odious comparisons. Neither do we intend to act, however, as if Judaism has nothing unique to contribute to the making of a good marriage. We shall call upon Christian authorities themselves to express the attitudes of their faith. The first historic truth to which they will attest is that through much of its development Christianity has been negative and suspicious in its approach to sex. It is not without significance that Jesus—unlike nearly all his contemporaries among the leaders of Judaism—was never married. According to Christian theology, moreover, he was born to a virgin. Judaism and modern science agree that this is impossible; the only way a new human life can be initiated is through the fertilization of an ovum by a spermatozoon. Without the deposit of male sperm in or very near to her vagina, a woman cannot be impregnated.

Paul, who was the founder of Christianity, looked upon sexual desire and especially coitus as evil. He expressed the explicit wish that all men might be capable, as he was, of remaining permanently celibate. Because they were not, as a concession to human weakness he said: "It is better to marry than to burn."[1] Theologians have disputed whether he meant better than to burn with sexual desire or to burn in hell for indulging in intercourse without marriage. But there can be no doubt that he considered normal sexual relations to be evil.

The disdain of Paul persisted through most of early Christian Church history. Summarizing his view and that of the New Testament generally, one Christian religious authority has written:

> In this idea of marriage as an accommodation to human weakness and a hindrance to the fullest service of God there is but little appreciation of its dignity and high calling; nor do the writers of the New Testament show much sense of the joys and privileges of family life. . . .[2]

The same writer, commenting on the preponderant Christian attitude in the centuries following completion of the New Testament, has said:

> While none denied that marriage, relatively speaking, was a good thing, it was nevertheless tolerated rather than commended. . . . Of the joys, privileges, and opportunities of home and family life we find little appreciation, while hardly more than lip service is paid to the blessing of children.[3]

From time to time a voice of protest or disagreement was raised within the Church, but for the most part sex was disparaged and intercourse even within marriage was reluctantly accepted only as a concession to human weakness and a biological necessity. Additional evidence of this attitude is to be found in the fact that in some Christian denominations to this day—most notably but not exclusively in Roman Catholicism—religious leadership is limited to those who remain celibates or virgins.

In the extreme Christian view sexual desire and its fulfillment were scarcely more ethical within marriage than outside it. St. Jerome, for example, wrote: "He who loves his own wife too ardently is an adulterer." The Church Fathers condemned the use of cosmetics and other adornments by all women, whether married or not, on the ground that it might increase their sexual attraction for men. According to Tertullian, even the natural, unadorned beauty of women "ought to be obliterated by concealment and neglect, since it is dangerous to those who look upon it."[4]

No one was more immoderate or intense in the expression of such views than St. Augustine. Psychiatrists would find it very significant that in his youth Augustine's sexual behavior was extremely debauched and depraved. Later in life he himself wrote, regarding his earlier years: "I boiled over in my fornications." He is alleged at one point to have intoned this prayer: "Lord, make me chaste—but not yet!" When Augustine reacted, it was from one extreme to the other, condemning all intercourse that was not directly intended to produce progeny.

He said: "Intercourse even with one's legitimate wife is unlawful and wicked where the conception of offspring is prevented." He also decreed: "It is good for a man not to touch a woman." His rejection of all intercourse not intended to impregnate was described, fifteen centuries later, by Pope Pius XI as "an uninterrupted Christian tradition." Meanwhile, in the thirteenth century St. Thomas Aquinas agreed that "every carnal act done in such a way that generation cannot follow is a vice against nature and a sin ranking next in gravity to homicide."

Many modern Catholic authorities have echoed these views. Thus a prominent Jesuit, Father William J. Gibbons of Fordham University, has said that the church "does not wish to see sexual expression regarded as an independent good."[5] Some voices within the Roman Church have commenced to question this stand but they still appear to be much in the minority.

Augustine even attempted to read his own new view of sex back into the minds and lives of the Hebrew Patriarchs—Abraham, Isaac, and Jacob—saying that they would have preferred to fulfill God's commandment to "be fertile and increase" without indulging in intercourse, but this was manifestly impossible. Therefore, he concluded, they must have experienced coitus with their wives only reluctantly and out of duty.

This transference by Augustine of his own later contempt for sex to the Patriarchs was ridiculous. There is not the slightest shred of evidence that they actually felt as he did. Indeed, as we shall see very shortly, biblical Judaism is characterized by an honest, open, at times almost lusty acceptance of sex.

Our brief résumé of Christian attitudes toward sex would be neither adequate nor fair if we failed to add that in more recent times the views summarized above have been appreciably altered, if not altogether abandoned, by many Christian individuals and denominations. It is now increasingly accepted in

Christian circles that an active sex life in marriage is commendable even when it is not intended to produce children. Insofar as this is true, however, it is important to recognize that these Christians have renounced their own historic approach to sex and have approximated that of Judaism. It is also essential to bear in mind that large numbers of Christians even in our own day have been educated to accept a theological stigma against sex.

A Different View

What does Jewish tradition say about marriage and sex? To begin with, it sees marriage not as a necessary evil or a concession to human frailty, but as a primary good. The only purpose for which the sale of a Torah scroll was permitted was to make marriage possible for an orphan who would otherwise have been too poor to marry. Despite the immense importance which Judaism has always assigned to study, the Talmud is explicit in saying: "A man shall first take unto himself a wife and then study Torah." In ancient Temple times the High Priest was not permitted to perform the most sacred rites of the year, those of atonement on Yom Kippur, unless he was married.[6] It was decreed also that if marriage and funeral processionals happened to approach an intersection simultaneously, the former was to proceed first.

Our rabbis were convinced that whatever freedom an individual had to relinquish because of marriage was more than counterbalanced by what he gained. They made this clear in their parable about the emperor who said one day to Rabbi Gamaliel: "Your God is a thief, because it is written [in Genesis]: 'The Lord God cast a deep sleep upon Adam and he slept; and He took one of his ribs. . . .' " Rabbi Gamaliel's daughter, who had overheard the conversation, asked her father to let her handle the matter. The next day she entered a complaint with the emperor that thieves had broken into her home the night before, taking a silver vessel and leaving a gold one. "Would that such a thief visited me every day!" exclaimed the emperor. The rabbi's daughter at once continued: "Was it not, then, a splendid thing for the first man when a single rib was taken from him and a wife was supplied in its stead?"[7]

Judaism looks with emphatic favor on marriage and on sex within marriage. It believes that intercourse between husbands and wives is desirable and wholesome; that God intended it not only as a means to propagate the human species, but also to fortify and reinforce their love. There is an occasionally discordant opinion among the authentic spokesmen of Judaism, but such is clearly an exception, not the rule. That which has been the major motif in Christianity is but a minor and incidental melody in the symphony of Judaism. The following observation of Maimonides is astonishing in its departure from a more normal Jewish view, even from other opinions articulated by the Rambam himself: "We ought to limit sexual intercourse altogether, hold it in contempt, and desire it only rarely. . . . The act is too base to be performed except when needed."[8]

Much more typical of normative Judaism is the following effective rebuttal to Maimonides, attributed to Nachmanides in the thirteenth century. Some authorities doubt whether he was in fact its author. Even if not, however, the fact that he was alleged to have authored these words and that they have been cited to illustrate the authentic Jewish point of view is significant:

> It is not true, as our rabbi and master asserted in his *Guide for the Perplexed*, praising Aristotle for teaching that the sexual urge is a source of shame to us. God forbid that the truth should be in accordance

> with the teachings of the Greek! . . . The act of sexual union is holy and pure. . . . The Lord created all things in accordance with His wisdom, and whatever He created cannot possibly be shameful or ugly. . . . When a man is in union with his wife in a spirit of holiness and purity, the Divine Presence is with them.[9]

Both Bible and Talmud discuss matters pertaining to sex with uninhibited honesty. King David is portrayed as having indulged in adultery and being severely punished for it. One of the shorter books of the Bible is devoted in its entirety to the physical side of love. True, Jewish tradition considered Song of Songs to be an allegory depicting the mutual love between God and the Jewish people. But this was undoubtedly a later sublimation of what had originally been a beautifully poetic series of passionate love songs. The fact that such literature was included in the very canon of Holy Scripture, however it may have been reinterpreted by the rabbis, discloses much concerning the wholesome approach of ancient Judaism to sex. From Song of Songs come the very beautiful words of the modern Israel song, often engraved on wedding rings: דודי לי ואני לו (*dodee lee va-anee lo*)—"my beloved is mine and I am his." Here also are to be found descriptions of a woman in pursuit of her lover (3:1-4), of her physical beauty as seen by him (4:1-5), and of his physique as it impresses her (5:8-16).

The Talmud contains an interesting discussion on the best time for husband and wife to experience intercourse. Our tradition even suggests a prayer of great meaning and beauty, to be recited by a man before cohabiting with his wife. Rabbinic literature recognizes that the sex urge varies from individual to individual, that consequently one man may require intercourse more frequently than another. The Shulchan Aruch, sixteenth-century compendium of religious law by which Orthodox Judaism is governed to this day, states:

> . . . each man is obliged to perform his marital duty according to his strength and according to his occupation. Gentlemen of leisure should perform their marital obligation every night. Laborers who are employed in the city where they reside should perform their duty twice weekly, but if they are employed in another city, once a week. Donkey-drivers [should have marital relations] once a week; camel-drivers, once in thirty days; sailors, once in six months. As for scholars, it is obligatory for them to have intercourse once a week, and it is customary for this to be on Friday nights.[10]

It is clear from this quotation that the frequency of intercourse was to be governed both by the basic nature and physique of the individual and by the intervals of travel imposed upon him by his vocation. Even more indicative of how Jewish tradition felt about sex is the remarkable fact that precisely the Sabbath was chosen as the night most appropriate for intercourse by a scholar and his wife!

Women's Needs Too

The statement just quoted from the Shulchan Aruch may seem to relate the frequency of coitus only to the nature and need of the husband. Elsewhere, however, Judaism recognized that women too are active partners in the sexual relationship and that their needs must also be met. Even though, in early times, marriage was more often than not arranged for a girl by her parents, the rabbis insisted that her consent was indispensable before the nuptial contract could be executed. One of the greatest of the talmudic authorities, Rav, severely punished any man who married without first obtaining the consent of his prospective wife.[11]

This awareness of the emotional and sexual needs of women was all the more notable for having been achieved in a patriarchal society and at a time when most cultures supposed that only men have strong sexual desires. It was decreed that a husband must not leave on a long journey without first having intercourse with his wife and must do so again as soon as possible after his return. Refusal to cohabit was accepted by Jewish law as grounds for divorce at the initiative of either husband or wife. The bridegroom was bidden to be sensitive to his wife's natural timidity in their first performance of coitus: "The Torah teaches gentle manners: the bridegroom should not enter the marriage chamber until the bride gives him leave."[12] That women share in the sexual responsibilities and opportunities of marriage and should play an active role in them is implied in the following admonition by Meir of Rothenburg, the outstanding rabbi of thirteenth-century Europe. Contrary to the strictures of early Christianity against the use of cosmetics, he asserted: "Let a curse descend upon a woman who has a husband and does not strive to be attractive."[13] The Shulchan Aruch decrees that a married woman may enhance her appearance with cosmetics even during the thirty-day mourning period for a close relative (that is, after the first week), "so that she does not become repulsive to her husband"! A mourning bride is permitted to adorn herself even during the first week.[14]

Judaism looks upon intercourse in marriage not as something sinful, not as a regrettable necessity, but as a beautifully meaningful experience which enhances the love of husband and wife. Every form of sex play which leads to that end was approved. The same Maimonides whose curiously un-Jewish statement on sex has already surprised us said elsewhere:

> The sexual union should be consummated only out of desire and as the result of the joy of the husband

> and wife. . . . He must not approach her when he thinks of another woman and certainly not when he is under the influence of alcohol or while they are quarreling, and hatred divides them. He must not approach her against her will or force her to submit to him out of fear.[15]

The final sentence of this statement reiterates a view which the Talmud had expressed many centuries earlier: "He who coerces his wife will produce unworthy children."[16]

Another talmudic authority urged that each act of coitus in marriage be as exciting and fresh as the first.[17] Finally, Judaism acknowledged and accepted the fact that intercourse serves more than the purpose of propagation when it decreed that even the marriage of a couple who are incapable of producing children is legally valid.

Clearly, then, there has been a major divergence between the historic attitudes of Judaism and Christianity pertaining to sex. In most faiths the mystics were especially prone to withdraw from active sex life into monastic celibacy. In Jewish tradition even the mystics refrained from such asceticism. The biblical Nazirites, denied so many other luxuries and pleasures of normal life, were not pledged to celibacy. For a long time it was supposed by scholars that the ancient Essenes, a small mystical group which lived in Palestine at about the time of Jesus, consisted only of men. Recent discoveries in the area of the Dead Sea lead us to suspect now that even this numerically insignificant group of mystics may have lived normal sex lives, with men and women together in the community. The eighteenth-century Jewish mystical movements—unlike similar tendencies in most other faiths—never repudiated or rejected an active sexual partnership in marriage.

Dr. Gershom Scholem has written the following in his monumental study of Jewish mysticism:

> There is, however, one important respect in which Chasidism differs from its Christian contemporaries: it does not enjoin sexual askesis; on the contrary, the greatest importance is assigned in the *Sefer Chasidim* to the establishment and maintenance of a normal and reasonable marital life. Nowhere is penitence extended to sexual abstinence in marital relations.[18]

A word of caution is in order here. Without detracting in any way from the foregoing, it must be honestly acknowledged that many contemporary Jews are unaware of what Judaism teaches about sex; many, moreover, who know these things intellectually are emotionally incapable of implementing them in their lives. A person who has been preconditioned by early childhood experience to regard sex with suspicion, contempt, or fear will need more than this chapter—or indeed, many such chapters—to absorb Jewish tradition into his heart as well as his mind. If his (or her) antipathy to sex is deeply rooted in repressions, some form of psychotherapy will probably be required. For most couples, however, this will not be needed. As they approach marriage, they can gain immeasurably from understanding the wholesome maturity with which their own faith has encouraged the proper enjoyment of sex.

A PRACTICAL APPLICATION

The differences between Judaism and Christianity on the legitimacy of sexual pleasure lead inevitably to a divergence of view with regard to birth control. If sex is evil and coitus is acceptable only for the purpose of procreation, it follows that deliberate contraception must be sinful. This has been precisely the historical logic of the Church. Originally both Catholics and Protestants were opposed to birth control. Among

Protestants there has been a steady inclination to relax this opposition; many leading Protestant denominations, as they have moved closer to our Jewish point of view on sex in general, have also come to accept birth control.

Though change in the Roman Catholic Church has been much slower and less substantial, it has appeared there too. At one time the Church insisted that under no circumstances should a married couple cohabit unless they intended pregnancy as a consequence. We have already examined the views of Augustine, Aquinas, and Father William Gibbons in this respect. Later the Catholic attitude shifted to approval of the so-called rhythm method, which was discussed earlier. This removes the stigma of sin from married couples who indulge in coitus for pleasure and love—even if they deliberately time themselves to avoid pregnancy—provided that their failure to conceive results from the incidental absence of an egg to be fertilized, not from any interference on their part with the normal processes of nature. Most Catholic theologians consider rhythm a *natural* method of family planning; as such, they accept it. All other devices for birth control they condemn as *artificial.*[19]

In very recent years there has been debate among Catholics on whether the contraceptive pill might not be approved as a natural method. Dr. John Rock, a nationally prominent gynecologist whose research contributed substantially to development of the pill, is a leading Catholic layman. He has urged upon his Church acceptance of this method. A few priests and bishops have voiced similar views. In the summer of 1968, after an exhaustive study of the entire question by a special commission he had previously appointed, Pope Paul VI vigorously reaffirmed the traditional Catholic opposition to all mechanical or chemical methods of contraception. Though his pronouncement stirred up a great deal of dissension within the Church, among both laymen and priests, it remains official Catholic doctrine.

One of several factors which have instigated the call for change among Catholics themselves is a recognition of the fact that large numbers of their communicants are in fact practicing birth control methods condemned by the Church. Convincing evidence of this comes from Massachusetts, one of two states in which the sale or use of contraceptive devices was long prohibited. A comparison of Catholic and non-Catholic birth rates in that state is instructive. In the seven most Catholic cities in Massachusetts, where the Catholic proportion of the population amounted at the time to 62 percent, the average annual birth rate between 1935 and 1940 was 14.0 per thousand. In the seven least Catholic cities of the Commonwealth, with an average of only 25 percent adhering to that faith, the comparable rate was 13.9 per thousand![20] This insignificant difference would have been statistically impossible if most Catholic couples had followed the teachings of their faith.

A more recent study by the Population Reference Bureau disclosed similar evidence in Europe. Eleven Catholic countries produced 18.1 babies per thousand population; fifteen non-Catholic countries produced 18 per thousand. The bureau concluded: "The big difference between high and low birth rates is not whether they are Catholic or non-Catholic but whether they are economically underdeveloped or advanced.[21]

A survey, published in *The New York Times* of December 3, 1966, substantiates the trend among Catholic wives. It indicates that the number relying exclusively on the rhythm method declined from 27 percent in 1955 to 25 percent in 1965. In 1955 43 percent used no method of birth control; by 1965 this figure had been reduced to only 22 percent. The percentage of Catholic wives complying with the teaching of their Church on contraception is represented in the following:

1955 .... 70 percent
1960 .... 62 percent
1965 .... 47 percent

These data have led many Catholics to the conclusion that it is injurious to insist on doctrines which the average individual is either unable or unwilling to observe, that it produces a massive burden of guilt, and generates disrespect for religious law in general. Hence the ferment on this subject within the Church.

It should go without saying that whether or not Catholicism changes its attitudes still further is the business only of Catholics themselves. The foregoing comments on the subject have been introduced only to provide a background of contrast for exposition now of our Jewish attitude on birth control. We make no distinction between *natural* and *artificial* methods. For men to regulate conception by either mechanical or chemical means is to us no more reprehensible than to regulate or control other automatic processes of the body through medication or surgery. We believe God wants us to use our intelligence responsibly toward learning more and more about nature and to bring healing and health upon ourselves by regulating and abetting nature's autonomous procedures.

Judaism has always believed that the noblest fulfillment of marriage is the birth and rearing of children. We are reminded by our ancient rabbis that the very first positive commandment given by God to man was: "Be fertile and increase, fill the earth . . . !" No marriage is deemed complete unless it produces children. Among many rabbinic sayings to this effect is the following:

> A man is not a complete man if he has no son and daughter. . . .[22] A man without children is like a piece of wood, which though kindled does not burn or give out light. . . . A man with children eats his bread in joy; a man without children eats it in sadness.[23]

Yet the emphasis our ancestors placed on parenthood did not blind them to the fact that intercourse serves functions other than just procreation. They believed that God has endowed us with sexual desires and needs because He considers these to be good. Partners in marriage, therefore, should live as full and active a sex life as they wish, utilizing their choice of birth control methods, in order that they may continue to express and enrich their love through intercourse, without producing more children than they can properly love.

Orthodox Jewish tradition has approved only those methods of contraception practiced by women, not those used by men. This is a matter now of no more than academic interest, since it happens that by the dictates of modern science the most reliable contraceptive methods in any event are those employed by women.

God's commandment that Adam and Eve be fertile, reported in Genesis, lent itself to an interesting rabbinic dispute. The rabbis asked how many children a man must have before he is deemed to have fulfilled this requirement. The disciples of Shammai said two sons; the followers of Hillel insisted that even a son and a daughter absolved one of further obligation. Obviously neither group held that God imposes a lifelong responsibility to continue having children.

No less than four times, in different tractates of the Talmud, we find the following statement:

> There are three women who, when experiencing sex relations with their husbands, may (or must) take the precaution of using an absorbent to prevent conception: a minor, a pregnant woman, and a woman who is still nursing her baby.[24]

What were our teachers really attempting to tell us in this passage? Three things: that the prevention of pregnancy in a minor was permissible to safeguard the health of the prospective mother; that it was legitimate in the case of a woman already pregnant, for her sake as well as that of the child she carried; that it was acceptable when a mother was still nursing, for the welfare of a child already born. The explanations of Rashi and other commentators on this passage allow no room for doubt. The only area of potential disagreement is whether, under any of the foregoing circumstances, a woman *may* or *must* use a contraceptive device. It is also clear from the opinions of medieval and premodern rabbis that contraception was deemed permissible in cases where a woman had given birth to children who were mentally retarded or suffered an incurable congenital disease.

Social conditions of emergency proportion were also accepted even by our most Orthodox rabbinic authorities as justification for the practice of birth control. Thus during the Nazi persecutions Jewish women were permitted by their rabbis to live normal sex lives with their husbands while preventing pregnancy. The hazards to both mother and child were considered beyond reasonable risk. The very reverse of this reasoning is used by some Jews today. They say that—despite the permissiveness of Jewish law regarding contraception—to compensate for the brutal destruction of six million Jews by Hitler and the alarming reduction of world Jewish population due to our relatively low birth rate, we ought not restrict the size of Jewish families. While there is no doubt merit to this argument, it does not refute the fact that only a tortuous kind of logic can twist Jewish tradition into a blanket prohibition of birth control.

Turning to the Present

After exhaustive study of all the pertinent talmudic references, Dr. Jacob Z. Lauterbach, formerly professor of Talmud at the Hebrew Union College, summarized his own views as follows:

> ... according to the opinion of all the teachers, it is not forbidden to use a contraceptive in cases where conception would bring harm either to the mother or to the child born or unborn. And I cannot see any difference between the protection of a minor from a conception which might prove fatal to her and the protection of a grown-up woman whose health is, according to the opinion of physicians, such that a pregnancy might be fatal to her. Neither can I see any difference between protecting a child from the danger of being deprived of the nourishment of its mother's milk, and protecting the already born children of the family from the harm which might come to them due to the competition of the larger number of sisters and brothers.[25]

A modern extension of the talmudic view is to be found in the following statement, adopted by the Biennial Assembly of the Union of American Hebrew Congregations in November of 1959:

> We fully recognize the right of all persons, for religious reasons or otherwise, to abstain from or to practice birth control as they see fit. However, the failure of large sections of our population to plan their families effectively is due neither to conscience nor to free choice, but rather to legal and official obstacles imposed upon many Americans with the result depriving them of knowledge and medical assistance in this field. . . . When government responds to the theological beliefs of any religious group by interfering with the dissemination of birth control information to all who desire it, such interference represents an improper imposition of such religious beliefs upon the community at large. Therefore, be it resolved that:

> A. We favor the elimination of all restrictions and prohibition against the dissemination of birth control information and of rendering birth control assistance by qualified physicians, clinics, and hospitals.
>
> B. We favor the wider dissemination of birth control information and medical assistance, both by private groups, such as the Planned Parenthood Association, and health agencies of local, state, and federal government as a vital service to be rendered in the field of public health.

The pressure of population throughout the world today is such that, unless effective birth control be practiced on every continent, the consequence in a relatively short period of time will be disastrous. Our immediate concern with the Jewish point of view on contraception, however, derives from the harmful effect of unwanted children on the success of marriage and family life. The married couples who prefer not to have children are depriving themselves of inestimable happiness. By the same token, the couples who produce more children than their physical and emotional resources can decently support are jeopardizing not only their own future but equally the welfare and health of their offspring. This is the unmistakable conviction of our Jewish faith.

It would nevertheless be both misleading and unfair to leave the impression that all modern Jews are, without exception, agreed on the subject of birth control. We have already indicated that on sex in general there is often a great gap between intellectual understanding and emotional acceptance. Some Orthodox Jews, therefore, will use tradition selectively to justify a position on contraception which scarcely differs from the Catholic view. Their attitude must not be confused, however, with that of authentic Jewish tradition. Paradox though it be, there are some situations in which a knowledgeable Reform or Conservative Jew may grasp the intent and spirit of Jewish tradition more accurately than an Orthodox Jew!

«««««««11»»»»»»»

Made in Heaven?

SEXUAL INTERCOURSE AND CONTRACEPTION ARE BY NO MEANS the only aspects of love and marriage on which Jewish tradition has spoken. Long before the advent of modern psychology and marriage counseling, the founders and expositors of Judaism had worked their way to many of the insights on love described in earlier chapters of this volume. They knew, for example, that love means a total sharing of life between husband and wife, that it provides a fulfillment together for each that would be impossible for either alone. Thus one of the ancient rabbis said: "He who has no wife remains without good, without a helper, without joy, without a blessing. . . ." To which a colleague added: "He is not a whole man." Still other rabbis proclaimed: "The unmarried man diminishes the likeness of God." In a similar spirit, a medieval Jewish mystic declared: "The שכינה (*Shechinah*)—God's Presence—can rest only upon a married man, because an unmarried man is but half a man, and the שכינה does not rest upon that which is imperfect."[1]

The completeness which husband and wife should bring to each other was further emphasized by our ancient teachers in their comments on the ineffable sadness of either mate's losing the other. Thus, according to the Talmud: "The widower lives in a darkened world."[2] The Midrash adds that when a man's wife dies, his steps are shortened, his spine becomes bent, and it is as if the Temple had been destroyed in his time. To which Rabbi Samuel bar Nachman added: "For everything there is a substitute except for the wife of one's youth."[3]

The association of love with God is of special consequence. In Chapter IV we mentioned the legend which recounts that God creates each soul in two parts—one-half to be placed in the body of a male, the other in the body of a female. Marriage means that the two halves of a single soul—created together, originally meant for each other—are reunited in accordance with God's plan. In another rabbinic tale we are told that God thought His creation of the universe was completed after He had formed Adam. He was disturbed, however, by a note of discord which marred the harmony of the spheres. An angel whom He sent to investigate reported that the disturbing sound was Adam's sigh of loneliness. Then God created Eve as Adam's partner; the discord disappeared and the work of creation was really finished. Along the same vein, we noted in an earlier chapter that an ancient rabbi, when asked by a Roman woman how God has occupied Himself since He completed creation, replied that He spends His time matching couples for marriage!

Yet another rabbinic passage elaborates charmingly on the great concern of God with marriage:

> The wedding of the first couple was celebrated with pomp and ceremony never repeated in the whole course of history since. God Himself, before presenting Eve to Adam, attired and adorned her as a bride. Then He appealed to the angels, saying: "Come, let us perform services of friendship for Adam and his helpmate, for the world rests upon friendly services, and they are more pleasing in My sight than the sacrifices Israel will offer upon the altar." The angels accordingly surrounded the marriage canopy, and

> God pronounced the blessings upon the bridal couple, as the *chazan* does under the *chupah*. The angels then danced and played upon musical instruments before Adam and Eve in their ten bridal chambers of gold, pearls, and precious stones, which God had prepared for them.[4]

We return here to a point raised earlier: Does the repeated association in Jewish tradition of God with love mean that Judaism holds marriages to be made in heaven?

That depends on the specific meaning assigned to these words. If they are assumed to imply that for each man there is only one woman—and for each woman only one man—with whom either could be happy, the thought surely is one we today cannot accept. The truth is that for each of us there is no doubt a certain type of person with whom he could conceivably enjoy a successful marriage, but there are surely numbers of individuals who come at least reasonably close to that type. Aside from much other evidence, the fact that so many men and women, after the death of a first mate, are able to achieve happiness later with a second would dismiss the notion that God literally sets aside only one specific individual for each of us.

Yet there is valid truth to the quaint, poetic ways in which our fathers identified love with God. They thus expressed their conviction that love is part of the very plan of the universe, not just an incidental relationship conjured up by man on his own. The mutual love of husband and wife reflects something basic and integral within the very nature of the universe and life. This truth can be observed and expressed in the lexicon of modern science too. We tend to think of nature as harsh and cruel. Often it is that. What we too frequently forget, however, is that the primal beginnings of love may be seen in nature too. For example: protons, neutrons, and electrons must all remain in the proper proportion and relationship with each other in order for atoms to exist. It can almost be said that they must serve certain purposes for each other, rather than each existing only for itself. Atoms must follow a similar pattern if there are to be molecules. Molecules, in turn, must relate to each other in a manner which could almost be called "cooperative" if there are to be cells, cells if there are to be whole organisms, individuals if there are to be tribes and nations, nations if a peaceful world is to survive.

Once the human level has been reached, all quotation marks and qualifications can be removed from the word *cooperative*. Prior to the appearance of man, admittedly it is only by stretching our imagination that we can use such terms. We do not mean to infer that there is any conscious or direct parallel between the behavior of matter's most elementary particles and that of men. Nor that love exists anywhere in prehuman forms of life. Only that nature itself provides a paradigm for the kind of relationship among components which is destined later in the evolutionary process to emerge into love.

This can be seen most dramatically in the relationship between cells. The first forms of life on earth consisted of only a single cell. That isolated cell had to perform for itself all the functions necessary for the maintenance of life: digestion, respiration, locomotion, elimination—these and many other processes had to be encompassed by each cell. In the course of evolutionary time, however, large numbers of cells "learned" to remain together as parts of a larger organism. Again quotation marks must be used for the word *learned* because there was nothing deliberate or conscious about the change; it took place automatically, as part of nature's steady development, without either knowledge or choice on the part of the cells involved.

As cells developed the capacity to form multicellular organisms, they also began to specialize. At the risk of deliberate oversimplification, it could be said that one group of cells undertook the responsibility of digestion for the entire organism, thus freeing another group to take over respiration, still another to handle locomotion, yet another to meet the needs of elimination, etc. In short, individual, hitherto isolated cells were developing the ability to perform together essential services for other groups of cells and for the whole organism. Thus each separate cell was able to realize its own potentiality to a far greater degree than any of them could have done alone.

You will observe that the language used in the last sentence comes close to that with which we defined love in an earlier chapter. Surely it would be stretching the truth to call the relationship between cells—or, for that matter, even between animals—love. Yet here, on the crudest, most elementary level of simple biology, we recognize nature's preliminary pattern for what later becomes love. The potentiality for love was inherent in nature from the beginning; evolution has moved perceptibly toward its realization. Human love developed out of these earlier relationships just as truly as the human arm and hand developed from the foreleg and paw of animals. Our Jewish ancestors were not aware of all these scientific details. Yet, by uncanny intuition they understood that the love which unites husband and wife is, at its best, a reflection of something which lies close to the very heart of reality.

Means to the End

Because they appreciated the nature and value of love, our rabbis understood also that, like everything precious, it would deteriorate if it were not cherished and tended. Therefore they pronounced a great many choice epigrams in which advice was given to husbands and wives on how to treat each other. The fact that most of their directives were addressed only to men should not mislead us. These passages were written exclusively by men, to be read almost entirely by men. But the advice they proffer is no less valid for wives. Here are a few of the rabbinic recommendations addressed to married couples:

> Thy wife has been given to thee in order that thou mayest realize with her life's great plan; she is not thine to vex or grieve. Vex her not, for God notes her tears.[5]
>
> A wife is the joy of man's heart.[6]
>
> A man should eat less than he can afford, and should honor his wife and children more than he can afford.[7]
>
> A man should be careful not to irritate his wife and cause her to weep.[8]
>
> If your wife is short, bend down and hear her whisper.[9]
>
> He who loves his wife as himself; who honors her more than himself; who rears his children in the right path, and who arranges for them to be married near the period of their puberty, concerning him it is written: "And thou wilt know that thy home is peace." (Job 5:24.)[10]
>
> Man should ever be mindful of the honor of his wife for she is responsible for all the blessings found in his household.[11]
>
> A man must not cause his wife to weep for God counts her tears.[12]
>
> Strive to fulfill your wife's wishes for it is equivalent to doing God's will.[13]
>
> When the husband is blessed, his wife is also blessed thereby.[14]
>
> A wife who receives love gives love in return; if she receives anger, she returns anger in equal measure.[15]

It was recognized by these wise teachers of Judaism that in a good marriage important decisions are made by husband and wife together. The Talmud therefore decrees that the choice of a new place of residence or a new profession must be made jointly. The only circumstance, significantly enough, where this did not hold was if one mate wanted to live in Palestine and the other did not. In that event, the desire of the one who wanted to live there was given priority.

Jewish tradition also recognized many centuries ago that husband and wife must be sensitive to each other's moods and needs, must be able to perceive them even without a word from the other. Thus a chasidic rabbi related this incident:

> A commander-in-chief received a message telling him that his main line of defense had been broken by the enemy. He was greatly distressed and his emotions showed plainly on his countenance. His wife heard the nature of the message, and entering her husband's room, she said: "I too at this very moment have received tidings worse than yours."
>
> "And what are they?" inquired the commander with agitation.
>
> "I have read discouragement on your face," replied the wife.
>
> "Loss of courage is worse than loss of defense."[16]

Many of these ancient insights will at once be recognized to have anticipated some of the steps toward a happy marriage which were suggested in our chapter entitled "No Blueprint, But–."

NO OTHER LOVE?

Most of the foregoing quotations from Jewish tradition seem to assume monogamous marriage. Yet it would be idle to pretend that through substantial spans of Jewish history polygamy was not practiced. The fact that Adam is described in Genesis as having been given only one wife has been adduced as evidence that monogamy was always the ideal in Judaism. The prophets and virtually all the rabbis mentioned in the Talmud also had, each of them, but one wife.

Yet in this respect, as in many others, the ideal was not always realized. There are numerous biblical instances of polygamy; these include Kings David and Solomon. The most we can say is that polygamy was not practiced as widely among ancient Jews as among their contemporaries.

Talmudic law accepts the validity of polygamous marriage. One rabbi sanctioned a man's marrying as many women as he could support; a colleague countered that a woman could claim a divorce if her husband married a second wife.[17] Regardless of legal permissiveness, the fact that a Jewish husband was required, as part of the marriage ceremony, to guarantee financial support for his wife in the event of divorce deterred all but the wealthiest from undertaking multiple marriages.

It was not until the beginning of the eleventh century that Rabbi Gershom ben Yehudah, known as "the Light of the Exile," issued his famous prohibition of polygamy. Even under his decree, however, a man whose wife was either insane or rebellious was permitted to marry a second woman. Rabbi Gershom's edict was accepted only by the Ashkenazic or Western Jews; Sephardic and Oriental Jews continued to practice polygamy, though on a limited basis. In Africa the following declaration was inserted in the marriage contract: "The said bridegroom . . . hereby promises that he will not take a second wife during the lifetime of the said bride . . . except with her consent."[18]

The State of Israel has had to deal with some remnants of polygamy, especially among immigrants from North Africa. While Israeli citizens are legally restricted to monogamy, a man who brings two wives with him into the country may keep them. If either wife subsequently requests a divorce, the state will support her. I myself, while visiting the apartment of a Moroccan Jew in Ashdod, have met his two wives. The bitter enmity between them, which was immediately evident, attested to the wisdom of monogamy.

It becomes apparent, then, that although polygamy was not proscribed until about nine hundred years ago, and despite the vestigial remnants of multiple marriages today among a very small number of Jews, monogamy has long been a cherished ideal in Judaism, an ideal which is now almost universally achieved.

A Final Difference

In the preceding chapter we discovered how Judaism differs from other faiths in its attitude toward love, marriage, and sex. There is one more difference to be discussed at least briefly before we can in good conscience bring this part of our consideration to its close. Throughout the centuries our faith has also evolved a unique and interesting stance on the subject of divorce. Here again, a background of contrast will be instructive. Some religions are unalterably opposed to divorce. It is ironic that in many instances precisely those faiths which have historically looked upon marriage with jaundiced eye are the ones that have insisted that it is too sacred ever to be dissolved. And Judaism, which has always approved marriage enthusiastically, is far less rigid in recognizing the possibility of failure and in allowing room for the correction of mistakes.

There are religions which prohibit divorce altogether, others which reluctantly accept divorce but do not permit either partner to marry again. While Judaism recognizes that marriage is a sacred enterprise, not to be undertaken lightly or tentatively, it nevertheless provides for the possibility of human error. The Talmud stipulates that "a man should not marry a woman with the thought in mind that he may divorce her."[19] It further recognizes divorce to be a pathetic tragedy, in saying: "He who puts away the wife of his youth, for him God's very altar weeps."[20]

A beautifully poignant and poetic story is told in our tradition concerning one couple who contemplated divorce. It is based on the talmudic law that a husband whose wife has not conceived in a decade of married life may divorce her.

> There was a woman in Sidon who lived ten years with her husband and had borne no children. They went to Rabbi Simeon b. Yohai and asked to be divorced. He said to them: "As your coming together was with a banquet, so let your separation be with a banquet." They agreed and prepared a large banquet at which the wife made her husband drink more than enough. Before he fell asleep he said to her: "Pick out what is most precious to you in my house, and take it with you to your father's house." What did she do? When he had gone to sleep, she beckoned to her servants and said to them: "Carry him on his mattress to my father's house." In the middle of the night he awakened and said to her: "Whither have I been brought?" She said: "To my father's house." He said to her: "Why have I been brought here?" She replied: "Did you not tell me last night to take what was most precious to me in your house and go with it to my father's house? There is nothing in the world more precious to me than you." They went back to Rabbi Simeon b. Yohai and he prayed for them and they had a son.[21]

There can be no doubt, then, that in Judaism marriage is deemed to be a permanent, sacred bond, not to be terminated for slim cause. Yet our tradition does permit divorce. It recognizes that even more tragic than the separation of husband and wife is their living a life of pretense and deceit.

Often couples who have reached the end of the road remain nonetheless together out of consideration for their children. No one can afford to minimize the tragic consequences of divorce on children; in order to maximize their chance for wholesome development, they need a unified home, with discipline and love from both parents. But a home kept ostensibly intact physically after it is already broken spiritually—which means to say, a home which is maintained though husband and wife no longer love each other or perhaps have even come to hate each other—can injure children even more devastatingly than divorce. In the 1950's a Washington State study of schoolboys revealed that intact but quarreling families were more likely to produce delinquents than broken families.[22] Because it understood this long centuries ago, Judaism has provided the justification and machinery for honorably ending a marriage that has failed.

The conditions which warrant divorce are first described in the Bible:

> A man takes a wife and possesses her. She fails to please him because he finds something obnoxious about her, and he writes her a bill of divorcement, hands it to her, and sends her away from his house. . . .[23]

The matter, however, was not quite so simple or easy as it appears to be here. As in so many other instances, a complicated garment of talmudic law was woven from a solitary biblical thread.

The rabbis were uncomfortable, to begin with, over the fact that Deuteronomy seems to extend the right of divorce only to husbands. They therefore provided that under certain circumstances a wife could petition the court for a divorce and, if right were on her side, the court could pressure the husband to assent. Maimonides articulated this principle of Jewish law as follows: "If a woman says, 'My husband is distasteful to me, I cannot live with him,' the court compels the husband to divorce her, because a wife is not a captive."[24]

What were the circumstances which entitled a wife to sue for divorce? The court considered her request to be justified if her husband refused to have sexual intercourse with her, if he contracted a loathsome disease which she could not endure, or—as we have already seen—if his occupation contaminated his person with an odor she found intolerably offensive. Also if he treated her cruelly, prohibited her from visiting her parents, changed his religion, or was notoriously immoral.

A husband, in turn, could seek a divorce if his wife were guilty of adultery, insulted him or his father in his presence, was morally indecent in public, disregarded the ritual laws pertaining to women, or refused to have intercourse with him. If the two agreed mutually that they wished to terminate their marriage, no further justification was required; the court had to grant their request. No matter what the circumstances of separation, however, the financial protection promised the wife as part of the traditional wedding ceremony had to be provided.[25]

In Orthodox and Conservative Judaism it is necessary for a couple to obtain a religious as well as a civil divorce. The religious divorce, called a גט (*get*), is issued by a rabbi or a rabbinical court. In Reform Judaism the civil divorce is sufficient. In all branches—provided the divorce was valid—there is no objection to a second marriage. This discrepancy among the several branches of Judaism sometimes poses a perplexing problem. No Orthodox or Conservative rabbi will officiate at the marriage of a divorced person unless he has obtained a גט. If, then, a divorced Reform Jew who did not receive this religious decree wishes to marry into a Conservative or Orthodox family, only a Reform rabbi will be able to oblige.

The גט is frequently a vexing matter even for those who believe in it. There have been many cases—especially if divorce proceedings have left a residue of rancor—where a husband will refuse to grant his former wife a religious divorce to facilitate her remarriage. Even unsavory instances of attempted blackmail have been known. Responsible religious authorities are eager to eliminate all such abuses.

We see, then, that Judaism accepts divorce. But only as a last resort. The most prodigious effort must first be made to mend whatever imperfection mars the couple's happiness. Indeed, reconciling a quarreling couple is adjudged a great virtue in Judaism. The story is told of Rabbi Meir, who lectured to the public each Friday evening. A certain woman attended these sessions regularly. Her husband, who was not interested in them himself, objected to the fact that she returned home every week later than he wished. Finally he banished her from the house in a temper, saying that she could not return until she had publicly spat in Rabbi Meir's eye. She spent the week with a neighbor and returned the ensuing Friday to hear the rabbi's lecture. Meanwhile, Rabbi Meir had heard of her husband's unreasonable demand. He called the woman to him before the assembled audience and said: "My eye pains me; spit into it and it will be relieved." It took considerable persuasion before the woman was willing to comply, but she finally did. When her husband heard of it, he permitted her back into their home. The Midrash which recounts this tale concludes with the following:

> "Learn, then, that no act is disgraceful that tends to promote the happiness and peace of husband and wife."[26]

We Jews believe that marriage is the most sacred relationship in human experience. It should never be undertaken without very serious contemplation; it deserves and demands a deep sense of commitment on the part of both mates, an unswerving determination to work hard at it and resolutely to surmount all obstacles to success. But so long as men and women are fallible, mistakes will be made. If a couple discovers that in the case of their marriage such an error has in fact been compounded and that, despite the most diligent efforts of both, there is no realistic chance for happiness together, our faith looks upon this as a lamentable failure but accepts it as such and recommends divorce under the most civilized conditions possible.

«««««««« 12 »»»»»»»»

Generation to Generation

SOCIOLOGISTS HAVE LONG MARVELED OVER THE VIRTUES OF Jewish family life. Both formal studies and informal observation testify that family ties are stronger among Jews, that divorce, infidelity, and juvenile delinquency are rarer. Some scholars are convinced that this superiority is a compensatory device, resulting from the fact that for centuries Jews were denied many of the satisfactions and pleasures which others received from their larger social life; therefore Jews concentrated on their families. Although there is undeniably a measure of truth to this claim, it would be superficial in the extreme to attribute the whole of Jewish family strength to hostile external pressure.

Even as we have already discovered in our tradition unique insights on sex, love, and marriage, there is also a large body of Jewish teaching on the family. What we know today as Judaism is the result both of external and internal factors. It has been shaped in part by discrimination, but in large part also by the inner direction of our ideals. In a sense each newlywed couple forms a bridge between the generations of past and future. Bride and groom are products of family syndromes, while at the same time they establish together a new family of their own. Our Jewish ideals of family life can help them in two ways: in understanding their respective pasts and in commencing to build a happy future.

One of the most idyllic descriptions of wholesome family life encompassing three generations to be found anywhere in literature is that of Psalm 128:

> Happy is the man that revereth the Lord,
> That walketh in His ways.
> When thou eatest the labor of thy hands,
> Happy shalt thou be, and it shall be well with thee.
> Thy wife shall be as a fruitful vine, in the innermost parts of thy house;
> Thy children like olive plants, round about thy table.
> Behold, surely thus shall the man be blessed
> That revereth the Lord.
> The Lord bless thee out of Zion;
> And see thou the good of Jerusalem all the days of thy life;
> And see thy children's children.

For countless generations this noble ideal was the goal of most Jewish families and was in fact realized by many of them.

I recall the time when a student in my Confirmation class asked to discuss some personal problems with me. "We don't really have a home," he said with considerable emotion, "just a group of people living in the same house." He proceeded to tell me that his parents paid very little attention to his wishes or his younger sisters', that he had to go home alone each Sunday from religious school to get lunch for himself and the girls because his mother and father always spent the whole day at their club. During the week, too, they were generally too busy to spend much time with the children; their concern was limited to the pronouncement of rules, followed by grim scoldings when these were violated.

This was obviously not a very attractive or desirable pattern of family life. It could scarcely be said to square with our traditional Jewish ideals. The probability is that this boy's parents weren't even aware of what Judaism teaches about the ideal family. Our purpose in this chapter is to make sure that, as you approach your marriage, you are familiar with these values and their practical application to some of the problems you will face.

OBLIGATIONS OF PARENTS

It is a source of continual astonishment to discover how many of the principles of modern pedagogy were apparently known to the ancient rabbis. They were acutely aware, for example, of how important it is for parents to agree on major matters pertaining to the rearing of their children. A chasidic rabbi said: "If husband and wife quarrel, they cannot raise good children."[1] It is possible to carry this injunction to the unhealthy extreme of insisting that husband and wife must agree on all things in the presence of their children. The consequence of this can be to arouse in youngsters the suspicion that the adult world is engaged in a massive conspiracy against them. Voicing honest differences in the presence of children can be an intelligent way for parents to demonstrate how divergent opinions can be lovingly accommodated to each other. But total agreement is imperative on all important aspects of child rearing itself. If mother and father argue, for example, on discipline, they openly invite indecision and instability into the lives of their children. This is why we suggested, in an earlier chapter, that an engaged couple should discuss their respective ideas on disciplining children. Too wide a difference may disclose fundamental incompatibilities of personality and presage later trouble both for the couple and their offspring.

The ancient and medieval teachers of our faith also knew how dangerous and destructive it is for parents to play favorites among their children. Several of them attributed the strong animosity Joseph's brothers bore him to the fact that he was the recipient of special attention from their father. The Talmud states explicitly: "Show no partiality among your sons. Treat all of them alike."[2]

Many modern parents are confused with regard to discipline. Reacting against what may have been excessive discipline in their own childhood, they have attempted to exercise none toward their children. They make a grievous mistake. A total absence of regulations and rules in favor of permissiveness can be as harmful in the home as rules which are too restrictive. For one thing, psychiatry has helped us understand that children are often frightened by some of their own impulses and desires. If these are not controlled by teachers and parents, a corrosive accumulation of guilt may accrue. There is also the fact that life itself imposes disciplines. Nature and human nature are such that immoral conduct very often carries its own punitive consequences. The child who is led to believe, early in life, that he can do whatever he wants, without fear of being disciplined, is inadequately prepared for the realities of life. So far as possible discipline should be fair, should grow out of the offense committed and be proportionate to it in severity. But the absence of all discipline is no favor to the child.

As long ago as Bible times our ancestors understood this. In the Book of Proverbs they urged:

> Train up a child in the way he should go.
> And even when he is old, he will not depart from it.
> Withhold not correction from the child;
> For though thou beat him with the rod, he will not die.

In similar vein the Midrash says:

He who rebukes not his son leads him into delinquency.[3]

Notwithstanding the recommendation of corporal punishment just quoted, it was not an unreasoning or unloving discipline which Judaism approved. It was implicitly assumed that the love and tenderness which prevailed between husband and wife would pervade their relationship to their children too. Thus rabbinic literature tells us that when God spoke to Moses from the burning bush, fearing lest he be frightened, He spoke in the voice of his father. We are also enjoined by the rabbis never to promise either punishment or reward to a child unless we truly mean to follow through.

The greatest responsibility of Jewish parents by far was to teach their children Torah, which means to say, the history, literature, theology, liturgy, and ethics of the Jewish people. Countless are the aphorisms and epigrams establishing this obligation:

A home where Torah is not heard will not endure.[4]

If a man does not teach his son Torah, it is as if he had merely created an image.[5]

He who teaches his sons and grandsons Torah is as if he had received it himself at Mount Sinai.[6]

Rabbi Hiyya ben Abba saw Rabbi Joshua ben Levi hurrying one morning to take his grandson to school. He asked him: "Why the haste?" and Rabbi Joshua answered: "Is it a small thing to stand at Mount Sinai?"[7]

He who teaches Torah to children abides with the שכינה (*Shechinah*)—God's Presence.[8]

Rabbah, son of Rabbi Huna, ate no breakfast until he had taken a boy to school.[9]

> Jerusalem was destroyed only because the children did not attend school, and loitered in the streets.[10]
>
> One is immortal if his descendants study the Torah.[11]

It must not be assumed—merely because all these admonitions speak either to or concerning men—that only fathers were responsible for the education of their children. While it is true that formal education was deemed by our tradition to be within the purview of the male parent, Judaism nevertheless recognized that the religious tone of the home is set primarily by the mother's influence. The Midrash contains a convincing example:

> A pious couple lived together for ten years, and having no children, were divorced. The man married an impious woman and she transformed him into a man of wickedness. The pious woman married a man of wickedness and she transformed him into a man of goodness. Therefore the sages declared: "Woman determines man's behavior."[12]

The same basic thought was expressed many centuries later by the Zohar, the principal medieval sourcebook of Jewish mysticism:

> The chief influence transforming a man's house into his home is his wife. The שכינה (*Shechinah*) will not forsake his house if his wife keeps it according to the ways of Israel.[13]

The responsibilities of Jewish education, then, were clearly assigned to both parents.

Actions Speak Louder

As impressive as the foregoing quotations are, they constitute but the beginning of parental obligation for education. Not only can scores of similar statements be cited for each one given here, Judaism also recognizes that the example set by parental conduct is a much more effective instructor than even the most eloquent of words. Therefore fathers and mothers were urged so to order their deeds that they would offer the right example to their children.

> Every Jew should so conduct himself that his sons will rejoice to say: "The God of my father."

A chasidic rabbi expressed this truth with exceptional eloquence:

> The Belzer Rabbi commented on the verse in Exodus 10:2 "And that you may recount in the hearing of your sons and your sons' sons how I made a mockery of the Egyptians and how I displayed My signs among them—in order that you may know that I am the Lord." It may be remarked that the end of the verse would have seemed more correct if it had been expressed thus: ". . . in order that *they* may know that I am the Lord." But the verse was intentionally worded "you" instead of "they" in order to furnish us a lesson. Recount to your sons the wonders of the Lord, but remember that this will have a beneficent influence upon them only if you yourselves recognize that He is the Lord.[14]

Another chasidic rabbi addressed himself to the same point:

> A man asked the Kotzker Rabbi to pray for him in order that his sons might study the Torah diligently. He replied: "If your sons will see that you are a diligent student, they will imitate you. But if you neglect your own studies, and merely wish your sons to study, the result will be that they will do likewise when they grow up. They will neglect the Torah themselves and desire that their sons do the studying.[15]

A third rabbi of the same group demonstrated an admirable and effective sense of humor in this direction. He is reported to have seen a man and his son, both drunk, reeling together in the gutter. Turning to his own son, who was with him, he said:

> I envy that father. He has succeeded in his ambition to have a son like himself. But I do not yet know whether you will be like me. See to it that the drunkard does not have better success with his son than I with you.[16]

We shall shortly consider the responsibilities of children to their parents. First, however, it is imperative to recognize that all of them were contingent upon the ethical teaching and conduct of the parents themselves. The Talmud is unmistakably clear on this point:

> It is possible to think that even if the father ordered his son to defile himself or not to restore a lost article which he had found, he is to obey him; consequently there is a text to teach, "You shall each revere his mother and his father, and keep My sabbaths." (Lev. 19:3) All of you alike are bound to honor Me.[17]

It would be impossible to exaggerate the emphasis of Judaism on the moral responsibilities of parents toward their children. Only if they met these obligations–by deed even more than in word–did their children have to assume similar responsibilities toward them.

Too many parents in our own time have failed to match the understanding of our ancient teachers that the example of parental conduct is a far more efficacious instructor than the eloquence of parental words. Thus they urge restraint on their children while indulging in gluttonous exhibitionism themselves; they stress the virtues of ethical behavior in their homes while behaving with gross immorality in their business or professional lives; they insist that their children tell the truth while they themselves consistently lie to the government on their tax returns; they force their sons and daughters to attend religious school while they attend religious services only on the High Holy Days. Judaism emphasizes today, as it always has, that the primary obligation parents owe their children is a living example of the conduct they want them to follow.

Since this is not essentially a book on the rearing of children, we desist from further detail. It is, however, a book on marriage and the family. As such, it requires at least the foregoing instruction on the precepts of our faith concerning the duties of parents toward their children, duties which you yourself assume from the moment you contemplate having a family.

If we have discussed the familial responsibilities of parents before those of children, this is because, chronologically and psychologically, they come first. It might have been more productive had Moses phrased the Fifth Commandment not as "Honor your father and your mother," but rather as "Honor your daughter and your son." All other things being equal, parents who properly and lovingly respect their children will elicit similar respect from them. They stand a good chance of their children's fulfilling the obligations which Judaism has long enjoined upon the younger generation in a household.

OBLIGATIONS OF CHILDREN

The same Book of Proverbs which stipulated the responsibilities of parents was equally explicit on those of children. Thus:

> A son that dealeth shamefully and reproachfully
> Will despoil his father, and chase away his mother.
> Hearken unto thy father that begot thee,
> And despise not thy mother when she is old.

The Torah even went so far as to order that a son who is contemptuous of his parents is to be publicly stoned. While we can scarcely accept the undue harshness of the prescribed punishment, it is impressive nonetheless to perceive the importance our tradition has assigned to filial respect.

The Talmud expands the emphases of the Bible. It asks, for example: "In what does reverence for a father consist?" And immediately it answers:

> In not sitting in his presence and in not speaking in his presence, and in not contradicting him. Of what does honor for parents consist? In providing for them food and drink, in clothing them, in giving them shoes for their feet, in helping them to enter or leave the house. R. Eliezer said: "Even if his father ordered him to throw a purse of gold into the sea, he should obey him."[18]

Here again, we cannot accept literally every ancient or medieval prescription for behavior toward parents. We today would be inclined to doubt either the desirability or wholesomeness of forbidding a child ever to sit in his father's presence or to disagree with him. But we can learn from tradition that disagreement merely for its own sake is not valid and that the spirit in which a child acts toward his parents is the all-important consideration.

Are we stretching talmudic truth in saying this? Not if we understand the intent of the passage which tells us that if a father errs on a point of law, his son should not directly or bluntly charge him with having made a mistake. Instead, he should more subtly suggest: "Father, in the Law it is written thus"—proceeding to quote the proper biblical passage in order to spare his father avoidable embarrassment.[19]

Another talmudic passage underscores more explicitly that the spirit of one's actions toward his parents is even more important than the actions themselves. We are told that a man who feeds his father on fattened chickens may be treating him abominably, while one who orders his father to do the heavy work of treading the mill may be acting with admirable affection. How is this possible? In the first instance, if the father asks whence the chickens were obtained, the son may impatiently reply: "Eat, old man, eat and be silent!" In the second case, the government may have issued a decree that all millers report to the capital at once. The son, fearing that this presages a period of dangerous military duty for all who respond, directs his father to remain at home, doing the relatively safe work there, while exposing himself to the greater risk.[20]

The devotion and love due one's parents are manifest further in the comment that father and mother are partners of God in the proper rearing of their child.[21] It was said also that because God knew He would be unable to attend Himself to the needs of every child, He created parents to act in His stead. One rabbi even proposed that parents are entitled to more honor than God. This he deduced, in typical rabbinic style, from two biblical verses. One states: "Honor God with your substance," (Prov. 3:9) which he interpreted to mean that only if one possesses substance is he obligated to honor God. A different verse, however, reads: "Honor your father and your mother." (Exod. 20:12) Here there is no qualifying condition; one is to honor his parents regardless of whether or not he has possessions.[22]

With reference to children no less than to parents, the fulfillment of obligation is judged by Jewish tradition more on the basis of deed than of word. Rabbinic literature contains numerous illustrations of famous men whose behavior toward their parents is considered exemplary. One such man was Abimi who was said to have had five sons, all of them ordained rabbis. Yet whenever this man's father would summon him, he would run to open the door and exclaim: "Yes, yes, I am coming to you!" One day his father asked him for some water. By the time Abimi had come with it, his father had fallen asleep. So he stood there patiently until he awakened and then gave him the water.[23]

The mother of Rabbi Tarfon broke her sandal one day as she walked through a courtyard. In order to spare her from walking barefoot on the rough stones, Rabbi Tarfon bent down, putting his hands on the pavement ahead of each step. When he later fell ill, his mother asked the other rabbis to pray for him, saying: "Pray for my son, Tarfon, for he honors me more than I deserve." When she told them what he had done for her, they responded: "If he had done a thousand times more for you, he would not have shown half the honor for a parent which is commanded in the law!"[24]

A chasidic student is said one day to have observed in the midst of class that his rabbi was deeply engrossed in trying to unravel a certain verse. Knowing from past experience that such concentration was usually of long duration, the student ran home for lunch, assuming that he could easily return before his rabbi would be ready to resume the lesson. As he finished eating, his mother asked him to run an errand for her. He refused, giving as an excuse the fact that he had to hurry back to his studies. On the way back, however, it occurred to him that the chief purpose of studying was to perform good deeds, that helping his mother in fulfillment of a lesson he had already learned was more important than hastening to learn a new one. So he retraced his steps, did the errand for his mother, and then returned to the classroom. As he entered, the rabbi looked up from his concentration and said: "You must have done a good deed, for the moment you entered a complicated matter I had not previously understood became clear to me."[25]

Finally, the Talmud describes a Gentile whose respect for his mother was all the more noteworthy by virtue of the fact that she had apparently become demented. Once, while he was conducting a public meeting, for no reason at all she took off her slipper and hit him in the face. When her slipper fell to the ground, he bent down to pick it up for her. On another occasion she tore his silk robe, hit him on the head, and spat in his face—all in the presence of others. But he refrained from retaliation in order to spare her shame.[26]

It is clear, then, that in the eyes of Jewish tradition parents and children were mutually obligated to each other. Only if honor, respect, and love were abundantly demonstrated in both directions, could the full promise of marriage and the family be realized. This is no less true today than it was during the centuries when the Bible and Talmud were being recorded. The couple who understands our Jewish ideals of family conduct and who conscientiously strives toward the attainment of these ideals has a head start in the pursuit of marital happiness.

More to the Present Point

As important and impressive as the traditions of Judaism are on family responsibilities, they will be of doubtful value in your marriage unless we undertake now at least briefly to apply them to a few of the major familial problems you are likely to encounter. In reading the foregoing paragraphs, you may have been able to recognize some of your parents' virtues and failings. It is imperative in this connection to be aware of how frequently a generation in a given family repeats the pattern of mistakes perpetrated by its predecessors. Often the very person who has consistently complained about having been treated too severely by his parents becomes in turn an overly severe parent himself. Or, in the understandable effort to prevent such repetition, he may react to the opposite and equally damaging extreme of exercising no discipline in his home at all.

As you establish your own home, and in it start from the beginning to build foundations for your own family, a conscious effort should be made to avoid the mistakes of your parents both directly and by "over-reaction." You and your mate will be part of a continuing stream, flowing unbrokenly from the past to the future. Neither of you can altogether escape the consequences of the home in which you grew. By the same token, you will in due course have it in your power to shape the welfare of your own children. The more accurately and honestly each of you understands and appraises his feelings toward his parents, the greater will be the probability of working out a wholesome relationship with your children.

Whatever the emotional bonds have been between you and your parents, a difficult transition will be required from the moment of your marriage. If your parents have gradually and gracefully loosened their hold on you already, treating you in recent years more as an adult than still a child, the difference now will be one of degree rather than of kind. But if the emotional umbilical cord has not yet been completely severed, the change will be more radical and difficult.

The bond between each partner in a marriage and his parents is bound to affect profoundly the quality of the new marital relationship. The bride or groom whose parents have demanded that he be a submissive child—never asserting his own adult self, always submerging his own will to theirs—will carry this stunted self-image into his marriage. He is likely either to act as a thwarted, indecisive child, or to react so violently as to become an insufferable dictator. Neither attitude is calculated to enhance his posture as a spouse. The young person whose only personal experience with "love" has been at the hand of a martyr-mother who catered to his every desire may find it painfully difficult to realize that adult love sometimes means denial. In short, the success of your marriage will hinge substantially on whether both sets of parents grant you freedom to make your own mistakes, as they have undoubtedly made theirs. It is no less essential, however, that you and your mate both be ready to assume such freedom and to transfer your major love relationship from parents to each other.

Jewish tradition has long been aware of this. Immediately after the Bible tells of Eve's creation it adds: "Hence a man leaves his father and mother and clings to his wife, so that they become one flesh." To which one of the post-biblical rabbis added: "Before a man marries, his love goes to his parents; after he marries, his love goes to his wife."[27]

This statement should not be misinterpreted to mean that you face here a choice of "either-or." I do not stop loving my parents in order to love my wife. To the contrary, unless I am able to continue loving them—on a level appropriate to my age and my marital status—there is little chance that I shall love my wife healthily. We saw long ago that my love for my wife is qualitatively different in some respects from the love I bear all others, that it achieves a dimension beyond that which I continue to feel and express for my parents. To the degree that they coincide, however, and in the measure that life may from time to time force me to establish priorities, on or before the day of my wedding my wife became the number one object of my love. My parents had to be satisfied—indeed, satisfied and happy—to assume second place. The final successful consummation of the process came when, at the time of my daughter's wedding, and later my son's, my wife and I rejoiced to witness the new member of our family taking precedence over us. Fortunate is the person who never has to choose between parents and mate. But if such a choice becomes unavoidable, marriage can succeed only when one's wife or husband comes first.

This truth too was anticipated by Judaism centuries ago. A

thirteenth-century rabbi, Judah ben Samuel of Regensburg, wrote:

> If a father knows his married daughter to be busy and occupied with her husband's affairs, let him not suggest or order her to attend to his own, unless the husband allow of it, postponing his own interests for a while.[28]

But marriage obviously involves the relationship of each partner not only to his own parents but also to a new set of parents, his in-laws. We alluded briefly to this problem at an earlier point in urging, as a dimension of compatibility, that one give serious consideration to his probable relationship to future in-laws. It remains now to add that this can be an excitingly enriching experience or a depressively degrading one. Much depends on the maturity of the individuals involved, as well as their respective capacities to love.

The alertness of Jewish tradition to this problem is attested by the following talmudic extract:

> Three years had passed since the day that Abraham had sent Ishmael away. He longed to see him, and sought out his camp in the pasture-country of Paran. When Abraham came to his son's tent, he found Ishmael absent from home. He asked Ishmael's wife for a little water, but the ill-natured woman refused to give it to him. Abraham said: "When thy husband returns, pray tell him that an old man from Philistia came to visit him, and not finding him home, offered this advice: the pegs of your tent should be changed." Ishmael understood this allusion to his wicked wife and divorced her. He wedded another woman, named Fatima. The following year Abraham again wished to visit his son and again found him away from home. Without waiting for a request, Fatima offered him

> hospitality, and urged him to partake of food and drink. Abraham said: "When thy husband returns, tell him: his pegs are excellent and he should retain them." Ishmael thanked his gracious wife, and blessed the Lord who had sent him so admirable a mate.[29]

Not every instance of in-law interference works out so well. Apparently Abraham was right in his evaluation of Ishmael's wives, and fortunately Ishmael seems to have agreed with him.

In the ideal situation both husband and wife come in the course of time to feel about each other's parents as if they were their own, and this affection is reciprocated. To achieve or even approach this ideal, the young married couple must conscientiously work toward such a relationship and the parents on both sides must strive to avoid anything remotely resembling interference. Couples old enough to marry must be presumed to be old enough to manage their own affairs. This does not mean that parents have no right to offer suggestions or advice. But the couples themselves are the ones to evaluate all such advice and to accept or reject it according to their own wisdom.

Under One Roof?

Should a newly married couple live with either set of parents? The Talmud leaves no room for doubt. It asserts without equivocation:

> Can a goat live in the same barn as a tiger? In the same fashion, a daughter-in-law cannot live with her mother-in-law under the same roof.

There is seldom room for two adult generations in one household. Rare indeed is the parent who will not at least subtly take sides in any tension between married children with whom he lives; or the young husband or wife who will refrain from enlisting a parent on his side of an argument. Even if it means settling for a lower standard of living, the wisest course for couples is not to live with parents. Where such doubling up cannot be avoided, every effort must be made on both sides to maintain a maximum of privacy and to eschew interference in each other's business.

The couple who preserves its own integrity is precisely the one most likely to maintain love and respect for parents and in-laws. A recognition of this apparent paradox is implicit in two statements from the Apocrypha which may at first blush seem contradictory. The first reads: "I have carried iron and removed stones, and they were not heavier than for a man to settle in his father-in-law's house." The second statement: "Honor your father-in-law and mother-in-law, because henceforth they are your parents."

Judaism recognizes realistically that often life imposes on us a necessity for compromise. On the relationship with in-laws the Shulchan Aruch stipulates that if either husband or wife finds the visits of the other's family disturbing to the peace of their household, such visits are to be prohibited. Neither mate, however, has the right to deny the other visits with his or her parents in *their* home.[30] Needless to say, the very need for this kind of compromise would indicate that a sorry state of affairs had already developed.

So far we have had in mind the problem of couples living with parents immediately after their marriage. And we have without hesitation recommended that wherever possible this kind of arrangement be avoided. It occasionally happens, however, that many years later one parent dies and the survivor then wishes to move in with his children. There are, of course, situations in which either financial or emotional compulsions make it necessary for the couple to accede. Yet here too every alternative should be explored first. True, there are very rare grandparents who can, by their presence, enrich the lives of their children and grandchildren. But such enrichment is more likely to take place when the grandparents do not actually live in the same house. Aside from everything that has already been said, there is grave danger that children will come to feel they have two fathers or mothers, and will bitterly resent both. This is often true regardless of whether the two generations differ or agree in the discipline they exert on growing children.

Looking Ahead

It may at first seem premature to anticipate some of the problems we are about to discuss. After all, as you read this you are not quite even married; why rush ahead to issues you are not likely to face for a number of years? Our answer is that everything you do from the beginning of your marriage will be setting the stage for decisions to be made far in the future. Mistaken or misguided policies at the start can prejudge the choices you will want later. They can so corrupt the atmosphere of your home that in point of fact you may no longer have a truly free choice when the time for decision comes. Hence the following is not as premature as it may seem.

One altogether human danger to which attention should be called is the tendency to recognize our own faults more clearly in others than we do in ourselves. This applies especially to parents. When my son was a small boy, each time I became irrationally angry with him I knew I must have unconsciously discovered in him a failing I had not yet been able consciously to acknowledge in myself. Sometimes upon due reflection I was able to identify it, at other times not. But I knew that in every instance where my anger was disproportionate to whatever he had in fact said or done, it was probable that I was actually the target of my own resentment. This projection of one's own defects onto others can exist in the relationship between husband and wife too, though it is probably more common in the attitudes of parents toward their offspring. In either case, to be forewarned of the possibility is to be prepared to fend successfully against it.

How about the general organization and structure of the family? Who should make major decisions? Whose word should rule when there is vigorous disagreement? No one answer to these questions will satisfy every couple. We can say in general, however, that the patterns established from the outset of your marriage will probably prevail permanently. If you and your mate unite at the beginning to make important decisions together, with loving consideration for each other, when your children reach the age even of minimum understanding you will want to give them a voice too in matters which deeply concern them. If, on the other hand, one of you imposes his or her decisions on the other—which means to say, if your home from the start is an autocracy in miniature—your children too will eventually be dominated by a domestic dictator. The choice is yours. The quality of your marriage and family life will depend upon it.

Even in those areas of domestic life where most decisions will necessarily be made by one partner or the other, in setting policy there is room and need for mutuality. The wife should plan menus and market, but not without considering her husband's preferences. The husband, if mechanically capable, will take care of minor household repairs, but with loving attention to the comfort and convenience of his wife. And all major policy decisions—having to do with such matters as budget, place of residence, religious practice, and juvenile discipline—should be determined jointly.

The role of the father in the American family has caused deep anxiety among sober observers. There was a time when economic necessity forced fathers to be away from home so much that many mothers took over the duties of both parents more or less by default. Today, despite the fact that an increasing number of men need no longer be away from their families so much of the time for economic reasons, it is questionable whether the average American father is with his wife and children more than his predecessor was a generation ago. In some cases an obsessive compulsion to work longer hours than are really needed keeps him away from home. In other cases it may be a mania for golf or some other avocation or hobby which deprives the family of his presence. There is no denying the fact that, both for biological and economic reasons, the mother will continue to be the dominant influence during the child's earliest years. But children need both parents as active determinants of their future. The father who abdicates all domestic responsibility to his wife, who functions in the lives of his children only as a kind of supreme court or administrator of ultimate punishment, is doing both them and himself a gross disservice.

The appearance of their first child necessarily poses a whole new complex of problems for husband and wife. If they have already established a solid, loving relationship, these problems will be easily resolved. If the one-to-one involvement itself has never been satisfactorily resolved, the first baby can be a serious hazard. Where parents are secure in their love for each other, a child will strengthen the ties which already unite them. Where the relationship between husband and wife is unstable, the child can be an intolerable threat. I know of one lamentable instance in which a husband was so threatened by the appearance of his first child that he actually reverted to infantile forms of behavior himself in an unconscious but clearly discernible effort to compete with the newborn infant for his wife's attention. Each time the baby became ill, the father also took to bed. This, to be sure, was an extreme, psychopathic example. More often the competition between an infant and his insecure parents is subtler, though no less heinous. This is the primary reason for our earlier recommendation that a child not be conceived until the prospective parents are so sure of their love for each other that such a child will enrich their marriage.

Several chapters back we stressed the importance of spending much leisure time together if husband and wife are to deepen the ties that unite them. Here again, the same emphasis applies to the entire family after children have reached the age of doing even simple little things together with their parents. I know a man who attributed an emotional illness of long duration in his adult life to his feeling as a child that his parents loved each other with such exclusive concentration as to leave no room for him. He always felt pushed out to the fringe of their concern. Whether he was right or wrong with reference to his particular grievance is not the point at issue. The disastrous thing was that he *felt* that way. Wise parents will try to avoid even giving the appearance of shutting their children out of important aspects of their lives. They will discover that time spent constructively or creatively with their children can be as enriching to themselves as to the youngsters. Two authorities on marriage have written wisely on this matter:

> If most contemporary families no longer work together in the common task of operating a farm or small business, there are many leisure time projects in which they may engage as family groups. . . . The list of such projects is endless—building a vacation shack, a family orchestra, a trailer or camping trip in summer, a family basketball team, a vacant lot garden, a family art exhibit, barber shop harmony around the piano, father-son workshops in the basement, a family

> reading circle, the breeding of dogs or other animals, church activity, a golfing foursome, family games, a flower garden, or a small business as a side issue. . . . What the particular project may be depends naturally on the abilities, circumstances, and interests of the particular family, and in this connection is of somewhat incidental importance. What is important is that the family plans, works, thinks, laughs, succeeds, or even fails together. It is the family in action as a group.[31]

The celebration of our Jewish holidays in the home, and joint family preparation for such observances, can serve an invaluable function in giving both parents and children a feeling of comradeship and companionship which is the most essential ingredient of family loyalty. We shall have more to say about such celebrations later.

This chapter cannot be concluded without at least a brief word concerning the sex education of your children. Remember what was said earlier about such education's commencing even before a child is actually born. Your own attitudes toward sex and especially the sexual success of your marriage will vitally affect your child. Information about sex should be given to him at the proper time as freely and unself-consciously as information about any other matter. His interest in his own body and experimentation with it should not be frowned upon as something unnatural or dirty. Both boys and girls should be told about menstruation, wet dreams, and masturbation in a manner calculated to prevent undue apprehension or fear.

The most important principle governing sex education—indeed, all education—is truth. No child of any age should ever be told that storks bring babies unless his parents really believe it. Nothing should be taught as truth that will later have to be unlearned. It is often impossible to tell young children *the whole truth;* but whatever is taught must be *nothing but the truth!*

And it must be taught with wholesome attitude. A father who thinks all females are fit objects of conquest by males can truthfully transmit all the necessary facts about sex to his son, but only in a way which will lead to imbalance and distortion. A mother to whom the sex act is repulsive, who *feels* toward all men that they are beasts, can be ever so honest in relating information to her daughter, but she will probably also lead her perilously close to frigidity. Healthy attitudes are at least as important as accurate facts.

To the outer limit of his comprehension, a child at each age should be supplied with all the sex information he wants or needs. If the proper kind of parent-child relationship prevails, questions will be asked freely. If not, parents may have to take the initiative in extending openings which will encourage the asking of questions. Care must be exercised, however, not to inundate a child with more than he wants or is able at the moment to handle. You may have heard the classic story of a child who asked one day: "Mommy, where did I come from?" The mother, elated at finally hearing the question for which she had long been waiting and was so well prepared, proceeded to give her little daughter a forty-five minute lecture on the "facts of life." Upon reaching her nearly breathless conclusion, she inquired: "Tell me, honey, what made you ask this question today?" To which the child innocently responded: "Well, Francie told me this morning that she comes from Philadelphia, so I wondered where I came from." It is always a good idea to be sure of the real question before attempting an answer.

Parents must never lose sight of the difference between true sex education and just education for reproduction. A child who is old enough to learn the anatomical and physiological facts involved is also old enough to know the role of sex in the lives and love of his parents. It should come to him not as a rude shock, but as the revelation of beautiful truth, to learn how he himself was conceived. And when the time comes for discussions of premarital sexual chastity, the emphasis should be not on the dangers of promiscuity—though these cannot be entirely neglected—but rather on the advantages which can accrue to a marriage which is based on the chastity of both spouses. In no area do parents have a more priceless opportunity to influence the future happiness and welfare of their children than in this. And all other things being equal, the sexual happiness or unhappiness of your child is likely to follow the same pattern as your own.

«««««««« 13 »»»»»»»»

A House Divided?

THE HOUR WAS LATE—ALMOST MIDNIGHT. I HAD SAT SINCE 8:30 counseling with a husband and wife who had been married sixteen years and were the parents of five children. We were standing at the door of my study, about to terminate a far from satisfactory evening, when something prompted me to ask a final question. Turning to the wife, I began: "If you had known sixteen years ago what you know now. . . ."

I never finished the question. Misreading my intention entirely, the woman looked viciously at her husband and almost hissed: "If I had known then even half of what I know tonight, I would never have married him!" I am still uncertain who was more acutely embarrassed at her outburst, the startled spouse or I. We both were aware, however, that the problem of mixed marriage, which had been minimized or denied through so many years, had explosively ruptured their relationship. She was Protestant and he, Jewish. Neither had converted to the religion of the other. At the time of their marriage they had agreed their children would be sent in alternate years to a Reform Jewish religious school and a Protestant Sunday school. It was the breakdown of this Solomonic "solution" that had brought them to me.

Though the wife's vehemence was certainly exceptional, there was nothing rare about their problem. No kind of anxiety appears more frequently in the average American rabbi's study than that of mixed marriage, either contemplated or already consummated. Whether the rabbi wills it so or not, he soon becomes an expert. The sharing of my own experience in this area will naturally be most immediately compelling for those couples who are themselves of mixed religious background. Yet their specific situation illustrates so many of the considerations pertinent to all marriages that other couples too should find benefit in this chapter.

I begin with the assumption that no man is entitled to play God in another person's life. This is why I have never deliberately advised a given couple not to marry. Such attempts would in any event almost always be doomed to fail. Not even the most persuasive admixture of logic and fact is likely to triumph over the physical and emotional compulsions which bring two people to the point of marriage. Yet even if the rabbi has no right directly to dissuade them, he retains both the right and the responsibility to explore with them three crucial areas they may either have neglected or touched upon only casually.

The first of these is their motivation for having fallen in love with someone outside their own faith group. Our generation is so psychiatrically oriented that we look for ulterior motives and dynamics for every decision—especially for those of which we disapprove. Let it be honestly acknowledged, therefore, that it is possible for a Jew and a Christian to fall in love for no more complicated reason than that they are in most respects an uncommonly good match for one another and would like to live out the rest of their lives together. Part of the price we pay for living in a democracy is that our young people of high school and college age will enjoy increasing opportunities for social contact across religious and racial lines. This, in turn, is bound to increase the incidence of romance and love between

Christians and Jews, perhaps also between whites and Negroes.

Having said this much, however, it must also be added that a devious dynamic of some kind is more likely to prevail in a mixed marriage than in one within a given group. We have already had occasion to refer to the fact that one's choice of mate can be indirect rebellion against his parents. This is especially so when the proposed mate is of another faith. Nor is this a probability only in cases where the parents are intensely devoted to Judaism. By an odd paradox, sometimes those who have been most negligent in their own practice of Jewish life become most apoplectic at the prospect of a son's or daughter's marriage out of the faith. So the threat of such a match can be a devastating weapon in the hand of one who has need to reject his parents. When the motivation is unconscious, it becomes all the more difficult to resist and the probabilities of success for the marriage are correspondingly remote.

But it is not only parents against whom young people are sometimes in rebellion when they propose marrying outside their faith. It can also be the very idea of being a Jew. Despite the many advances of recent decades in the status of American Jews, the fact remains that we are a minority group and in some respects still an underprivileged group. Particularly for the individual Jew who has never experienced the joyous and fulfilling aspects of modern Judaism, the game may not appear to be worth the candle. He may—consciously or unconsciously—crave a social prestige or status which can be achieved, he thinks, only by admission to the allegedly superior majority class. And mixed marriage often seems to such a person to be a one-way ticket in the direction he wants to travel.

Two Christian authorities on marriage have written convincingly on this point:

> If you belong to a group which as such has low social status . . . you can escape, both for yourself and your children, by marrying a person who belongs to a

> higher status group. Particularly is this true of minority group members who are rebellious or have moved somewhat above the social station of their group. This is shown rather clearly in a study of Gentile-Jewish intermarriages, made some years ago by J. S. Slotkin, of the University of Chicago. He speaks of the rebellious and marginal as two personality types who "amalgamate with members of the dominant group in order to raise their own status."[1]

Other studies corroborate this conclusion. They show that among those who marry outside their own racial or religious groups is to be found a disproportionate number who are "unorganized or demoralized . . . detached . . . rebellious . . . marginal. . . ."[2] A rather curious fact should be noted before we move on from this point. As Jews in America move up the ladder of economic success, it is possible for the restiveness and ambition which often stimulate mixed marriage to operate in either direction. That is to say, a non-Jew of a lower socio-economic category may unconsciously interpret marriage to a Jew to be the same kind of improvement that a Jew desires through marriage to a socially superior Gentile.

Since such personality disorders and social ambitions are probably but not necessarily among the dynamics of mixed marriage, how can a couple contemplating such a match discover the truth in their own case? There is no easy or certain answer. They face the excruciating difficulty confronted by every person who struggles to uncover his own unconscious motivations. Certain clues, however, may be helpful. A man or woman who feels generally inferior or insecure, who has had persistent difficulty getting along with parents, who has been generally uncomfortable or unhappy in Jewish surroundings, who has followed a pattern of dating more non-Jews than Jews, who doesn't see any point to Jewish survival—such a person should indeed be wary of mixed marriage. He should at the very least postpone it, pending a most conscientious effort to examine his real motives. Unless he does this, the prognosis for his marriage leaves much to be desired.

Not a New Story

A second legitimate area of exploration as the rabbi counsels a couple contemplating mixed marriage is the probable effect of matches such as theirs on Jewish survival. Admittedly, this will be an item of major concern only to those who really care about the perpetuation of the Jewish people and their unique civilization. It may even be—in cases where unconscious rejection of Judaism has been a dynamic from the start—that introduction of this factor may strengthen the thrust toward immediate marriage. But in such instances it is doubtful whether any argument or tactic would make a difference.

Those to whom Jewish survival is important should be made aware of the fact that historically this has always been the basis for Jewish opposition to mixed marriages. The first biblical reference to the subject is to be found in Abraham's admonition to his servant when he sent him to find a wife for his son, Isaac: ". . . I will make you swear that you will not take a wife for my son from the daughters of the Canaanites among whom I dwell, but will go to the land of my birth and get a wife for my son. . . ." (Gen. 24:3)

If Abraham was less than explicit in identifying his reason for this instruction, no room is left for guesswork when Deuteronomy restates the matter in terms of legal directives. There our ancestors were warned that when they come to the land which God has promised them and become acquainted with its inhabitants—"you shall not intermarry with them: do not give your daughters to their sons or take their daughters for your sons; for they will turn your children away from Me to worship other gods." Clearly, then, it was the manifest threat to Jewish integrity and survival—not any foolish doctrine of inherent ethnic superiority—which prompted our ancestors to oppose the practice of mixed marriage. They were aware of the fact—as true then as it is now—that when members of a numerically small group intermarry with those of the predominant majority, the direction of assimilation will be overwhelmingly from the smaller to the larger.

Any doubt as to the motivation of ancient Jews is dispelled by two additional biblical books dealing with the subject of mixed marriage. Perhaps the strongest denunciation of this practice anywhere in Jewish literature is to be found in the Book of Ezra, written soon after the Jewish people had returned to their own land from Babylonian exile. The practice of mixed marriage had become quite common during the exile. Not only did Ezra speak against it in unequivocal language, he even went so far as to order that his Jewish contemporaries divorce their gentile wives. The danger of dissolution was grave; only extremely stringent steps could avert it. In Ezra's view, collective survival was entitled to priority over individual happiness.

Another biblical book, Ruth, speaks directly to the opposite side of the question. Here we read of a Moabite girl who becomes something of a heroine by virtue of her marriage to a Jew. Their marriage is described approvingly. No opposition or resentment is voiced. In fact, Ruth becomes in Jewish tradition a progenitor of King David himself! The apparent contradiction between these biblical views can be understood only in terms of the difference in historic context. First, Ruth represented a single instance of mixed marriage, not a wave which threatened to engulf the entire Jewish people. Second, she adopted Judaism as her own faith, living a dedicated Jewish life and even marrying a second Jew after her first husband had died. In short, it is not mixed marriage *per se* which Jewish tradition opposes, but mixed marriage which jeopardizes Jewish survival.

In order to arrive at an intelligent attitude toward mixed marriage in our own time, then, we must undertake to ascertain whether the historic setting today resembles that of Ezra's time or of Ruth's. There can be little doubt. The threat posed by mixed marriage today may not be quite so dramatic as it was for Ezra, but the ultimate consequences are of the same order. Our earlier speculation that in theory the freedom of democratic society would increase the incidence of such marriages has been verified in fact.

Research in the area of Washington, D.C., shows that the rate of such marriages among Jews in the latter 1950's was 13.1 percent. The true significance of these statistics rests in the fact that this was an average for the entire community. Among first-generation Jews in Greater Washington the rate was only 1.4 percent; among second-generation Jews it was 10.2 percent; by the third generation it had reached 17.9 percent.[3] The specific figures will vary from community to community, but there is no doubt that the general trend prevails throughout the country. The rate of mixed marriage a generation hence will most probably be even higher than it is now.

A further statistic compounds the danger to Jewish survival. There is every reason to believe that the vast majority of the children born to mixed couples are reared outside the fold of Judaism. More than just logic or common sense supports this assertion. The Washington survey disclosed that in at least seventy percent of the mixed marriage families, the children were not identified in any way with the Jewish people. This does not justify the assumption that close to 30 percent of these families were taking positive steps to educate their children Jewishly. Just telling the children they were Jews—without in any way reinforcing the statement—sufficed as Jewish identification for the purpose of this study. Other investigations verify the fact that at best less than a fourth of the children born to mixed couples are in any way identified as Jews.[4]

These figures assume their true significance only in light of the fact that the Jewish proportion of the total population in the United States has been steadily declining. In 1937 we were 3.7 percent of the whole, in 1963 only 2.9 percent. If current trends continue, it has been estimated that by the year 2000 no more than 1.6 percent of the American population will be Jewish. We do not mean to attribute all of this to mixed marriage. Other factors, such as a lower birth rate among Jews, are of great importance. Reference was made to this in our presentation of the Jewish point of view on birth control. But mixed marriage is undeniably an alarming part of the problem. The individual Jew who desires Jewish survival and feels a sense of personal responsibility for it cannot enter into a mixed marriage lightly.

ANY REAL DIFFERENCE?

Because this second consideration will count only for the Jew to whom the survival of Judaism matters, let us pause before resuming the mainstream of our thought to see whether Jewish survival is really important. We begin by recognizing that national and religious groups—like individuals—possess unique personalities. Each results from a whole complex of environmental circumstances and historic experiences which have shaped its attitudes and capacities. This is why French music differs from Italian music and German thought is by no means the same as Russian thought.

Civilization is an elaborate tapestry, into which each people has woven its own patterns and colors. If any major component were to be removed, the sum total would be diminished. This is as true of our Jewish people as of any other. We have made our own special kind of contribution to world thought, a contribution which no other group has made in exactly the same way. More persistently and successfully than any other historic culture, we have inquired into the essential meaning of human life and have probed the moral imperatives imposed upon man by the very nature of reality.

No knowledgeable person could doubt that this has been true in the past. Where some of us err, however, is in forgetting that it can be equally true in the future. Again, a comparison between individuals and groups is instructive. Mozart died at the age of thirty-five. Nothing less than the extinction of all civilization could ever impair his prodigious musical accomplishment. But how many works of incomparable genius remained uncomposed at the moment of his death? How much more might he have given mankind had he lived another decade? The wellspring of his creativity had not yet run dry, yet its flow was irretrievably stopped the moment he died.

Similarly, were the Jewish people as such to expire, the threads we have already woven into the fabric of civilization would remain, but the loom would henceforth be deprived of our future potential. No one who believes—as I do most profoundly!—that we Jews have even more to offer mankind in the future than we have given it in the past can view our possible disappearance with anything less than raw dismay.

What is the singular pattern which history has equipped us to weave into the total tapestry? Within the context of a book about marriage, my description of Judaic uniqueness must of necessity be brief. Yet it must be attempted. For what, then, does Judaism stand—especially, uniquely?

First, that the heart of all reality is spiritual, not physical.

It follows from this that if man is to be truly man, and not just the most complex of all animals, his primary pursuit must be after truth, after beauty, after moral goodness—not merely after pleasure and material wealth.

Second, there is a oneness about the universe and mankind. A physical oneness in the sense that everything emanated from the same creative beginning and that the same chemical components and natural laws are operative throughout all existence—from the remotest reaches of outer space to the minutest molecule within my body. There is also a spiritual oneness which inextricably binds each person on earth to every other person, each nation or religion or race to all others.

Third, our noblest ethical aspirations, which derive from the very nature of reality itself, must be applied to every segment of life. There can be no asceticism, no withdrawal, no denial. All of man's experience is susceptible to sanctification. Life is to be divided, as Martin Buber put it, not into the sacred versus the profane, but into the sacred and the not-yet-sacred.

Fourth, every human being on this earth is my brother. The same ethic by which my family life should be governed must be extended to the stranger whose language I don't understand, whose mores may even be entirely beyond my comprehension. I who am descended from oppressed strangers must be forever compassionate to all who are either strangers or oppressed.

Fifth, religion is not a separate compartment of life but is rather a lyric melody which recurs through all the movements of life's symphony, enriching and enhancing the whole. Which means to say: whatever I do as political man or civic man or biological man must be influenced by what I am as religious man.

Sixth, our greatest need today, if humanity is to survive, is a synthesis of the particular and the universal. We must learn to live as citizens of our respective nations, yet simultaneously as citizens of the world. No one is in a better position to succeed at this excruciatingly difficult task than we are. For only we Jews on the world scene today exist in part as a separate nation, living on a soil of its own, yet also as a universal people, scattered over most of the planet. In mankind's ineluctable, urgent, desperate pursuit of peace, we Jews constitute—whether we deliberately will it so or not—as we have in other contexts so many times in the past—an experimental human laboratory, testing for the whole human race concepts and ideals calculated to achieve salvation.

Are we Jews the only ones dedicated to the foregoing emphases? It would be foolish to reply affirmatively. One or another of these values may, of course, by now be found elsewhere, in other cultures and among other individuals. But Judaism originated them as a comprehensive, cohesive pattern. Judaism holds them bound closely together in an integrated, organic whole, which issues out of our collective historic experience. Judaism at its best expresses and reinforces them, without destructive reservations and without adulteration by other insights which are less than faithful to the spirit of these. Judaism, therefore, can best develop them as a pattern for the future. It can, that is, if it survives.

Even with reference to ideals which are universal, Judaism possesses its unique modes of expression. Take, for example, the ideal of freedom—certainly by no means restricted just to Jews. Freedom means something in Judaism that it means nowhere else. No event has been rehearsed more frequently in the telling of our people's history than the Exodus from Egyptian slavery. This could almost be called the seminal episode of our entire past. Out of it grows the ceremonial syndrome of the Passover seder and the intense preoccupation of Jews as such with the struggle of all minorities for emancipation. If the

Jewish people and culture were to vanish, the universal cause of freedom—celebration of its past accomplishment and encouragement for its future struggle—would thereby be diminished.

There is much, then, to be lost by assimilation. Civilization would be bereft of Jewish music, Jewish literature, Jewish art, and—above all—of the rich continuing possibilities of Jewish spiritual insight. Is it too much to ask the young Jew who is enamored of a Gentile to think of this? I hope not.

A Third Consideration

The rabbi who spurs a young couple to examine their own motives for desiring mixed marriage may be expecting more than most couples will be capable of achieving. His argument for Jewish survival will touch only those to whom this survival has already assumed importance. But his third proper area of concern—the probability of happiness in marriage—will be minimized or ignored by any prospective bride and groom only at their own peril.

The plain, unvarnished, inescapable fact is that couples of mixed religious background have a substantially lower prospect for success than do couples within a given group. This is true both religiously and racially. Everything we have said about interreligious marriages, as a matter of fact, applies with added emphasis to interracial marital partnerships. As our society is currently constituted and is likely to be for a long time to come, the odds faced by a Negro-white couple are even more formidable than those confronting a gentile-Jewish couple.

Let the truth be acknowledged: every marriage is to some extent a gamble against risks. The balance between maturity and love on the one hand, and tension and stress on the other, is often precarious. A construction engineer knows that if he imposes upon a steel beam greater weight than it was fabricated to carry, he takes a chance that his whole building will collapse. The same thing is true in marriage, though unfortunately the weight which can be carried by any specific couple cannot be calculated with anything like the precision available to the builder. The additional burdens inherent in an interreligious or interracial marriage—over and above those to be carried by every couple—increase the risk enormously. One of the most agonizing frustrations faced by every marriage counselor is the difficulty of impressing this upon the couple contemplating mixed marriage. Each such couple without exception, admitting the danger in principle, is firmly convinced of its own ability to surmount all obstacles. The fact that many of them return later to acknowledge the grim truth is of little consolation or help to the conscientious counselor in his effort to aid the next couple.

The statistical evidence is convincing. It discloses the divorce rate in cases of mixed marriage to be between three and four times that in other marriages. In one of the earliest authentic scientific studies of marriage, Burgess and Cottrell concluded that the chance for marital success is eleven times greater where husband and wife agree on all religious matters than where they differ. A study made some years ago by the American Youth Commission revealed the number of young people in several categories who were found to come from broken homes:

Both parents Jewish	4.6 percent
Both parents Catholic	6.4 percent
Both parents Protestant	6.8 percent
Parents from mixed religions	15.2 percent
Parents with no religion	16.7 percent

It is the fourth of these figures which concerns us most directly here. It confirms the conclusions of all other available surveys.

There is no need to exaggerate. No one at all conversant with the matter would pretend that no mixed marriages ever succeed. Religious background is scarcely the only factor adding up to failure or success in marriage. But it is one of the more important considerations. At an earlier point we emphasized the importance of cultural congruity and compatibility. Religion is an important aspect of culture, often far more important than is realized by a young couple about to be married. A host of religious experiences and impressions has already been absorbed into the total personality of both bride and groom, many more than either of them may consciously remember. These cannot easily be erased or expunged.

Religion involves more than theological doctrine. This is especially true of Judaism, which has always been more a way of life than of belief. Judaism involves one's attitudes toward the meaning of life, frames of reference regarding sex, patterns of family behavior, idioms and idiosyncracies of expression, peculiarities of food and holiday rituals. A Jew who is accustomed to observing Chanukah and Passover might find it painfully difficult to celebrate Christmas and Easter instead. A Christian who had been baptized and had regularly taken Communion could feel lost, even ineradicably guilty, in the absence of these practices. There are many subtle yet vital aspects of each person's life no less imperative for the fact that they may have been taken for granted—the absence or disruption of which can cause extreme unhappiness.

No couple can afford to ignore all this, not even if religion seems currently to bear no special importance to either of them. They perpetrate a gross injustice against themselves if they "freeze" their spiritual lives at what may well be only a temporary climate of indifference. We shall see in our next chapter that religion can and should be one of the most creative forces enriching the relationship between husband and wife. This often proves to be true even of couples who, at the time of their marriage, are still religiously neutral. At the very least, interreligious marriage precludes this entire area of sharing. It may also transpose what should be a positive, love-inducing phase of life into a cause of friction and hate.

Christian authorities have no need to be concerned with Jewish survival or with the persistence of their own religious traditions. Since the direction of assimilation will most often be toward rather than away from them, in strictly mundane terms they stand to gain, not to lose from mixed marriages. The fact that they are nevertheless so frequently and emphatically opposed is based on the danger such marriages pose to the couples involved. No doubt this is what motivated the General Conference of the Methodist Church to declare in 1956 that "recent research has emphasized the importance of common cultural and religious backgrounds as the foundation of successful marriage. . . . Ministers are urged to discuss with both youth and parents the likelihood of failure in mixed marriages."[5] In 1959 the Lutheran Church Missouri Synod adopted a statement affirming that " religious agreement between a husband and wife is undoubtedly one of the major factors in securing that peace and harmony that makes possible the normal functions and development of Christian family life."[6]

Secular experts on marriage are generally in agreement. Thus Dr. Clarence Leuba, professor emeritus of psychology at Antioch College, concludes:

> In every marriage there are bound to be some outstanding differences in interests, attitudes, and beliefs; but a marriage cannot stand too many of them. . . . Cultural, religious, or racial differences are of this sort; they are likely to have far-reaching effects on marital adjustments. . . . Where the marriage partners come from different religious, economic, political, or

social backgrounds, there are endless possible sources of irritation.[7]

INNOCENT VICTIMS

The foregoing considerations are true in the first instance in the immediate relationship between husband and wife. What gives them very special urgency, however, is the problem of children born to a mixed couple. If one wanted to be callous or crude, he could simply say that two people who disregard so many compelling factors in marriage deserve whatever of grief they thereby bring upon themselves. But their children are entirely innocent—they made no choice, they had no alternatives, they did not even ask to be born. Yet how often they are the most piteous victims of the religious divergence between their parents!

Orthodox and Conservative Jews subscribe to the traditional view that a child automatically follows the religion of his mother. With or without the conversion of a Christian husband to Judaism, then, so long as his wife remains Jewish, their children are considered Jews. Reform Judaism relies more on parental intention than on the mother's faith. In the eyes of Reform no matter which parent is Jewish, regardless of whether the Christian partner was converted, the fact that parents choose to enroll their children in a synagogue school and see them through to Bar Mitzvah and Confirmation qualifies these youngsters as Jews. But these fine distinctions among the several branches of Judaism have little to do with the gnawing insecurity from which the offspring of a mixed marriage are likely to suffer.

A child's most desperate need is to know where he belongs. If born to religiously mixed parents, he is not likely to achieve this security. He will probably be made to suffer certain disadvantages by virtue of the fact that one parent is or was Jewish—wondering from time to time why he cannot choose to be identified instead with the other who is not Jewish—oblivious to the positive pride which comes from knowledge of Judaism and which can provide an effective antidote to painful prejudice.

Again, this is more than just theory. I remember a woman who came to me years ago, insisting that I convert her to Judaism prior to officiating at her marriage to a Jewish man. Her unexpected vehemence elicited my curiosity. When questioned, she said: "Rabbi, I am myself the product of a mixed Protestant-Catholic marriage. I know in my own blood and bones the terrible uncertainty which afflicts such a child. Under no circumstances would I ever cause such pain to any child of mine. This is why I insist that my marriage be based on a religiously unified home!"

Where unity is not achieved, children often become hapless ropes in an emotional tug of war; if not between their parents, then perhaps between competing grandparents. It is extremely difficult for two families of divergent religious loyalties not to press their respective points of view, however subtly, upon their grandchildren. And the consequence—more often than some of us would like to contemplate—is a confused, neurotic child.

Sometimes even intelligent parents deceive themselves on this score. They act as if all the problems posed by interfaith marriage have been solved, but their children reveal the truth —in erratic behavior when they are young, or in confidential conversation with trusted advisors when they reach high school or college age. It is not uncommon for a clergyman, psychiatrist, or college professor to hear from the offspring of such marriages that even at a tender age they detected the religious animosity between their parents and felt a devastating war being waged through and over themselves.

Not only do parents often use their children as pawns in working out their unresolved religious conflicts, children also play their parents one against the other. Several of my colleagues have been confronted in recent years with adolescent, usually post-Bar Mitzvah children who refused to continue their religious education. Their justification was that since only one parent was Jewish, they reserved the right to follow the one who was gentile. The problem is serious and potentially disruptive enough even when it is thus expressed on a conscious level. When repressed to the unconscious, it becomes ever so much more explosive, both to the marriage and to the mental health of the youngsters.

Neat intellectual solutions agreed upon in theory before the wedding seldom stand up to the stubborn demands of life. The agreement of the parents cited at the outset of this chapter—to stagger their children's religious education between synagogue and church—would be funny if it were not so tragic. The cost to the children, in confusion and hopeless despair, is inordinately high. The crux of the difficulty is that not even the wisest and most perceptive of young people can anticipate in advance just how the experiences of parenthood will affect them. To agree intellectually in advance that one's child will be reared in no religious tradition, or in that of one's mate, may seem at the time like such a simple, sensible solution. But when the child is actually here, snuggling in one's arms, suddenly the whole experience becomes overwhelmingly emotional, not just intellectual. Circumcision and Bar Mitzvah and Confirmation for the Jew—Baptism and Communion for the Christian—no matter how little these seemed to mean to each at an earlier stage of his life, may now loom up as matters of utmost urgency.

A Lutheran in my community once came to see me. Or at least I had known him for several years as a Lutheran. Only after several highly charged false starts sitting at the opposite side of my desk did he reveal to me that he had been born a Jew. Religion had meant so little to him that he felt no sense of sacrifice at all in glibly agreeing with his Lutheran wife that their children would follow her faith. In the case of their elder child, a daughter, this hadn't seemed to pose any unusual problems. But he had come to see me in desperation now because his son was just six months short of his thirteenth birthday. "Rabbi," he blurted out sporadically between tears, "I have suddenly realized that this boy of mine will be the first male in our family for centuries not to celebrate a Bar Mitzvah. I haven't been able to sleep one night since this thought came to me. What can I do?"

No human being on earth can be immune in his early twenties from this kind of shattering experience a decade and a half later.

"What Can I Do?"

Have I betrayed my self-imposed charge not to play God in other people's lives? Have I come down so hard in intervening pages on the couple contemplating mixed marriage as actually to attempt dissuading them? I hope not, for this has not been my intention. I wanted rather, with all my mind and heart, to apprise them of the rough road ahead in the hope that I might help them prepare for their journey. If I knew the trip two people had planned for themselves was charted over a route scarred with ridges and pits, would I not be responsible for warning them in advance? I feel the same sort of responsibility toward the reader who may be on the threshold of a mixed marriage.

It was too late for an effective answer to my Lutheran friend's anguished "what can I do?" Had he asked me the same question sixteen years earlier, I might have been able to help.

How? First, by doing precisely what I have attempted in foregoing paragraphs: spelling out the kind of problems he would have to face. To proceed as if they didn't exist, or blithely to assume that "we're different, we'll be the exception, our love will be strong enough to surmount any obstacle . . ." is to invite disaster.

My second way of helping would have been to suggest the desirability of his non-Jewish sweetheart's studying Judaism, even considering conversion to Judaism, before their marriage took place. This is not an easy kind of advice to give. Not for one who is firmly convinced, as I am, that religious conversion should never be undertaken purely for purposes of expediency. My faith means far too much to me to permit that it be treated cheaply or lightly. The only person who has a moral right to convert, the only person whom I as a rabbi would ever be willing to help convert, is one who, after carefully studying Judaism, had arrived at the genuine conviction that it holds out a set of values and practices to which he is willing to commit the rest of his life.

Obviously I have this possibility in mind in suggesting that the prospective gentile mate of a Jew undertake the study of Judaism. But no commitment should be either expected or accepted until that course of study nears its completion. Even if it does not lead to conversion, it holds the patent advantage of helping the non-Jew understand the background of his mate and some of the problems with which their marriage will have to contend.

Every rabbi is confronted by couples who have agreed that their children will eventually be reared as Jews, but who stop short of actual conversion prior to being married. Such couples need to think through in greater depth the implications of their decision. Most cases of mixed marriage involve a Jewish groom and a gentile bride. For the traditionalist Jew, this immediately poses a problem; we have already seen that according to rabbinic law a child automatically follows the faith of his mother. But even those who no longer accept such laws literally must recognize that the religious flavor of the home is determined in most cases more by the mother than the father. One must wonder, then, just how feasible it is for a non-Jewish mother to succeed in rearing Jewish children. Even where the prospective husband is the gentile, however, the domestic tensions and competitions we have already discussed remain as potential aggravations unless conversion precedes marriage.

Why do I suggest only that the non-Jew consider conversion to Judaism? Why not conversion in the opposite direction? My first and primary reason emerges from our previous discussion on Jewish survival. One of my most sacred responsibilities as a rabbi is to do my utmost to increase the prospects for meaningful Jewish survival. It is only through a unified *Jewish* home that this becomes possible.

But there is another reason, perhaps even a more practical one, for thinking only in terms of a change to Judaism. Most couples of mixed religious background soon discover that in any event all or nearly all their social life turns out to be with Jewish friends. Their children, moreover, are generally considered by their peers to be Jews. This means that such couples and their families are Jews *de facto,* that they experience the superficial and often the negative aspects of Jewish life, whether or not they choose to participate in the positive and creative advantages of being Jewish.

A word is in order here concerning the couple who wishes to be married by a rabbi, despite the unwillingness of the gentile mate to become Jewish. No Orthodox or Conservative rabbi will officiate at such a ceremony; only a small minority of Reform rabbis will do so. The majority who will not are moved by their responsibilities both to Judaism and to the individual couple. To consent to exploitation as an expedient, to be "used" in order to make such a marriage more palatable to parents or grandparents, is less a favor to the insistent couple than to force a hard, penetrating confrontation with reality. The couple unable or unwilling to reach a definitive resolution of their many problems prior to marriage will not find it easier to do so afterward, when more than a few additional complications will have entered the picture.

Does the rabbi who refuses to officiate at a mixed marriage thereby reject the couple, driving them forever away from Judaism? Not if he is considerate and they are mature. Whenever possible, his reasons should be expressed not in a perfunctory telephone conversation or letter, but in a relaxed personal interview. He should make it clear that his refusal to violate his own professional conscience does not constitute personal rejection, that both he and Judaism are willing to accept the couple as human beings and to acknowledge the validity of their marriage even if it has been solemnized at a civil ceremony. Naturally, a rabbi is convinced that something important is lost when such a ceremony must replace the religious ritual. But couples who pose complicated problems must not expect the rabbi to be the kind of miracle worker who can always find a perfect solution for them. They may have to settle realistically for the best of several imperfect alternatives. It is they, after all—not the rabbi—who created the problem. His responsibility is limited to compassionate understanding, to truthful explanation, and to an open door policy which will encourage such a couple to return for continued discussion even after their marriage.

The Specifics of Conversion

In all three major branches of American Judaism the primary prerequisite for conversion is a thorough process of study. The curriculum and method of instruction will vary from branch to branch, even from rabbi to rabbi. In Orthodoxy the content of the candidate's instruction is likely to center mostly on the ritual laws involved in maintaining a Jewish home. In Reform these procedures will be less central than the study of Jewish history and thought. A Conservative rabbi will probably strike some degree of middle ground between the other two.

Both Reform and Conservative Judaism have established unified classes for conversion in most metropolitan centers. In smaller communities the instruction is more likely to be given by an individual rabbi. An appendix to this volume contains a reading list for any non-Jewish reader who is unable to consult a rabbi or class but desires to learn more about Judaism.

The ritual requirements for conversion vary among the branches of Judaism. Orthodox law demands that a male convert be circumcized and immersed in a מקוה (*mikvah*) or ritual bath; a female convert also requires immersion. These traditional procedures are waived by Reform practice. Most Conservative rabbis will probably approximate the Orthodox pattern. In Reform Judaism the ceremony itself consists of a brief prayer service, often held in the synagogue or chapel before the opened ark. The convert promises to accept Judaism, to cast his lot under all circumstances with the Jewish people, and to rear his children as Jews. Though Reform Judaism does not insist on the circumcision of adult males, it generally does expect a pledge that any male children born to the couple will be circumcized.

The conversion of a non-Jew to Judaism is frequently a traumatic experience for his Christian family. To a lesser degree, but sometimes in a troublesome way nonetheless, acceptance of a convert can be difficult for a Jewish family. Actually, it should not be. Our tradition is unambiguous on the matter. Though Judaism has not actively sought converts through the greater part of its history, it has always welcomed them warmly. Jewish law insists that a genuine convert is in nearly every respect a Jew. The only exception would be that a convert could not become a כהן (*kohane*), a priest. Maimonides was asked whether a convert to Judaism—in view of his biological background—should join the congregation in the prayer which commences, "Our God and God of our fathers. . . ." His answer was affirmative; he held that once a person has accepted our faith, he is to be considered as if even his ancestors had been Jews. We are enjoined, moreover, by Jewish tradition never to remind a convert of the fact that he was not born a Jew, lest he thereby be embarrassed.

It would be foolish to assume that, because of our tradition and law, every Jewish parent will immediately and fully accept a converted daughter- or son-in-law. Patience and love on the part of the involved couple can help; in some cases the assistance of a cooperative rabbi might also be sought. Both sets of parents should be treated respectfully and lovingly, unless they, by irrational and unreasonable behavior, make this impossible. Their needs are very real, often extremely urgent, and are not to be treated casually.

The Jew whose mate has converted for the sake of a happier marriage and a unified home assumes serious responsibilities as a consequence. The first of these is to study Judaism along with the candidate for conversion. Once or twice in the earliest years of my rabbinic career I experienced the unhappy suspicion that a man or woman whom I was converting may have known more about Judaism than the Jewish counterpart. To prevent this intolerable anomaly, I henceforth insisted that both parties study together.

The Jewish mate must accept also an obligation to practice a meaningful Jewish life, not to act indifferently toward that which his spouse has worked so hard to attain. I have been involved in two instances where a convert to Judaism desired many years later to revert to her original faith, simply because her "Jewish" husband seemed to have no use for Judaism, never observed the sancta of his faith at home, never attended public services of worship. Surely we have no right to expect of converts a greater regard for Judaism than we who were born to it are ready to exhibit ourselves.

A final word on the subject of mixed marriage. Conversion is not a perfect preventive against all abrasions. The varying backgrounds of the individuals involved obviously cannot be obliterated. In a sense, each of us is at any given moment the sum total of heredity plus all the experiences he has ever known. Not even a sincere conversion based on study and commitment can erase the digits which add up to what each individual is at the moment of marriage. What it can do is to influence the future, if not the past; it can pave the way toward a unified quest for the ultimate meaning of life and a spiritually harmonious setting for the rearing of happy children.

«««««««14»»»»»»»

Faith and Future

A RABBI WHO PROCLAIMS THAT RELIGION IS AN IMPORTANT INgredient of successful marriage may be suspected of special pleading. There is much evidence from impartial sources, however, to substantiate this view. Reference was made just a few pages back to the American Youth Commission study. Even more alarming than the proportion of divorces it revealed among couples of mixed religious background was the evidence of failure by those who claimed no religious affiliation. Among students born to Jewish parents, 4.6 percent came from broken homes; the comparable percentage among those whose parents practiced no religion was 16.7!

Bishop James A. Pike of the Episcopal Church calls our attention to surveys showing that the divorce rate among couples who are identified with neither synagogue nor church runs two and a quarter times that of couples who actively share a common religious tradition.[1] Evelyn and Sylvanus Duvall summarize a number of similar studies by saying:

> . . . those who rate high in religiousness in all of the faith groups have a high happiness rating in marriage and a low divorce rate. Success in marriage is closely related to whether the married couple have religious or nonreligious families.[2]

A survey made at the University of Southern California disclosed that among couples belonging to the same church 68 percent of the men were happily married; in a comparable group where neither husband nor wife was a church member only 31 percent of the men had achieved marital happiness.[3]

The Oklahoma City Family Clinic reached a similar conclusion. In attempting to reconcile 250 couples whose marriages were rocky, the clinic staff achieved much greater success with those who attended church services than with others. It was concluded that participation together in religious activities made reconciliation "almost a certainty."[4]

These impressive statistics should not be misinterpreted. They do not mean that active religious affiliation guarantees success in marriage. Certainly a religious identification which is only nominal—which amounts to no more than an annual payment of dues plus a semiannual antipasto of public worship—can exert little or no favorable effect on a marriage. What our studies do indicate is that, all else being equal, the active sharing of a religious life can be an important contribution to any couple's happiness. There seems to be almost an intuitive acceptance of this truth even among those who show no other evidence of religiosity. How else explain the fact that, despite the legal respectability of civil ceremonies, the overwhelming majority of Americans ask a clergyman to officiate at their weddings? Or that so many who seldom frequent a synagogue or church are nonetheless anxious to have their nuptials solemnized in a sanctuary?

The noteworthy correlation between religious affiliation and marital happiness should not surprise us. It can be explained in part by the fact that the personal characteristics which impel people toward the religious life coincide with those which make for good marriages. Even more significant, however, is our earlier conclusion that the more two persons share of cultural background and interests in general, the happier their marriage is likely to be. If this be true with regard to such man-made aspects of culture as literature, music, or art—how much truer in the cosmically oriented culture of religious faith! Two who share an active quest for the ultimate meaning of human life, who search together for their cosmic address, who strive to comprehend whether or not their love reflects an ineffable Source of Love in the universe—two such as these have touched together as deeply in their sharing as is humanly possible. Their marriage is likely to achieve a dimension which is attainable in no other way. Dr. James A. Peterson puts this point with exceptional clarity:

> Religious values, when sincerely believed and made a pivotal part of one's aspirations, must contribute to marital adjustment because these are the very values that are most necessary for it. . . . It matters in marriage whether a couple reach upward in their common interests toward that which is creative and lofty or whether they are content with that which is tawdry and inconsequential.[5]

Added Emphasis

It matters especially in Judaism. A religious civilization such as ours, which has always emphasized deed more than creed, must necessarily impinge on marriage at many points. Many centuries ago the Midrash recognized the importance of religion in marriage: "No man without a woman, nor a woman without a man, nor both of them without God."[6]

The rabbis indulged in an intriguing play on words to illustrate this truth. They observed that the Hebrew word for man is איש (*ish*), while that for woman is אשה (*isha*). The first of these words contains the letter י, which is missing from the second; the second contains the letter ה, which is not found in the first. These two letters together spell one of the Hebrew abbreviations for God. When they are removed from the Hebrew for *man* and *woman*, there remains in each case the word אש (*aysh*), meaning fire. From all this our rabbis deduced that when God is removed from the relationship between man and woman, nothing but consuming fire remains. Only if God is present in all they experience together, is it possible for their marriage to be fully human.[7]

Thus—and in many other ways—did the ancient teachers of Judaism emphasize the importance of religion to marriage. There are numerous contexts within which a sensitive person can feel a close personal relationship to God. We sense God in the beauty of the universe, in a mystical awareness of kinship between ourselves and the rest of nature, in the emergent thrust of life toward higher evolutionary goals, in our own moral aspirations and values, in the exquisite excitement of discovering a new truth, in our recognition of cosmic purpose to which, if we will, we can contribute.

But in the love of husband and wife—more than in any other experience accessible to human reach—we come close to the divine spirit which permeates the universe. And in the love act which unites both body and soul, through which they can initiate a new life—more than in anything else they do—a married couple becomes God's creative partners. To experience and appreciate this is to know marriage in its noblest dimension.

On almost every page of this volume we have encountered some insight of Judaism on love and marriage. It would be naive to assume that memorizing them will automatically assure your happiness. It is important to know the marriage and family ideals of Judaism, but also to realize that there is often a gap between intellectual understanding and emotional acceptance. It is naive to assume that the distance between head and heart is always twelve inches; sometimes it proves to be many miles. Not everyone is capable of achieving the kind of marriage envisaged by our tradition.

All of us are moved by unconscious as well as conscious factors. This is likely to be especially true in our sex lives. Most of us are ordinarily able to live comfortably without exploring our unconscious. We manage to keep our intentions and performances sufficiently aligned to maintain good health and self-respect. Where this is not the case, where even the most diligent effort seems unavailing in an individual's desire to implement the marital ideals of his faith, it may be that psychotherapy is indicated.

But this will be the exception rather than the rule. Just as most of us can go through life successfully without surgery, so most have no need of psychotherapy, which perhaps might be defined as a form of emotional surgery. The important thing to remember is that our conduct is motivated not only by the unconscious pushing us from below, but also by our conscious values and ideals, pulling us upward from above. It is here that the values emerging from Judaism can be of such vital help.

"My Beloved Is Mine"

Because our rabbis appreciated the immense importance of religion in marriage, they devised a marriage ceremony of singular significance and beauty. They called it קדושין (*kiddushin*), coming from the same root as קדוש (*kiddush*) and קדיש (*kaddish*) and expressing the idea of sanctity. Originally designating the betrothal ceremony, קדושין became the term most commonly used for the combined rituals as we know them today. The details of a Jewish wedding ceremony vary from group to group; the essentials are the same. There are seven Hebrew blessings which acknowledge God as the universal Source of Love and identify the couple being married with the whole of Jewish tradition. Bride and groom drink from either one or two glasses of wine, symbolizing the fact that henceforth they will taste together both the happiness and sorrow of life. As the groom places a ring on the bride's finger, he recites the following formula: הרי את מקדשת לי בטבעת זו כדת משה וישראל (*Ha-ray at m'ku-deshet lee b'ta-ba-at zu k'dat moshe v'yis-ra-ayl*)—"Behold, thou art consecrated unto me by this ring (as my wife), in accordance with the faith of Moses and of Israel." In traditional ceremonies the ring must be a plain gold band, without engraving or stones. Reform rabbis permit use of the ring the bride plans to wear permanently, even if it is adorned. The ring symbolizes a sum of money which earlier Jewish grooms handed to their brides during the ceremony.

Increasingly in modern times the bride also places a ring on her groom's finger. Apparently this practice was known even in ancient days, for the Talmud suggests a formula for her to recite.[8] That formula seems never to have been adopted, however, as common usage. Some rabbis today simply ask the bride to repeat the groom's declaration with a change of gender, making it: הרי אתה מקדש לי בטבעת זו כדת משה וישראל (*Ha-ray ata m'ku-dash lee b'ta-ba-at zu k'dat moshe v'yis-ra-ayl*)—"Behold, thou art consecrated unto me by this ring (as my husband), in accordance with the faith of Moses and of Israel." Other rabbis direct the bride to address her groom in words taken from Song of Songs: דודי לי ואני לו—"My beloved is mine and I am his."

Jewish tradition suggests that at the very end of the ceremony the groom break a glass by stomping on it with his foot. Most Reform rabbis deem this to be an optional part of the ceremony, following the wishes of the couple. This custom probably goes back to pre-Jewish primitive times, when among various nations and tribes it was customary to break a piece of ceramic or glass on happy occasions. People who were rejoicing over a birth or a wedding considered themselves to be especially vulnerable to attack by evil spirits. By breaking some object of value, they thought perhaps they could either frighten these spirits away or convince them that they were really suffering enough already and should be left alone.

Many religious rituals of modern faiths can thus be traced back to their origins in prehistoric superstition. This does not necessarily invalidate them. The important thing is not the inception of a given custom but the reason attributed to it later by a developing tradition. In this case our rabbis explained that a Jew should pause even in the happiest moment of his life to remember the destruction of the Temple in Jerusalem. Hence, the breaking of the glass.

Another explanation offered in the Talmud makes a point very much needed in our own time.

> Mar bar Rabina made a marriage feast for his son. He observed that the rabbis present were very gay. So he seized an expensive goblet worth 400 zuzim and broke it before them. Thus he made them somber. When Rab Ashi made a marriage feast for his son, he also noticed that the rabbis were rejoicing excessively. So he took a costly cup of white glass and broke it before them. This filled them with sorrow.[9]

We shall resume this thought in a moment. Suffice it to say for the present that if the rabbi is willing to leave the decision on the breaking of a glass up to the bride and groom, they should consider the reasons summarized above and decide in accordance with their own desires.

We return to the ceremony. Among Orthodox and Conservative Jews the couple stands beneath a marriage canopy known in Hebrew as a חופה (*chupah*). Sometimes in Reform or Conservative ceremonies a simulated חופה is used, made of flowers. As part of their ceremonies Orthodox and Conservative rabbis read what is known as a כתובה (*ketubah*), a contract in which the groom accepts certain legal obligations and financial responsibilities toward his bride. Reform rabbis generally replace the כתובה with a modified and abbreviated marriage certificate.

A Limit to Affluence

We may safely assume that what bothered Mar bar Rabina and Rab Ashi was not excessive joy as such but rather a lack of proper dignity and restraint. In many periods of our history this has been the concern of Jewish religious authorities. The eminent historian, Dr. Salo Baron, attests to this in the following paragraphs:

> Beginning with the fifteenth century, more and more communal organs, regional as well as local, felt the need of issuing a *pragmatica*, or some other ordinance, describing in great detail the articles of clothing which might be worn by various individuals on certain occasions, the number of guests and musicians who might be invited to certain functions, and the amount and type of food which might be served at such celebrations. Various reasons were advanced in justification of such sumptuary ordinances: the envy of ever suspicious gentile neighbors usually aroused by a display of costly garments or jewelry and by revelry in feasting; the attempt to keep up with the neighbors which led to the impoverishment of numerous families and converted many a celebration into a sorrowful occasion; the frequent indebtedness of extravagant

> celebrants to Gentiles and the ensuing enmity in the case of bankruptcy; the obliteration of what were considered legitimate distinctions between rich and poor or, on the contrary, the underscoring of such distinctions. . . .
>
> . . . The Castilian synod of 1432 . . . ordered the communities to call within thirty days, a meeting for the purpose of regulating expenditure for food "at the time of betrothals and weddings and the birth of a child and other seasons of rejoicing." The need for such regulation was felt most strongly in Italy, where the gay and colorful life of the general population invited imitation. . . . The Conference of Forli in 1418, acting for many North Italian communities and prompted by the consideration that the Jews spent on banquets "more than they could afford and more than the wealthy Christians among whom we live," reduced the number of guests who might be invited to a wedding to a maximum of twenty men, ten married women and five girls in addition to relatives up to the third degree (second cousins). Transgressors were to be punished by a fine of one ducat for each guest in excess of the permitted number. . . . The communities of the County Wied-Runkel thought that they were adopting "a truly profitable and acceptable ordinance" when they forbade the invitation of any guests except relatives to the third degree for weddings, to the second degree for other festivities. . . .[10]

There are intriguing contemporary overtones at various points in the foregoing; certain phrases sound almost as if they had been written today. Yet if our problems are quite similar, the circumstances surrounding them are vastly different. We no longer have Jewish communities with the power to issue compulsory decrees and to police them. Whatever restraint is exercised today, therefore, must be voluntary, resulting from the discipline and good taste of the individual rather than the power of the community. While there are one or two American cities in which rabbinical associations have imposed rules governing the locale of weddings and the outer limits of sumptuary embellishment, for the most part the influence of the rabbis is based only on education and persuasion.

Jewish religious authorities are agreed that the wedding ceremony should be one of simple dignity, that the spiritual significance of the occasion must not be obliterated or overbalanced by ostentation. The social celebration should augment the religious ceremony, not outshine it. So far as possible, we should strive to emulate the spirit of Jewish law, which insisted that if a prospective bride lacked the means for a respectable wedding gown, it became the responsibility of the community to provide one. Where bride and groom face financial problems in their early years of marriage, how much more appropriate and sensible it is for their parents to offer continuing assistance over a period of time in lieu of an extravagant splash following the wedding ceremony. Even where no financial worries are anticipated, an expression of family joy through contributions to important philanthropies in honor of the wedding is far more admirable than garish display. This paragraph should not be misinterpreted to be harshly critical of all wedding receptions; it is a plea only for proper proportion. The probability of achieving such balance is greater when the ceremony takes place in the bride's synagogue or home than when it occurs in a hotel or club.

Not an Island

The wedding ceremony is not an isolated event. Its religious flavor is likely to reflect that which has been characteristic of both bride and groom in the past and to foreshadow the quality of their religious life in the future. Jewish tradition provided a period of spiritual preparation preceding the marriage ritual. The bride was expected to visit the מקוה (*mikvah*) or ritual-bath, where her physical immersion in water symbolized an ethical and spiritual cleansing in anticipation of her nuptials. Both partners were obliged to fast on the wedding day itself and to seek atonement for their sins. Despite the fact that literal observance of these customs has been discarded by all but the most Orthodox among American Jews, we would do well to prepare for the marriage ceremony in the spirit dictated by the Shulchan Aruch:

> It is essential that the groom and bride upon entering the nuptial ceremony, purify themselves before God, by repenting of their sins, by reviewing all their deeds from the day of their birth up to that day, by confessing their sins and beseeching Him, blessed be His name, to grant them pardon, forgiveness and atonement.
>
> They should firmly resolve thenceforth to devote themselves to the worship of God, truly and sincerely, and to be holy and pure, and thereafter they should enter under the nuptial canopy and pray unto the Holy One, blessed be His name, that He may make His divine presence rest among them, as the wise, of blessed memory, said: "The Divine Presence rests between a husband and his wife."[11]

How thoroughly appropriate and constructive it would be if the hilarity—sometimes even vulgarity—which often attends the separate celebrations held for the bride and groom on the night preceding their wedding were to be replaced by a joint חשבון הנפש (*cheshbon hanefesh*), a spiritual audit of the past and solemn dedication of themselves to the future. Here again Jewish tradition is instructive. For centuries it has been common practice for the prospective groom to be called to the Torah on the Sabbath before his wedding. In many modern synagogues a prayer for the welfare of bride and groom is incorporated in the Sabbath service and they are invited respectively to recite the Torah blessings and kindle the Sabbath candles. Hopefully, this augurs well for their future participation in the life of the congregation.

After the ceremony, too, prayer can play an important role. A moment at the end of each day for quiet reflection together, an opportunity to express their gratitude for the love which unites them, a reappraisal of their relationship and its enhancement for the future—all this, accomplished through daily prayer, can add a dimension of richness to every marriage. The prayers voiced together by husband and wife in times of crisis or stress will be ever so much more meaningful if they are already accustomed to regular prayers of appreciation and inventory. And the silent communion of each with God—where there is no need to win an argument or save face—can add immeasurably to the compassion and consideration demonstrated to his mate the next day.[12]

Public affiliation of a young married couple with the synagogue is no less important than the private practice of prayer. Most congregations today sponsor special clubs or groups for such couples and offer lower rates of membership dues for those who cannot yet afford the normal higher levels. There is a good chance that the pattern of synagogue affiliation or indifference which you establish at the very outset of your married life will prevail permanently. Hence the extreme importance of a good beginning. In a large city which offers a variety of congregations, many newly-weds will want to attend religious services in several places and meet a number of rabbis before deciding upon the group with which they wish to become affiliated.

Suppose bride and groom originate from different types of congregations—one from a Reform background, the other from either a Conservative or Orthodox group? We have already indicated in an earlier chapter that this can cause difficulties of adjustment. What is required under such circumstances is an acceptance of each other's habits and needs, coupled with a willingness to maintain an open mind and heart as they seek together for a solution which comes closest to satisfying the religious needs of both. The very least such a couple should do is to attend services in both types of synagogue, always with the objective of welcoming a new learning experience and attempting to appreciate novel religious values. While there is no formula which will cover all such cases, the husband and wife who possess in all other respects the prerequisites for a good marriage will be able, by mutual understanding and love, to solve this problem.

The subject of synagogue membership should not be closed without brief comment on the value of such association prior to the wedding ceremony. The couple who can approach their officiating rabbi as a personal friend, who can seek premarital counsel from one who knows them and has perhaps taught and confirmed them, who can be married by a spiritual leader whose ceremony is personal because he knows them, has every advantage over those for whom the rabbi, as a stranger, can be only a professional officiant.

RITUAL OR ROTE?

Before approaching the importance of religious ritual in the home of the newly married couple, it would be wise to comment on the subject of ritual in general. For many, the word itself has unfortunately acquired a pejorative connotation, implying either the performance of meaningless rote or acting out neurotic compulsions or attempting by magic to influence the fates. It would be foolish to deny that ritual has indeed sometimes degenerated to all of these immature manifestations. But the fact that any form of human behavior is subject to abuse should not blind us to its possible value. Patriotism and parental love have also been disastrously distorted. Yet who would seriously propose that they therefore be totally contemned? Our task, then, must be not to repudiate ritual but rather to inquire into its creative role.

At its best, ritual is a poetic symbol, through which we undertake to express in movement a value, an attitude, a feeling, an ideal which words alone are unable fully to articulate. Shaking hands is a ritual. Though we have long outgrown what appears to have been the original reason for this custom—demonstrating that one is not carrying a concealed weapon in his hand—it still symbolizes our openness to friendship, our readiness to accept the person by whom we would ourselves like to be accepted. By a firm and affectionate handshake one friend can communicate to another far more than he can express with even the most eloquent of words.

Saluting the flag is a ritual. Whether it is an empty gesture or a meaningful symbol depends on the experience and intent of the individual. I served during World War II as a chaplain in the United States Marine Corps. My combat duty was with the Fifth Marine Division on Iwo Jima. At the very moment when the famous flag-raising occurred on Mt. Suribachi I was officiating at burials in our Division Cemetery at the foot of the mountain. For the rest of my life I shall never again salute an American flag anywhere without feeling again something of the spine-tingling emotion I experienced when I just happened to look toward Suribachi's top that morning and saluted as I witnessed the flag being hoisted on a piece of temporary piping.

The man standing at my side during a parade may be indulging in the very same physical movements perfunctorily, with no awareness of what undergirds his raised hand. For him the salute is mere rote; for me it is a poetic symbol of surpassing value.

Within a single fortnight several years ago the role of ritual was demonstrated by two events of international importance. One was the inauguration of Lyndon B. Johnson in 1964 as President of the United States. If, as a nation, we had wanted to be coldly practical, all that was necessary would have been for the Chief Justice of the Supreme Court to swear in the new President and Vice-President privately, in his office or one of theirs. Instead, an elaborate and memorable ritual was performed. Members of the Cabinet and Congress entered in an impressive processional. Clergymen of four faiths offered prayers. The United States Marine Corps Band played appropriate music. In the afternoon there was an elaborate parade, reviewed by the President and other officials from a specially constructed stand. Millions of citizens interrupted their normal routines to watch the proceedings on television.

Ten days later even greater numbers of individuals throughout the world witnessed the funeral of Winston Churchill. Again, from a strictly utilitarian point of view, a simple, private ceremony would have sufficed. Instead, there were massed troops, processionals of distinguished international leaders, bagpipes and bands, trumpeters and choirs, and the slow, mournful cadence of the funeral march.

Both rituals were indescribably impressive. In poetic, dramatic manner they symbolized the ideals of the American and British peoples. The movements and motions expressed more than any words alone could have articulated. The day following Churchill's funeral, James Reston, one of America's most eminent journalists, speculating on whether we may not have become so practical a people as to be almost sterile, wrote that the rich ritual of the preceding day "reminded Washington of the imponderables of life. It suggested that sentiment and history, that ideas and philosophy, are also powerful. . . . The ceremony, for a few hours, brought . . . the past and the present together, and made men here wonder whether, in this computerized modern world, they were not casting aside something from the older world that was essential to the future."[13]

In both its secular and its religious forms, ritual serves indeed as a bridge from past to present. It also helps to guarantee the future. The specific rituals employed for the Johnson inauguration and the Churchill funeral were not just arbitrary or artificial choices; they emerged through the years as fruits of the respective civilizations they enhance. So it is with our Jewish religious rituals too. They are indigenous to Jewish history. The breaking of a glass to conclude the wedding ceremony, for example, as a reminder of the destruction of the Temple in Jerusalem would be meaningless to any people except our own, for no other people ever had a Temple in Jerusalem which was demolished as was ours. The סדר (*seder*) on Passover makes sense only for the one people in the world which has a tradition of having escaped Egyptian slavery. Through the intelligent performance of such rituals, Jewish couples associate themselves with their people's past, as well as with every Jew who has ever lived on this earth, who lives on it now, or will in the future.

The best of our Jewish rituals identify us also with the universe and its inherent Creative Power. The husband and wife who precede each meal in their home with the מוציא (*motzee*) blessing are symbolizing their gratitude for a universe which provides both their physical and spiritual needs, and are reinforcing their sense of personal responsibility for the proper use of nature's gifts. Thus does religious ritual enhance their lives theologically no less than sociologically and psychologically.

A word should be added regarding the pedagogic value of ritual. The intelligent domestic practice of religious ceremonies can effectively remind both parents and children of important episodes and ideals out of their people's past. It can also spur them to live by the noblest of our ethical values. Couples who jointly observe שבת (*Shabbat*) at their dinner table are reminded weekly of their marital responsibilities and opportunities. This can provide no small impetus to their quest for a happy marriage.

YOUR CHOICE

We Jews are especially fortunate with respect to ritual. No religious tradition supplies its people with a richer treasury of ceremony and symbol. The most important moments and emotions of life—birth, growth, adolescence, love, marriage, death—are encompassed and expressed by rituals which emerge from the Jewish past and establish a foundation for its future.

Over and above their enormous value for all Jews, our religious rituals—precisely because, as poetic symbols, they appeal mostly to the emotions—can do much to enrich the relationship between husband and wife. The Jewish bride and groom associate themselves with their people and its ideals when—standing before the rabbi at their wedding—they repeat words and enact a drama in which Jewish couples have participated for centuries. In a sense they thereby invite all Jews—past and present—to share in their life, to give it a richness and strength they would be unable to evoke by themselves. The same deep dimension can prevail throughout their life together to the degree that the rituals of Judaism become part of their home.

True, the married couples who practice Jewish ritual are contributing to the survival of Judaism and the Jewish people.

But they simultaneously add experiences of indescribable beauty and meaning also to their marriage.

Which traditional rituals should a young Jewish couple observe? For the Orthodox Jew, the answer will include everything that has been sanctified by usage. The Conservative and Reform Jew will wish to be selective, retaining some traditions while rejecting others. The choice in terms of specifics must be made autonomously by each couple. Before a particular custom is cast aside, however, every honest effort should be made to understand its original significance and how it can be reinterpreted for modern meaning. I, for one, would not want to catalogue for others the specific religious customs and ceremonies which are worthy of being observed. I would prefer that each young couple go through its own process of evaluation and selection. The one point I would urge, however, is that there should be enough overall flavor of Judaism and Jewishness in their home so that they, their friends, and one day their children will have no difficulty in identifying them as a Jewish family. This is more important by far than their acceptance or rejection of any specific ritual.

Should the newly-wed Jewish couple maintain a kosher home? This is as good an example as any of the type of ritual choice which I believe must be made by each husband and wife on their own. For those who are Orthodox, the decision has already been made by tradition. Conservative and Reform couples will decide on the basis of contemporary criteria. Some will feel that כשרות (*kashrut*) is a discipline which can sanctify their homes; others will look upon it as an onerous burden. Some will be convinced that the dietary laws provide us with a superb mechanism for distinguishing the Jewish home, thus enlarging the probability of Jewish survival; others will view these same laws as nothing more than an archaic remnant of the past. Some will want to insure that any Jew of any persuasion—including, perhaps, their own parents or grandparents—will be able to eat in their homes; others will rely on the willingness of even the most Orthodox guest to eat dairy foods from paper plates. It is on the basis of alternatives such as these that each couple can decide for themselves. The answer will be relatively easy to reach where both bride and groom come from either a kosher or non-kosher background. Where their familial homes differ in this respect, the dilemma regarding כשרות can be an effective testing ground of their ability to achieve major compromises. Such a decision should in every instance, however, be confronted and resolved prior to their wedding. A bride emanating from a non-kosher home can always receive instruction on how to observe כשרות from a Conservative or Orthodox rabbi, from her future mother-in-law, or an observant friend.

A word should be added concerning one syndrome of ritual, that which is associated with the Sabbath. A proper observance of שבת (*Shabbat*) can immeasurably enhance a marriage. This can and should become the family day *par excellence*. The religious rituals of the Friday night dinner table bring all the members of the family together more closely than any other occasion. Saturday itself can be utilized for a variety of enterprises calculated to increase family unity and affection. These would, of course, include synagogue worship but by no means be limited to that. The husband and wife who strive to spend שבת together—reading, walking, listening to good music, attending the opera, visiting museums—any spiritual activity is proper —will find the beneficent effects of this one day flowing over into the remaining days of the week. What a pity it is that so many husbands and wives pick precisely שבת to be apart—going their respective but isolated ways on golf course or at luncheons. Nothing is potentially more enriching for marriage and the family than a modern observance of the Sabbath in the spirit of hallowed Jewish tradition.

The הבדלה (*havdalah*) ceremony which concludes the Sabbath is no less inspiring than the קדוש (*kiddush*) which commences it. Unfortunately הבדלה is one of the more neglected ceremonies in contemporary American Jewish life. For the sake of a beautiful Jewish home as well as marital happiness, it is worth reviving.

Frequently newly married couples agree that many advantages can accrue from the performance of Jewish ritual, yet because they have not been accustomed to such usages in the homes of their parents, they feel self-conscious and awkward. Many congregations sponsor adult classes precisely for this purpose. For those who may not have access to such assistance, appendices to this volume provide suggested home ceremonies for שבת (*Shabbat*), חנוכה (*Chanukah*), and פסח (*Pesach*)

Parents and Children

Sometimes a prospective bride and groom accept the importance of religious ritual but say they intend to wait until their first child is old enough to understand before practicing these ceremonies. More often than not, this is a serious mistake. For one thing, the domestic patterns established at the outset are likely to prevail permanently. A decision to practice the rituals of Judaism only in some indefinite future will most probably remain forever in the realm of unrealized intention.

Even more important, however, is the quality of the rituals practiced and how they will come through to the offspring of such a couple. Ceremonies and holidays observed only "for the sake of the children" become something of an artificial act. Even the youngest boys and girls possess an uncanny, intuitive ability to distinguish the genuine from the spurious in the behavior of their parents. They are likely to resent an *act* instituted primarily to impress them, but to cherish an invitation to share in something which has long since become a precious part of their parents' lives. The best time to commence the practice of religious ritual, therefore, is at the very beginning.

Needless to say, religion is a crucial area for agreement between husband and wife. One parent to whom religious belief and practice are meaningful and one who is indifferent or antagonistic to them will probably produce a child who is spiritually confused. This is far more crucial than mere intellectual disagreement between mother and father. Because religion is so largely a matter of emotion, because it involves not just facts, but loyalties, values, and ultimate goals, the child who constitutes a battleground for spiritual conflict between his parents is profoundly to be pitied. This is more than speculation or theory. Each year my heart goes out to youngsters in my Confirmation class who invariably attend religious services with one parent, never with the other. Or even worse: with neither parent. Often I can see the consequences of such conflict in the child and his work.

But suppose husband and wife honestly disagree on religion? Is it fair to demand that one capitulate to the other? If the parent whose attitude to religion is genuinely negative be expected to participate nonetheless, doesn't this smack of hypocrisy? Isn't it the kind of play-acting for the benefit of children which has just been decried?

These are valid questions—not to be dismissed easily or lightly. They underscore our earlier recommendation that an examination in depth of religious attitudes and convictions be an integral part of the courtship experienced by every couple. If their convictions about the ultimate meaning of life and the value of religious practice are so divergent as to rule out any agreement short of enforced hypocrisy, there is reason to wonder whether they ought to marry in the first instance. There can be religious reasons to doubt the advisability of a given marriage even where both prospective partners issue from the same background of faith.

Where the religious gulf between two Jewish parents appears to be beyond easy reconciliation, at the very least an honest effort should be made toward cooperation. A nonreligious father can without personal hypocrisy say, both by action and in word: "I don't agree with mother in this matter, but I must allow room for the possibility that I am wrong. In any event, since religion means so much to mother, I love her and you enough to cooperate. We'll celebrate the holidays together and I'll attend religious services with you—as far as I can, with an open mind. We'll search together as a family; only at the end of such searching can we know whether or not something like substantial agreement will be possible." If it becomes a jagged bone of contention, a jarring issue for relentless controversy, religion can jeopardize a marriage. If it serves as at least a common search, undertaken together in a spirit of love, it can provide immense reinforcement and strength.

A few practical problems about parents and children remain. They should at least be briefly mentioned even in a book which does not purport to cover such matters systematically. There is, for example, the question of the ברית מילה (*breet milah*), the circumcision ceremony for male children. Orthodox parents will insist that this be done by a מוהל (*mohel*), a specially trained religious functionary who can conduct both the surgical and religious phases of the ceremony with competence. Even in Orthodox tradition the surgery may be performed by a Jewish physician if no מוהל is available; the religious ceremony would then be conducted simultaneously by a rabbi. There can thus be no real objection on religious grounds to the increasing practice among Conservative and Reform Jews of asking a Jewish surgeon to remove the foreskin.

What is deplorable, however, is the tendency among some young Jewish parents to treat circumcision as a purely hygienic procedure, ignoring the religious emphasis entirely. It is true that circumcision is a medically recommended practice and that the vast majority of boys born in American hospitals these days are circumcised. But for Jews circumcision should be something more than that. According to our tradition it was enjoined upon all Jewish parents as a sign of the covenant between each individual male Jew and his God. It initiates the child into a whole cycle of identifications with his people and its faith. The מילה begins a spiritual process which continues through the observance of his first day of Jewish education, his Bar Mitzvah, his Confirmation, his marriage, his becoming a parent himself. During the circumcision ceremony a most meaningful prayer is recited:

זה הקטן גדול יהיה. כשם שנכנס לברית כן יכנס לתורה לחופה ולמעשים טובים.

(Zeh hakatan gadol yi-h'yeh; k'shem she-nich-nas lab'reet, ken yi-ka-nes la-Torah, la-chupah, ul-ma-aseem toveem.)

"May this little one grow in vigor. As he has entered into the covenant of Abraham, so may he in due course enter into the study of Torah, into a fulfilling marriage, into the performance of good deeds."

This is too precious a heritage to be lightly contemned. The Jewish parent who ignores it, who loses a priceless opportunity to emphasize the beauty of holiness on the birth of a child, thereby impoverishes himself, his marriage, and his family. Most American congregations today make provision for impressive public naming prayers for both boy and girl infants. The birth of a boy should also be marked by a meaningful religious ceremony for ברית מילה, conducted either by a מוהל or a rabbi. No statistical studies are needed to establish that parents who celebrate the circumcision of their sons in an appropriate religious manner are more likely to enjoy a rich life of ritual in their homes on other occasions too, while those who make light of circumcision will probably minimize ritual in general.

A brief word is in order here also regarding the naming of children. It is both appropriate and desirable for a Jewish child to be given a Hebrew name. This is another means of identifying the child Jewishly, of giving him from the very beginning a living relationship to tradition. But the naming of a child becomes a travesty when there is no intelligible relationship between his Hebrew and English names. If משה (*Moshe*), which should be Moses, is translated Montgomery—if שרה (*Sara*), properly transposed into Sarah, becomes Cynthia—it would be better for the Hebrew name to be skipped. To name a child after a revered parent or grandparent simply by using the same initial is also foolish. Either a closely related name should be given, or the entire pretense had better be dropped. The translation of names from Hebrew into English and vice-versa is not always simple. Where the name is one commonly used during the biblical or talmudic periods, a direct equivalent can be found. Otherwise, however, sometimes the best we can accomplish is a reasonable approximation.[14]

The naming of a newborn child is often an extremely sensitive area in the relationship between the infant's parents and grandparents. The latter have every right to express their preference, but none to dictate or insist. They had their chance to choose names for their own offspring. It is the baby's own parents who—after listening with respect and love to any suggestions the grandparents desire to make—have the right and duty to decide.

Central to the hopes and dreams of nearly every couple on their wedding day is the eventual establishment of a family. This is as it should be. Let them know, then, from the outset that children reflect the quality of their parents' marriage. All other factors being equal, parents who enjoy a wholesome, sensitive, loving relationship with each other will rear wholesome, sensitive, happy children. There is no other master key to successful parenthood. This is why at least these few paragraphs on parents and children are appropriate for consideration by the couple just contemplating marriage.

Alexander Magoun was perceptive and wise when he wrote:

> The child who cannot find God in his parents will not have an easy time finding God anywhere. The parent who cannot see God in the face of his child has never known God.[15]

«««««««« 15 »»»»»»»»

Bright Promise

How happy will your marriage be?

NO SURER ANSWER CAN BE GIVEN THIS QUESTION NOW THAN when it was asked at the outset. But at least we should be more aware of the important conditions on which the answer will depend. Neither the supreme happiness which comes to some married couples nor the abject misery which attends others is as inexplicable as we sometimes make them out to be. Over three decades of counseling many hundreds of couples have led me to associate certain factors with success, others with failure. Individuals differ. So do circumstances. The complex of attitude and behavior which works well with one couple may be quite inappropriate for another. Yet there are rules, and those who strive to learn and follow them will, on the average, enjoy a far greater degree of success than those who don't care or don't try.

I never face a couple during their wedding ceremony without wondering what their future will be. Because I refuse to officiate at all without one or more premarital conferences, usually I have at least some idea of the factors operating for and against them. But the eventual balance of these factors is beyond the power of any man exactly to anticipate. There are, of course, elements of luck in every marriage, as there are in every life. One couple may be fortunate in never facing at any one time a combination of tensions and stresses too onerous for their love to sustain. Another, with pretty much the same carrying power and endurance, may have such heavy burdens heaped upon them that even their strongest beams of support snap and crumble.

Yet it would be a massive mistake to conclude that the balance in marriage hinges exclusively on luck. The incidence of failure is very much greater among those who trust only to luck than among those who calculate as carefully and accurately as they can and who then act in accordance with their calculations. A happy marriage doesn't just *happen.* It is always the result of intelligent planning and wise action, planning and action which must come both before and after the wedding ceremony.

How happy will your marriage be?

That depends on how well the two of you understand the meaning of love and how capable you are of giving and receiving love, on how mature each of you is as an individual and whether the relationship between you is a mature one, on the breadth and depth of your compatibility, on the effort you expend year by year to enhance and enrich your marriage, on whether your sex life is arrested on the level of animality or is truly and beautifully human, on how wisely you have used your courtship as preparation for marriage, on your familial affection for your parents and for your children, on the religious dimensions of your life.

We can ask the question now. Only the future will reveal an answer, and you two will be partners in determining what that answer is to be.

When Help Is Needed

Almost every marriage is characterized by occasional crises. Most couples are able to survive them—even to learn and gain from them—without benefit of professional help. But the husband and wife who find their own combined resources inadequate should no more hesitate to seek assistance than to approach a physician or attorney for medical or legal aid. It is often a grievous error to assume that time will on its own take care of all problems. Time can either hinder or help. Time is worth only as much as the individuals involved put into it, as the constructive use to which they put it. A serious problem left to itself is like an internal infection, insidiously secreting poison which may soon contaminate the whole body. The longer it is allowed to fester unattended, the less likely does ultimate recovery become.

Where does one go for help when a marriage is sick? There are many sources of relief. The one a given couple will select depends on their personal preference, on the severity of their difficulty, and on availability. Sometimes lectures or books are useful; the reading lists in the supplements at the end of this volume will be helpful. In large cities family agencies and clinics can be consulted. Fortunate indeed is the troubled couple who feels close enough to its rabbi or physician—and confident enough of his competence—to approach him. He may feel it advisable, in turn, to refer them to a professional marriage counselor, a psychologist, or psychiatrist. All of these can help, but none can succeed without the utmost effort of the two people involved. Of the *two* people! Not infrequently a person who comes to me with marital difficulties will reveal that his or her mate is adamant in refusing all outside "interference." Little or nothing can be accomplished in such cases. Marriage is for two: its success depends upon two; the correction of its deficiencies demands the cooperation of two. It demands hard work too. Unless each partner is willing to concede that part of the fault may be his, and that changes must be made by both, the prognosis for improvement is poor.

Periodic inventory is good for a marriage. What better, more productive use for each wedding anniversary than to evaluate the past and plan for the future? Not in a ponderous, oppressive manner—nor in a mood of criticism and complaint—rather in a spirit of gratitude for the good things which have already issued from the relationship, of appreciation for the values and strengths already made manifest, of hope that yesterday's failures can be transposed into tomorrow's success. The table below is one which I have worked out for discussion groups of young married couples who are attempting to measure the success of their marriages. It should be filled out first by each mate alone; only after both have finished should their answers be compared. There will be no profit from this procedure unless both spouses respond with total truth. A further word of caution: better that the whole idea be forgotten than that these questions be utilized to secure ammunition for contention. If there appears to be danger in that direction, the likelihood is that this particular couple is already in need of aid more substantial than cooperative self-analysis.

HOW SUCCESSFUL IS OUR MARRIAGE?

(Check one response for each item—1 through 17.)

1. I love my mate today:
   - more than on our wedding day. ______
   - as much as on our wedding day. ______
   - less than on our wedding day. ______

2. If I knew a couple in the identical circumstances we were in during our courtship, I would advise them to:
    marry sooner than we did. ______
    marry the same time we did. ______
    wait a little longer than we. ______
3. Alexander Magoun has divided marriages into three categories. Check the one you think most accurately describes your marriage:
    Some marriages are sheer hell. ______
    Most marriages are pretty mediocre. ______
    A few marriages are positively delicious. ______
4. My marriage has more than met my expectations for happiness. ______
   My marriage has just about met my expectations. ______
   My marriage has not met my expectations. ______
5. I believe myself to be:
    emotionally very mature. ______
    reasonably mature. ______
    quite immature. ______
6. I believe my mate is:
    emotionally very mature. ______
    reasonably mature. ______
    quite immature. ______
7. Most of our major decisions are made by:
    me. ______
    my mate. ______
    both of us. ______
8. We resolve most of our disagreements:
    easily. ______
    fairly well. ______
    with difficulty. ______
9. In comparison to what I thought when we were

married, today I think my mate and I have:
- more in common. ______
- less in common. ______
- as much in common. ______

10. Our financial problems have been:
- serious. ______
- not serious. ______
- nonexistent. ______

11. Our sex life has been:
- excellent. ______
- good. ______
- fair. ______
- not so good. ______

12. To my mate sex has been:
- too important. ______
- of proper importance. ______
- not important enough. ______

13. Our progress toward marital adjustment has been:
- excellent. ______
- good. ______
- fair. ______
- poor. ______

14. With reference to rearing our children, we agree:
- always. ______
- most of the time. ______
- occasionally. ______
- seldom. ______

15. We spend our leisure hours together:
- always. ______
- occasionally. ______
- seldom. ______

16. The role of religion in our marriage has been:
- important. ______

casual. ______
insignificant. ______

17. On religious matters my spouse and I are:
    in strong agreement. ______
    in mild agreement. ______
    in mild disagreement. ______
    in strong disagreement. ______

(For items 18 through 22 mark True or False.)

18. I now see virtues in my spouse of which I was not aware when we were married. ______
19. I now see faults in my spouse of which I was not aware when we were married. ______
20. My parents have interfered in our marriage. ______
21. My spouse's parents have interfered in our marriage. ______
22. I have had moments of doubt as to the wisdom of our marriage. ______

(Fill in answers to items 23 through 28.)

23. Our most serious problem in marriage thus far:

24. The things I know now which I wish I had known before we were married:

25. I wish my mate would improve in the following respects:

26. I wish I could improve in the following respects:

27. Marriage has helped me grow in the following ways:

28. Marriage has helped my spouse grow in the following ways:

A loving and responsible comparison of the answers recorded separately by husband and wife should enhance most marriages. It would be wise also to compare the answers given one year to those of the preceding year. If this is done, however, the previous replies should not be consulted until after the new ones have been written.

FINALLY

I have tried in these pages to describe the ideal marriage, aware of the fact that very few couples will fully achieve it. There are no perfect marriages because there are no perfect human beings. Woodrow Wilson is said to have reflected that the value of having a goal is in knowing by how far one has failed to attain it. The couple striving to approximate an ideal beyond accomplishment will reap richer rewards by far than if they were satisfied just to improvise year by year. It is as destructive to be entirely without a plan or goal as to castigate oneself for falling short of perfection.

No wise person would venture upon a professional career without adequate preparation and diligent effort. These are also essential components of the good marriage. The effort to improve one's marriage—to realize more of its latent potentiality—should continue so long as husband and wife remain alive.

Each experience adds up to the sum total of marriage. Every word spoken by husband and wife to each other accumulates, for good or bad, to affect the balance. Whenever an expensive mahogany table is polished, its luster becomes more luminous. When a nail is driven into its surface, then extracted, not even the most skilled finisher can disguise the fact that damage has been done. So it is with marriage. Every rude, thoughtless, insensitive word spoken by either husband or wife leaves its permanent impression. Apologies can repair the harm but seldom obliterate its entire effect. Every act of sweetness and consideration is as rich wax, rubbed softly on the finest of woods. No one can live one kind of life and expect to reap a different kind of marriage.

Is there a secret to marital happiness?

Surely no simple or easy one. Perhaps the closest anyone has come to an all-embracing formula for success is reflected in the story of Abraham's faithful servant, whom he sent back to his native land to find a wife for Isaac. The servant's responsibility was heavy. Abraham had specified only one criterion: the girl must come from his own stock. He had said nothing about any other standard of choice. En route to discharge his franchise, the servant voiced this significant prayer:

> O Lord, God of my master Abraham, grant me good fortune this day, and deal graciously with my master Abraham. As I stand here by the spring and the daughters of the townsmen come out to draw water, let the maiden to whom I say, "Please, lower your jar that I may drink," and who replies, "Drink, and I will also water your camels"—let her be the one whom You have decreed for your servant Isaac. . . . (Gen. 24:12 ff.)

Was this just an arbitrary sign which Abraham's servant requested? A careful reading of his words will disclose that it was not. What he really sought was a girl who would immediately offer to do more than was requested or expected of her. He would ask for water only on his own behalf; she would volunteer at once to provide drink both for him and his camels.

The husband and wife who do only the normally expected

things for each other can probably get along all right. They may even enjoy a modest kind of success in their marriage. But the highest levels of happiness are reserved for those who give each other more than the norm.

There are no guarantees. Neither for you nor for any couple. There is only the bright promise of immeasurable happiness . . . and knowledge enough within your grasp for that promise to be fulfilled.

SUPPLEMENT A

A Home Service for Shabbat Evening

Adapted from material prepared by Rabbi Harvey J. Fields

(In this and the succeeding services, Hebrew passages are transliterated into English. The Sephardic pronunciation is used. Those who prefer Ashkenazic Hebrew may ask their rabbi or anyone who knows Hebrew to write out transliterations for them. Even persons who do not know Hebrew can manage, with a reasonable amount of instruction and practice, to pronounce the words correctly. It is recommended, however, that every effort be made to learn enough Hebrew to read or chant these selections from the original. The longer Hebrew responses may be read only in English if it should prove impossible to do them in Hebrew.)

LIGHTING OF CANDLES

(Recited by wife.)

Come, let us welcome the Sabbath. May its beauty illumine our hearts as we kindle these tapers.

Light is the symbol of the divine within us.

Light is the symbol of God's law.

Light is the symbol of our divine mission, of our covenant to be a light unto the nations.

The week of work has now ended. The Sabbath with its peace has come. Together we pause, that its meaning may enlarge our lives.

May our Sabbath lights reflect the love and devotion which brighten our home. May they inspire us toward the fulfillment of our sacred aspirations.

(The candles are kindled by the wife, aided by daughters old enough to do so. In some homes, each daughter lights her own set of candles. Then all the girls recite the following blessing with their mother.)

ברוך אתה יי אלהינו מלך העולם אשר קדשנו במצותיו וצונו להדליק נר של שבת:

Ba-ruch atah Adonai, elo-hay-nu melech ha-o-lam, asher kid'sha-nu b'mitz-vo-tav, vitzi-va-nu l'had-lik nayr shel Shabbat.

Praised be the Eternal our God, Ruling Spirit of the universe,

who has sanctified us by His commandments and ordered us to kindle the Sabbath lights.
May the Lord bless us with Sabbath joy, with Sabbath holiness, and with Sabbath peace. Amen.

PRAYER

(One of the following selections may be recited by the husband each week.)

ברוכה הבאה בשם יי

B'ru-cha ha-ba-ah b'shaym Adonai

Blessed be the Sabbath, which comes in the name of the Lord.

I.

Joyfully, O Lord our God, do we welcome the Sabbath, our sanctuary in time. Another week of our lives has passed; we thank Thee for the accomplishments we have enjoyed, for the lessons we have learned.
Help us, O Lord, to sanctify this precious day and to be sanctified by it. May it deepen our love for one another and enrich our lives through the acquisition of knowledge. Thus may Shabbat help us fulfill our richest potential.
May the inspiration and insight we gain now illumine the coming week, providing purpose and direction for all our endeavors. And may the love which now binds us together continue to crown our home with joy and peace. Amen.

II

Lord our God, in the beauty and peace of this moment we renew our sacred covenant with Thee. Like our forefathers before us, we lay aside the struggles of daily living now and lift our hearts to Thee.
O Eternal our God, make us more sensitive to the love crowning our home, to the friendships filling our lives, and to our heritage which gives purpose and meaning to everything we do.
May we strengthen our commitment to the covenant of our people. Let its demands for freedom and justice, for peace and truth, shape our lives. Thus shall Shabbat provide us with renewal and perspective to meet the challenges of the coming week. Amen.

III

(To be recited responsively, led by the husband.)

The Sabbath is the most cherished creation of the Jewish spirit; it mirrors the essence of the Jewish soul.

The Sabbath is a symbol of liberation, a symbol of triumph, the triumph of the holy over the profane, of spirit over matter.

In every age the Sabbath afforded the Jew a holy retreat, a haven of safety, a fountain of new strength and perpetual self-renewal.

The Sabbath is our hope, the calm haven where all the weary find repose; with the coming of the Sabbath, redemption and peace enter the world.

The Sabbath uplifts men from the gloomy depths of the earth into the splendor of the heavens, that they may know the God of truth and become seekers of truth and doers of right.

(From Sabbath Prayerbook—Jewish Reconstructionist Foundation.)

KIDDUSH

(In some homes, each member of the family lifts his own kiddush cup; in others, only the father does so, then passes his cup around for all to sip. In either event, all join to recite or chant the following.)

Let us praise God with this symbol of joy and thank Him for the blessings of the week that has passed.

ברוך אתה יי אלהינו מלך העולם בורא פרי הגפן:

Baruch atah Adonai, elo-hay-nu melech ha-olam, boray p'ri hagafen.

Praised be the Eternal our God, Ruling Spirit of the universe, who creates the fruit of the vine.

ברוך אתה יי אלהינו מלך העולם. אשר קדשנו במצותיו ורצה בנו ושבת קדשו באהבה וברצון הנחילנו זכרון למעשה בראשית. כי הוא יום תחילה למקראי קדש זכר ליציאת מצרים. כי בנו בחרת ואותנו קדשת מכל העמים ושבת קדשך באהבה וברצון הנחלתנו. ברוך אתה יי מקדש השבת.

Ba-ruch atah Adonai, elo-hay-nu melech ha-olam, ashair kid-sha-nu b'mitz-vo-tav v'ratzah vanu, v'shabbat kawd-sho b'aha-vah uv-ratzon hin-chee-lanu, zika-ron l'ma-a-say v'ray-sheet. Ki hu yom t'chee-lah l'mik-ra-ay ko-desh, zay-chair lee-tzee-at mitz-ra-yeem. Ki vanu va-char-ta v-otanu ki-dash-ta mi-kawl ha-ameem, v'shabbat kawd-sh'cha b'aha-vah uv-ratzon hin-chal-tanu. Ba-ruch atah Adonoi, m'ka-daysh ha-shabbat. A-mayn.

Praised be the Eternal our God, Ruling Spirit of the universe, who has sanctified us by His commandment and freely, lovingly given us His holy Sabbath as a heritage, a remembrance of Creation and of the Exodus from Egypt. It is the most important of all our sacred days, an evidence of the distinction God has conferred upon our people if we but search for Him with all our hearts. Praised be the Lord, who hast sanctified the Sabbath. Amen.

(All drink wine.)

BLESSING OF THE CHILDREN

(Either mother or father gathers the children at his place. The parents may alternate each week in pronouncing the following blessing.)

For boys: ישימך אלהים כאפרים וכמנשה—y'seem-cha eloheem k'eph-ra-yeem v'chee-m'na-sheh.

May God make you like Ephraim and Manasseh.

For girls: ישימך אלהים כשרה רבקה רחל ולאה —y'see-maych eloheem k'sarah, rivkah, ra-chayl v'layah.

May God make you like Sarah, Rebecca, Rachel and Leah.

For all: May the God of our fathers bless you. May He who has guided us unto this day lead you to be an honor to our family, a blessing to Israel and to all mankind. Amen.

HAMOTZEE

(Each person lifts a piece of bread, then all recite together.)

ברוך אתה יי אלהינו מלך העולם המוציא לחם מן הארץ.

Baruch atah Adonai, elo-hay-nu melech ha-olam, hamo-tzee lechem min ha-aretz.

Praised be the Eternal our God, Ruling Spirit of the universe, who brings forth bread from the earth. Amen.

BLESSING AFTER THE MEAL

(Recited by all.)

ברוך אתה יי אלהינו מלך העולם הזן את הכל.

Baruch atah Adonai, elo-hay-nu melech ha-olam, ha-zan et ha-kol.

Praised be the Eternal our God, Ruling Spirit of the universe, who provides food for all. Amen.

SUPPLEMENT B

Havdalah Service

(Members of the family gather in their home Saturday at dusk to bid the Sabbath farewell. The following ritual objects may be secured from any firm selling Jewish religious symbols: kiddush cup—as used Friday evening; ornamental spice-box—to be filled with sweet-smelling spices; special havdalah candle and candle-holder. Parents and older children may alternate in leading the service.)

All Sing

אליהו הנביא
אליהו התשבי
אליהו אליהו
אליהו הגלעדי
במהרה בימינו
יבא אלינו
עם משיח בן דוד
עם משיח בן דוד

Aylee-ya-hu ha-na-vee, Aylee-ya-hu ha-tish-bee,
Aylee-ya-hu, Aylee-ya-hu, Aylee-ya-hu ha-giladee.
Bim-hay-rah v'ya-may-nu yavo ay-lay-nu,
Im mashee-ach ben David,
Im mashee-ach ben David.
(Repeat first verse.)

Reader

Just as the Sabbath is ushered in by prayer and song, so, when the Sabbath departs, we bid her farewell with this Havdalah service. The Havdalah service is an old and honored ceremony in the Jewish faith. The word *havdalah* means *separation;* through it we would symbolize the conclusion of the Sabbath, as it separates itself from the rest of the week. This ceremony emphasizes for us the separation of light from darkness, the holy from the unholy, the sacred from the profane.

Unison

Lord our God, we thank Thee for the Sabbath, which brings us closer to each other and to Thee. May it also strengthen our commitment to Judaism. We pray that Thy spirit will fill our hearts, and that Shabbat will bring us a renewal in faith and understanding. May it serve to separate us from what is vain and unworthy. May it change the days that lie ahead into days of consecration and inspiration.

Reader

An ancient Jewish legend tells us that when God was about to give the Torah to our ancestors, He summoned them and said: "My children, I have a good article in the world, and I would like to give it to you forever—if you will accept my Torah and observe my commandments."

The people asked: "Master of the Universe, what good article will you give us if we keep your Torah?" The Holy One, blessed be He, replied: "It is the world to come!" The people of Israel answered: "Show us a sample of the world to come." The Holy One, blessed be He, said: "The Sabbath is a sample of the world to come. For that world will be a long Sabbath day."

Unison

For us, "the world to come" means the world men are capable of achieving if they observe the ethical ideals of Judaism. It will be a world without poverty, prejudice, or war—a world of justice, of love and of peace. Shabbat is a sample of that world, not only because it is a day of peace, but also because it renews our dedication to the building of a better future. In this sense Shabbat can symbolize "the world to come" in our home too. The special tenderness and affection we feel and express toward each other on the Sabbath can be a model for the rest of the week as well.

Reader

Wine is a symbol of gladness and is frequently used in religious ceremonies to express our heart's joy. As wine is used to welcome the Sabbath, so is it a part of this Havdalah service. We fill the cup to overflowing, praying that God's blessings may overflow our lives throughout the days of the week ahead. Grant, O God, that we may use those days, not just for selfish aims, but for the deepening of faith and the service of others.

Unison

ברוך אתה יי אלהינו מלך העולם בורא פרי הגפן.

Ba-ruch atah Adonai, elohaynu melech ha-olam, boray p'ree ha-gafen.

Praised be the Eternal our God, Ruling Spirit of the universe, who creates the fruit of the vine. Amen.

Reader

Our teachers have emphasized the importance of the Sabbath by saying that on it a man receives an "additional soul," a *n'shama y'tay-ra*. This added soul makes the Jew a different person on the Sabbath day. It transforms his being, touching him with serenity and peace. Here in our family each of us has experienced this spiritual enrichment during the past twenty-four hours. May it remain with us. May something of the "additional soul" accompany us in the new week, that the inspiration of Sabbath may be ours every day.

It is to symbolize this hope that our fathers made this spice-box part of the Havdalah ceremony, adding the fragrance of the spice to the very air we breathe. So do we pray that the fragrance of the Sabbath may suffuse the days that lie ahead.

Unison

ברוך אתה יי אלהינו מלך העולם בורא מיני בשמים.

Ba-ruch atah Adonai, elohaynu melech ha-olam, boray meenay v'sa-meem.

Praised be the Eternal our God, Ruling Spirit of the universe, who creates various kinds of spices. Amen.

(The spice-box is passed around for all to smell.)

Reader

The Sabbath is ushered in with the kindling of lights, and the Sabbath takes its leave with the kindling of a light, a specially woven taper called the Havdalah candle. May this Havdalah light illumine our way; may it scatter every darkness; may it cause us to walk in confidence and to trust that God will not forsake us nor leave us in the confusion of the night.

Unison

ברוך אתה יי אלהינו מלך העולם בורא מאורי האש.

Ba-ruch atah Adonai, elohaynu melech ha-olam, boray me-oray ha-aish.

Praised be the Eternal our God, Ruling Spirit of the universe, who creates the light of the fire. Amen.

(The Havdalah candle is kindled.)

Reader

ברוך אתה יי אלהינו מלך העולם המבדיל בין קדש לחול בין אור לחשך בין ישראל לעמים בין יום השביעי לששת ימי המעשה ברוך אתה יי המבדיל בין קדש לחול.

Ba-ruch atah Adonai, elohaynu melech ha-olam, hamavdeel bayn kodesh l'chol, bayn or l'cho-shech, bayn yis-ra-ayl la-ameem, bayn yom hash'vee-ee l'shay-shet y'may ha-ma-a-seh. Ba-ruch atah Adonai, hamavdeel bayn kodesh l'chol.

Unison

Praised be the Eternal our God, Ruling Spirit of the universe, who distinguishes between the sacred and the profane, between light and darkness, between Israel and other peoples, between the seventh day and the six days of labor. Help us, too, we pray Thee, to distinguish between that which is real and enduring, and that which is fleeting and vain. May we value affection and helpfulness more than power and possession, that the joy of a good deed may be our greatest delight, and our zeal for justice outweigh all selfish pursuits.

Praised be the Lord, who distinguishes between the sacred and the profane.

Responsive Reading

What do we mean when we say that the sacred is distinguished from the profane?

That physically man is an animal. He has evolved through the animal kingdom; his anatomy and physiology are similar to those of the beast. In this respect, man is profane.

What, then, is sacred about man?

We are like the animals, yet profoundly different. Only we are able to create and appreciate the true, the beautiful, and the good. This capacity constitutes our soul. In this respect, human life is sacred.

Does this mean that the mundane and profane are contemptible—that the pleasures of the body are to be scorned?

No. Judaism teaches that man must accept both aspects of his being, that the profane must emerge into the sacred, while the sacred must be infused into the profane. Judaism insists that no act is too vulgar to be sanctified, that the real distinction, therefore, is between the sacred and the not-yet-sacred.

And what does all this have to do with Shabbat?

Shabbat is the day dedicated above all others to the cultivation of the sacred. It is the day on which we intensify our divine heritage by reminding ourselves of who we are and what we can become. Unless something of Shabbat survives this ceremony, to permeate and inspire the week ahead, our observance of Shabbat will have failed.

What do we mean when we praise God for distinguishing between Israel and other peoples? Are we innately superior to the rest of mankind?

No. Our uniqueness is a possibility engendered by God, but its realization depends on ourselves. To be a God-chosen people means to be a God-choosing people.

Then should we not say—instead of אשר בחר בנו, who has chosen us—? אשר בחרנו בו, whom we have chosen?

Perhaps so. We have been chosen not for privilege but for responsibility. More than any other historic people, we have probed into the essential meaning of existence and have accepted the moral imperatives imposed upon us by the nature of reality.

And what does *this* have to do with Shabbat?

On Shabbat especially, each Jew is obliged to ask whether his actions during the preceding week entitle him to consider himself the object of divine choice.

Unison

ברוך אתה יי המבדיל בין קדש לחול.

Praised be the Lord, who distinguishes between the sacred and the profane.

Reader

We follow tradition now by extinguishing the light of our Havdalah candle in the overflow of wine which symbolizes the abundance of God's blessings.

May the inspiration of this Sabbath day enrich the week which now begins. May the effect of Shabbat be to draw us ever closer to one another, to all whom we love, to our friends everywhere, to the whole human race, and to God. And may the day dawn soon when all men will recognize that they come from one Source and yearn for one Goal.

Unison

ביום ההוא יהיה יי אחד ושמו אחד.

Ba-yom ha-hu yi-hi-yeh
Adonai echad ush-mo echad.

On that day the Lord shall be one and His name shall be one.

Reader

Eternal God of the universe, may we—all of us—be blessed with a good week, a week of courage and devotion, a week of health and strength, a week of love and of peace. Amen.

All Sing

שבוע טוב Shavua Tov—A Good Week.

SUPPLEMENT C

Home Service for Each Night of Chanukah

Adapted from material prepared by Rabbi Harvey J. Fields

(The following is the order of each service: opening prayer, lighting of Shamas—the serving candle—recitation of Chanukah blessings, lighting of candles, closing prayer. Kindle the candles from left to right. In addition to the Shamas, on the first night one candle is kindled, on the second night, two, etc.

The opening and closing prayers for each night focus on a significant value of Judaism. On the fifth night, designated Righteousness, each member of the family may make his contribution. The family may send the total to an institution of its choice, or bring it to the temple to be added to the Keren Ami fund.)

CHANUKAH BLESSINGS

ברוך אתה יי אלהינו מלך העולם אשר קדשנו במצותיו וצונו להדליק נר של חנכה.

Ba-ruch atah Adonai, elohaynu melech ha-olam, asher kid-sha-nu b'mitz-vo-tav, v'tzi-va-nu l'had-leek nayr shel Chanukah.

Praised be the Eternal our God, Ruling Spirit of the universe, who has sanctified us by His commandments and ordered us to kindle the Chanukah lights.

ברוך אתה יי אלהינו מלך העולם שעשה נסים לאבותינו בימים ההם בזמן הזה.

Ba-ruch atah Adonai, elohaynu melech ha-olam, she-asa ni-seem lavo-tay-nu ba-ya-meem ha-haym baz-man ha-zeh.

Praised be the Eternal our God, Ruling Spirit of the universe, who inspired the heroic deeds of our forefathers in times past, at this season.

(The following for first night only.)

ברוך אתה יי אלהינו מלך העולם שהחינו וקימנו והגיענו לזמן הזה.

Ba-ruch atah Adonai, elohaynu melech ha-olam, she-he-che-ya-nu, v'kee-ma-nu v'hi-gee-a-nu laz-man ha-zeh.

Praised be the Eternal our God, Ruling Spirit of the universe, who has granted us life, sustained us, and permitted us to celebrate this joyous festival. Amen.

First Night—25 Kislev
Freedom

(opening prayer)

We kindle these Chanukah lights in memory of the dedication and courage of the Maccabees. Believing that they should be free to worship God as their hearts and minds dictated, they willingly gave their lives for freedom. Now, kindling these candles, we rededicate ourselves to work for the equal rights of all men, and for a society of democracy and freedom.

CHANUKAH BLESSINGS

(closing prayer)

Our God and God of our fathers, on this eve of Chanukah we rededicate ourselves to Thee. Let these lights shine forth brightly, reminding us that all men are equal in Thy sight. Inspire us anew, that we may serve the cause of freedom as valiantly as did our ancestors before us. Praised be the Lord, who has implanted within us the love of freedom. Amen.

Second Night—26 Kislev
Family

(opening prayer)

Tonight as we celebrate Chanukah together we are conscious of our precious gift of family. So often we take one another for granted, forgetting to express our love and devotion. Let us now, as we kindle these festive lights, rededicate ourselves to sharing our interests and time with one another. Like the Maccabees of old, let us always face the tribulations and the joys of life united by our family bonds. Kindling these lights, we pray that through kindness and thoughtfulness our love for one another will increase from strength to strength.

CHANUKAH BLESSINGS

(closing prayer)

Eternal our God! We give thanks unto Thee for preserving us in health and joy. We pray that all families everywhere may experience the love for one another which we share. Praised be the Lord, who turns the hearts of the children to their parents and the devotion of the parents to their children. Amen.

Third Night—27 Kislev
Study of Torah

(opening prayer)

On the third night of Chanukah we rededicate ourselves to the study of our tradition. As the Maccabees courageously fought to preserve our faith, we too are duty-bound to sustain our heritage by deepening our understanding of it through study. As we increase our knowledge of Judaism, we become more sensitive to its abiding values, more aware of our responsibility to realize these values. Study opens our minds and fortifies us against tyranny. Learning secures our freedom. Let us, as we kindle these candles, rededicate ourselves to the study of Torah.

CHANUKAH BLESSINGS

(closing prayer)

O Lord, may we ever recognize our obligation to learn. Increase in us the desire to pursue knowledge as an instrument which strengthens our way of life. Humbly we realize how little we know of our world and our faith. Let these Chanukah lights serve to remind us of our need to study and to increase our understanding. May they inspire us to enlighten and use our minds for the benefit of all mankind. Amen.

Fourth Night—28 Kislev
Hope

(opening prayer)

Our forefathers have taught us that in hope man's future is illumined and made creative. Ours are times when many men live in fear and great despair. Like the Maccabees, we need to build our lives on hope—hope that ultimately truth will triumph over falsehood, that knowledge and understanding will finally depose superstition and tyranny. As we kindle these Chanukah lights, may our lives be strengthened by the highest hopes and visions of our faith.

CHANUKAH BLESSINGS

(closing prayer)

Eternal our God, Source of man's upward striving, inspire us with hope to face courageously the trials and challenges which confront us. Founded upon truth and honesty, may our efforts bring the fulfillment of our highest aspirations. We yearn for the day when all men will be free, when war will no longer delay the dawn of justice and peace. Praised be the Eternal our God, who encourages our desire for a better tomorrow and our steadfast hope in the future. Amen.

Fifth Night—29 Kislev
Righteousness

(opening prayer)

Our tradition tells us that during the Maccabean war for freedom all Jews, both children and adults, contributed toward the cause of defeating the oppressor. The Hebrew language contains no word for charity. The word צדקה (*tzedakah*), used for this purpose, really means righteousness. The Jew who contributes to charity deserves no special praise; he is merely doing what is right, what is expected of him in fulfilling his human responsibility.

There are still many forms of oppression in our world today. There are people afflicted by sickness, hunger, ignorance, and prejudice. Tonight we, like our forefathers, offer our gifts in order that we too may help bring an end to oppression. We pray that we may thus help to provide food for the hungry, medicine for the sick, knowledge for the ignorant, and equal opportunity for those afflicted by prejudice.

(Each member of the family gives his gift of charity.)

Now as we kindle our Chanukah lights, let us rededicate ourselves to the ideal of צדקה of righteousness found in our Jewish tradition.

CHANUKAH BLESSINGS

(closing prayer)

Our God and God of our fathers, we have been taught that the more צדקה there is, the more secure does peace become. May our Chanukah candles symbolize for us the light of happiness and hope which our gifts will bring to those oppressed by need. Aid us, O Lord, to be compassionate and generous toward our fellowmen. Praised be the Lord, who inspires within us a concern for the welfare and dignity of all men. Amen.

Sixth Night—30 Kislev
Peace

(opening prayer)

The candles of Chanukah remind us of our most sacred mission as Jews. The Maccabees are remembered not for their military victory, but for their rededication of the Temple and restoration of peace. Even so must we seek to rededicate ourselves to the service of God.

Today one of our foremost tasks is to secure peace in our troubled world. When we end disagreements through mutual understanding, when we seek to eradicate inequality and injustice, we are doing our part in making peace a living ideal. As we kindle our Chanukah candles, let us rededicate ourselves with renewed strength to the task of securing peace.

CHANUKAH BLESSINGS

(closing prayer)

O Lord our God, show the pathway of peace to all mankind. Teach us that only acts which flow from brotherliness and goodwill can bring enduring peace. Help us to realize that hate and prejudice bring nothing but strife and chaos into the world. Let all men recognize that only through cooperation and honest negotiation can the blessings of peace be made secure. Plant the love of peace in every heart, and may the bonds of friendship among all the inhabitants of earth be strengthened. Praised be Thou, O Lord, Source of peace. Amen.

Seventh Night—1 Tevet
Brotherhood

(opening prayer)

Brotherhood is founded upon a total respect for the liberty and freedom of all men. The Maccabees of old sought to protect themselves when their rights were violated. Our Chanukah lights serve as a reminder that brotherhood is secure only when we honor the precious rights of our fellowmen. As we kindle these candles, let us rededicate ourselves to the cause of brotherhood which alone can bring dignity to all men.

CHANUKAH BLESSINGS

(closing prayer)

Our God, teach us to be sensitive to the feelings of our friends and neighbors. Help us to understand their failings, and grant us the humility to praise and applaud their achievements. May our Chanukah candles remind us that all men are created equal in Thy sight. Praised be the Lord, who would have every human being cherish the brotherhood and unity of all mankind. Amen.

Eighth Night—2 Tevet
Faith

(opening prayer)

Tonight we kindle all the candles of our Chanukah menorah. Throughout the centuries the menorah has been a symbol of our faith, Judaism. Like the Maccabees, when they celebrated this festive holiday, we rededicate ourselves to the living of a more meaningful Jewish life. We pray that throughout this coming year we may fulfill the ideals of freedom, righteousness, family, study, hope, peace, and brotherhood, all of which are symbolized by the candles of our menorah.

CHANUKAH BLESSINGS

(closing prayer)

Our God and God of our fathers, may we be sustained and strengthened by our faith. Through our study of it, and through our devotion to its ideals, we pray that we shall speed the day when all men will recognize that they are brothers. Then will Thy kingdom be established, and peace on earth be made secure. Praised be Thou O Lord, for the faith of our forefathers, and for the opportunity to celebrate our holiday of Chanukah. Amen.

SUPPLEMENT D

Passover Seder Service

Adapted from material prepared by Rabbi Harvey J. Fields

(These selections supplement whatever Haggadah the family prefers to use. Their proper place in the סדר (*seder*) is indicated in each case either by the title or the note which follows it.)

1. THE NARRATIVE

(From *The New Haggadah*, Behrman House, 1942–to be inserted after the Four Questions have been asked.)

I am glad you asked the questions you did, for the story of this night was just what I wanted you to know. Although the Haggadah we are reading tells this whole story, and if you listen carefully you will surely learn it, I should like to tell you here, in a few words, the answers to your questions.

Indeed, this night is very different from all the other nights of the year, for on this night we celebrate one of the most important moments in the history of our people. On this night we celebrate their going forth in triumph from slavery into freedom.

Why do we eat only *matzah* tonight? When Pharaoh let our forefathers go from Egypt, they were forced to flee in great haste. Now, they had prepared dough for bread to take on their journey, but the Egyptians pressed them to hasten out of the land. So they snatched up their dough and fled, and had no time to bake it. But the hot sun, beating down on the dough as they carried it along with them, baked it into a flat, unleavened bread which they called *matzah*. This is why we eat only *matzah* on Pesach.

Why do we eat bitter herbs on Pesach night? Because our forefathers were slaves in Egypt, and their lives were made bitter. That is why we eat bitter herbs on Pesach night.

Why do we dip the herbs twice tonight? You have already heard that we dip the parsley in salt water because it reminds us of the green that comes to life again in the springtime. We dip the *maror*, or bitter herbs, in the sweet *haroset* as a sign of hope; our forefathers were able to withstand the bitterness of slavery, because it was sweetened by the hope of freedom.

Why do we recline at the table? Because reclining at the table was a sign of a free man in olden times; and since our forefathers were freed on this night, we recline at the table.

2. THE FOUR SONS TODAY

(Following Haggadah passage on Four Sons.)

As there are four types of sons traditionally mentioned at our seder, so there are four kinds of Jews in our own time.

The Jew who devotedly lives as a Jew says: "I find great fulfillment through practicing Judaism and by participating in the Jewish community."

The Jew who considers being a Jew his misfortune says: "If only I could assimilate." He is probably not even here with us tonight. There is little we can do to reach him.

The Jew who esteems all knowledge except that of his own heritage says: "Why should I trouble myself with this small group? The wisdom of all humanity lies open before me." To him you should say: "Study the contributions of our people and faith. We still have our own unique contribution, with which to enrich the wisdom of all humanity."

The Jew who has thoughtlessly drifted away from his faith and people asks: "What can I do to return?" Him we should answer by seeking to teach and inspire him with the historical experiences and accumulated wisdom of our people.

3. A TEAR OF SORROW

(Either following or instead of the Haggadah passage about the plagues.)

Tradition tells us that when the Egyptian hosts were drowning in the sea, the angels in Heaven were about to break forth in songs of jubilation. But the Holy One, blessed be He, silenced them with the words: "My creatures are perishing, and ye are ready to sing?"

Thus it is fitting for us to diminish our joy in sympathy for those who have suffered. "We do not rejoice at the punishment meted out to an enemy; we have been taught by our faith to have human sympathy." (Philo, Flaccus, 14)

In our day men continue to suffer. We hear their voices crying out from lonely trenches on far off battlefields. We see them torn by man's cruel inhumanity to man. And we mourn the loss of human potential, the utter waste of human life, the sorrow and spoil of war. In keeping with our tradition, we diminish our joy tonight by spilling now a drop of wine from our cups—showing thereby that we are caught up in the suffering of our fellowmen.

(Each person spills a drop of wine from his cup.)

4. THIS IS THE מצה (MATZAH) OF OPPRESSION

(The American Jewish Conference on Soviet Jewry urges that the following passage be read after *Ha Lachma Anya*—this is the bread of affliction.)

We set aside this לחם עוני (*lechem onee*)—this מצה (*matzah*) of oppression—to remember the three million Jews of the Soviet Union. Most of them cannot have מצה on their seder tables tonight. Conceive of Passover without מצה—without this visible reminder of our flight from slavery.

Think of Soviet Jews! They cannot learn of their Jewish past and hand it down to their children. They cannot learn the languages of their fathers and hand them down to their children. They cannot teach their children to be their teachers, their rabbis. They can only sit in silence and become invisible. We shall be their voice, and our voices shall be joined by thousands of men of conscience aroused by the injustice imposed on Soviet Jews. Then shall they know that they have not been forgotten, and they that sit in darkness shall yet see a great light.

5. LET MY PEOPLE GO

(From *The New Haggadah*, Behrman House, 1942,—to be inserted anywhere in the Haggadah.)

We have dedicated this festival tonight to the dream and hope of freedom, the dream and the hope that have filled the hearts of men from the time our Israelite ancestors went forth out of Egypt. Peoples have suffered, nations have struggled to make this dream come true. Now we dedicate ourselves to the struggle for freedom. Though the sacrifice be great and the hardships many, we shall not rest until the chains that enslave all men be broken.

But the freedom we strive for means more than broken chains. It means liberation from all those enslavements that warp the spirit and blight the mind, that destroy the soul even though they leave the flesh alive. For men can be enslaved in more ways than one.

Men can be enslaved to themselves. When they let emotion sway them to their hurt, when they permit harmful habits to tyrannize over them—they are slaves. When laziness or cowardice keeps them from doing what they know to be the right, when ignorance blinds them so that, like Samson, they can only turn round and round in meaningless drudgery—they are slaves. When envy, bitterness, and jealousy sour their joys and darken the brightness of their contentment—they are slaves to themselves and shackled by chains of their own forging.

Men can be enslaved by poverty and inequality. When the fear of need drives them to dishonesty and violence, to defending the guilty and accusing the innocent—they are slaves. When the work men do enriches others, but leaves them in want of strong houses for shelter, nourishing food for themselves and their children, and warm clothes to keep out the cold—they are slaves.

Men can be enslaved by intolerance. When Jews are forced to give up their Jewish way of life, to abandon their Torah, to neglect their sacred festivals, to leave off rebuilding their ancient homeland—they are slaves. When they must deny that they are Jews in order to get work—they are slaves. When they must live in constant fear of unwarranted hate and prejudice—they are slaves.

How deeply these enslavements have scarred the world! The wars, the destruction, the suffering, the waste! Pesach calls us to be free, free from the tyranny of our own selves, free from the enslavement of poverty and inequality, free from the corroding hate that eats away the ties which unite mankind.

Pesach calls upon us to put an end to all slavery! Pesach cries out in the name of God, "Let my people go." Pesach summons us to freedom.

6. PASSOVER TODAY

(To be inserted anywhere in the Haggadah. All passages recited in unison are biblical quotations.)

Reader

Why should we celebrate Passover? What is its message for us today? Let no one here think that this holiday speaks of ancient days alone. Passover reminds us also of the cruel slavery which exists in our day. It sensitizes us to the plague of human oppression and reminds us that like our forefathers, we are committed to overcome it.

Company

And the Lord said, "I have marked well the plight of My people in Egypt and have heeded their outcry because of their taskmasters; yes, I am mindful of their sufferings. . . . Come, therefore, I will send you to Pharaoh, and you shall free My people from Egypt."

Reader

God is the will toward freedom manifest in human destiny. He works through man—every man. When, through our efforts, we help our fellowman achieve dignity and equality, we are acting in harmony with God. This our prophets recognized and taught.

Company

It has been told you, O man, what is good,
And what the Lord requires of you:
To do justly, to love mercy,
And to walk humbly with your God.

Reader

Yet there are those in our midst who brazenly destroy the rights of others. Like Pharaoh of old, they refuse to recognize the dignity and equality of all men. They have crushed freedom and perverted the cause of justice.

Company

Have we not all one Source?
Has not one God created us?
Why do we deal treacherously
Each man against his brother?

Reader

There are those in our own nation scarred forever by the cruel slander of their fellowmen. There are those whose liberty is limited by the silence of citizens who don't care enough. Apathy endangers the freedom and welfare of our society.

Company

You shall not go about slandering people:
Neither shall you stand idly by
When your neighbor's life is in danger.

Reader

Today all life is in danger. The threat of extinction hangs over us precariously. War and weapons, power and hate combine to signal annihilation, and the prophetic warning may be our only salvation.

Company

I have set before you life and death, blessing and curse.
Choose life.
Seek peace and pursue it.

Reader

The time of awakening has come. Passover signals the will of justice, peace, and love at work in the universe. It calls us to action —it reminds us of our responsibilities.

Company

Seek justice, relieve the oppressed.
Hate evil and love what is good.
Let justice well up as water,
And righteousness as a mighty stream.

Reader

Let us ever remember that liberty, justice, and love are indivisible.

That whenever and wherever they are denied to the few, they wither for the many.

Company

One law shall be among you for all alike.
Hate not your brother in your heart;
Love your neighbor as yourself.

Reader

Thus shall we overcome the hatred that afflicts us.

Thus shall we overcome the poverty which plagues us.

Thus shall we overcome the oppression and cruelty which set man against man.

And thus, through human love, shall we break the fetters which bind us—and let human dignity prevail.

7. THE SPIRIT OF THE MESSIANIC

(To be read when the door is opened for Elijah.)

Elijah cannot be seen. He symbolizes the goodness that is in the hearts of men. He is justice. He is brotherhood. He is peace. Only as his spirit prevails in the deeds of men and nations, will mankind come nearer to the messianic day. God grant that next year all men may live together in freedom as brothers. With this hope in our hearts, we open the door for Elijah, welcoming him into our midst.

(The door is opened.)

ברוך אתה בבאך, וברוך אתה בצאתך

Ba-ruch atah b'vo-echa u-varuch atah b'tzay-techa.

Blessed are you, O Elijah, in your coming. Blessed be you in your going. We hope for the realization of your day as we sing together:

אליהו הנביא
אליהו התשבי
אליהו אליהו
אליהו הגלעדי

במהרה בימינו
יבא אלינו
עם משיח בן דוד
עם משיח בן דוד

Aylee-ya-hu ha-na-vee, Aylee-ya-hu ha-tish-bee,
Aylee-ya-hu, Aylee-ya-hu
Aylee-ya-hu hagee-la-dee.
Bim-hay-rah v'ya-may-nu yavo ay-lay-nu,
Im mashee-ach ben David,
Im mashee-ach ben David.

(Repeat first verse.)

(The door is closed.)

8. THE CLOSE

(From *The New Haggadah*, Behrman House, 1952)

Now we come to the close of our seder service.

Once again we have recited the age-old epic of Israel's liberation from bondage.

Once again we have chanted our psalms of praise to God, the Redeemer of Israel and of all mankind.

We have learned the message of the Exodus for our day.

And we have rededicated ourselves to the cause of man's freedom from tyranny and oppression.

As we have celebrated this festival tonight, so may we celebrate it, all of us together, next year again, in joy, in peace, and in freedom.

(All say in unison.)

לשנה הבאה בירושלים

La-shanah ha-ba-ah bee-ru-sha-la-yeem

May the coming year witness the further rebuilding of Zion and the redemption of Israel. Amen.

SUPPLEMENT E

Reading List on Judaism

Holy Scriptures, Jewish Publication Society, 1930

The Torah (A New Translation), Jewish Publication Society, 1963

M. Adler: *The World of the Talmud*, B'nai B'rith Hillel Foundations, 1958

B. Bamberger: *The Bible—Modern Jewish Approach*, B'nai B'rith Hillel Foundations, 1955

———: *The Story of Judaism*, Union of American Hebrew Congregations, 1957

S. Belkin: *In His Image* (Orthodox), Abelard-Schuman, 1960

S. Caplan and H. Ribalow (ed.): *The Great Jewish Books*, Horizon Press, 1952

A. Cohen: *Everyman's Talmud*, E. P. Dutton, 1949

J. Cohen: *The Case for Religious Naturalism*, Reconstructionist Press, 1958

M. Davis (ed.): *Israel: Its Role in Civilization*, Jewish Theological Seminary of America, 1956

I. Eisenstein: *What We Mean by Religion*, Reconstructionist Press, 1959

R. Gittelsohn: *Man's Best Hope*, Random House, 1961

J. Goldin: *The Living Talmud*, New American Library, 1954

R. Gordis: *A Faith for Moderns*, Bloch Publishing Co., 1960

———: *Judaism for the Modern Age*, Farrar, Straus and Cudahy, 1955

S. Grayzel: *History of the Jews*, Jewish Publication Society, 1953

———: *A History of the Contemporary Jews*, Meridian Books, 1960

M. M. Kaplan: *Judaism as a Civilization*, Yoseloff, 1934

———: *The Meaning of God in Modern Jewish Religion*, Behrman House, 1932

———: *Questions Jews Ask*, Reconstructionist Press, 1956

H. Orlinsky: *Ancient Israel*, Cornell University Press, 1954

W. G. Plaut: *The Rise of Reform Judaism*, World Union for Progressive Judaism, 1963

———: *The Growth of Reform Judaism*, World Union for Progressive Judaism, 1965

A. Sachar: *A History of the Jews*, A. A. Knopf, 1951

H. Sachar: *Aliyah*, World Publishing Co., 1961

———: *The Course of Modern Jewish History*, World Publishing Co., 1958

M. Samuel: *Certain People of the Book*, Knopf, 1959

H. Schauss: *The Jewish Festivals*, Union of American Hebrew Congregations, 1938

———: *Lifetime of a Jew*, Union of American Hebrew Congregations, 1950

L. Schwartz (ed.): *Great Ages and Ideas of the Jewish People*, Random House, 1956

_____ (ed.): *Golden Treasury of Jewish Literature*, Farrar and Rinehart, 1937
A. H. Silver: *Where Judaism Differed*, Macmillan and Co., 1956
M. Sklare: *Conservative Judaism*, Free Press, 1955
M. Steinberg: *A Partisan Guide to the Jewish Problem*, Bobbs Merrill, 1945
_____: *Basic Judaism*, Harcourt Brace, 1947
A. Vorspan and E. Lipman: *Justice and Judaism*, Union of American Hebrew Congregations, 1956
C. Weizmann: *Trial and Error*, Harper & Bros., 1949

SUPPLEMENT F

Reading List on Marriage

(Items marked * are especially recommended for the prospective bride and groom.)

D. S. Bailey: *Sexual Relation in Christian Thought*, Harper & Bros., 1959

*J. H. S. Bossard and E. S. Boll: *Why Marriages Go Wrong*, The Ronald Press, 1958

_____: *One Marriage, Two Faiths*, The Ronald Press, 1957

E. W. Burgess and L. S. Cottrell: *Predicting Success or Failure in Marriage*, Prentice-Hall, 1939

E. W. Burgess and P. Wallin: *Engagement and Marriage* J. P. Lippincott, 1953

*M. Davis: *The Sexual Responsibility of Woman*, Dial Press, 1956

S. Duvall: *Before You Marry*, Association Press, 1949

*E. Fromm: *The Art of Loving*, Harper & Bros., 1959

R. Gittelsohn: *Consecrated Unto Me*, Union of American Hebrew Congregations, 1965

*M. Hilliard: *A Woman Doctor Looks at Love and Life*, Doubleday, 1957

L. Kirkendall: *Premarital Intercourse and Interpersonal Relations*, Julian Press, 1961

C. Leuba: *Ethics in Sex Conduct*, Association Press, 1948

*F. A. Magoun: *Love and Marriage*, Harper & Bros., 1956

J. A. Peterson: *Toward a Successful Marriage*, Charles Scribner's Sons, 1960

I. L. Reiss: *Premarital Sexual Standards in America*, Free Press, 1960

L. M. Terman: *Psychological Factors in Marital Happiness*, McGraw-Hill, 1936

Notes

Chapter 1
A Many-Splendored Hope

1. Study at Pennsylvania State College, reported in *New York Herald Tribune*, October 23, 1949
2. F. A. Magoun: *Love and Marriage*, p. 346, Harper & Bros., 1956

Chapter 2
"This Funny Thing"

1. F. A. Magoun: *Love and Marriage*, pp. 4 f., 7
2. E. Fromm: *The Art of Loving*, pp. 22 ff., Harper & Bros., 1956
3. For the full account of this tender, poignant tale, see Goodman: *The Jewish Marriage Anthology*, pp. 38 f., Jewish Publication Society, 1965
4. Price: *Dialogues of Alfred North Whitehead*, p. 11, Little, Brown & Co., 1954
5. Herbert Weiner: "A Wedding in B'nai Brak," *Commentary*, July 1965
6. *Midrash Aseret Ha-dibrot*
7. K. Menninger: *The Vital Balance*, pp. 346 f., Viking Press, 1963

Chapter 3
Ready for Marriage?

1. *Zohar Chadash* 1:4b
2. J. H. S. Bossard & E. S. Boll: *Why Marriages Go Wrong*, p. 101, The Ronald Press Co., 1958
3. *Ibid.*, p. 110
4. *Ibid.*, p. 118
5. *The New York Times*, October 31, 1965
6. S. Duvall: *Before You Marry*, pp. 10 f., Association Press, 1949
7. *Zohar Chadash* 1:5a

Chapter 4
Right for Each Other?

1. P. & H. Goodman: *The Jewish Marriage Anthology*, p. 46
2. Yevamot 63a
3. L. Freehof: *Third Bible Legend Book*, pp. 80 f., Union of American Hebrew Congregations, 1956.
4. Pesikta Buber 11b–12a
5. Sotah 2a
6. Zohar I:91b
7. Pesachim 49a

8. S. Caplan & H. Ribalow: *The Great Jewish Books*, p. 229, Horizon Press, 1952
9. Yevamot 63a
10. Kiddushin 70
11. Pesachim 50
12. *The New York Times*, May 11, 1966
13. Sanhedrin 76
14. Yevamot 101b
15. Baba Batra 110a
16. F. A. Magoun: *Love and Marriage*, p. 229
17. J. E. Crawford & L. E. Woodward: *Better Ways of Growing Up*, p. 222, Muhlenberg Press, 1948.

Special Note: Unless otherwise stipulated, all talmudic references are to the Babylonian (Bavli) Talmud. The letter Y preceding a tractate indicates use of the Jerusalem (Y'rushalmi) Talmud.

Chapter 5
No Blueprint, But—

1. F. A. Magoun: *Love and Marriage*, p. 32
2. L. Newman: *The Talmudic Anthology*, p. 269, Behrman House, 1945. Menorat Ha-moar, quoting a midrash
3. F. A. Magoun: *Ibid.*, p. 318
4. Bereshit Rabbah 54
5. *Being Male and Female: Summary of a Campus Institute*, Kansas State University, Manhattan, Kansas
6. J. A. Peterson: *Toward a Successful Marriage*, p. 98, Charles Scribner's Sons, 1960
7. Aaron Rutledge: *Pre-Marital Counseling*, p. 237, Schenkman Publishing Co., 1966.
8. *Ibid.*, p. 236

Chapter 6
Of Matters Mundane

1. J. A. Peterson: *Toward a Successful Marriage*, p. 112
2. Kohelet Rabbah 7
3. L. Newman: *Hasidic Anthology*, p. 304, Charles Scribner's Sons, 1935
4. Erich Fromm: *Man for Himself*, p. 189, Rinehart and Co., 1947
5. J. A. Peterson: *Ibid.*, p. 130
6. For an extended discussion of this subject, see "Stop Being 'Just a Housewife,'" Ch. 7 of M. Hilliard: *A Woman Doctor Looks at Love and Life*, Doubleday and Co., 1957
7. Y. Ketuvot 5, 6

Chapter 7
God or the Gutter?

1. E. Fromm: *The Art of Loving*, pp. 88 f.
2. E. M. Duvall: *Love and the Facts of Life*, pp. 78, 81 f., Association Press, 1963
3. For further fascinating examples of this kind, see Ch. IX of R. Cabot and R. Dicks: *The Art of Ministering to the Sick*, The Macmillan Co., 1947

4. A beautifully poetic description of childbirth from the infant's point of view, as it were, may be found on pp. 8 ff. of A. N. Franzblau: *The Road to Sexual Maturity*, Simon and Schuster, 1954
5. J. Huxley: *New Bottles for New Wine*, pp. 218 f., Harper & Bros., 1957
6. For a more detailed description of coital positions, see F. A. Magoun: *Love and Marriage*, pp. 273 ff., and H. & A. Stone: *A Marriage Manual*, pp. 229–234, Simon and Schuster, 1939
7. Valuable suggestions dealing with feminine sex hygiene may be found in Chapter XIII of M. Davis: *The Sexual Responsibility of Woman*, Dial Press, 1956
8. W. H. Masters & V. E. Johnson: *Human Sexual Response*, Ch. V, Little, Brown & Co., 1966; also A. Rutledge: *Pre-Marital Counseling*, pp. 175–186

CHAPTER 8
Sex and Love

1. Trident Press, New York, 1968
2. *Saturday Review*, September 26, 1953
3. E. Fromm: *The Art of Loving*, p. 92
4. E. M. Duvall: *Why Wait Till Marriage?* p. 75, Association Press, 1965
5. Readers interested in a more extensive treatment of premarital chastity are referred to Chapters X, XI, and XII of the author's book for high school students, *Consecrated Unto Me*, Union of American Hebrew Congregations, 1965. For an excellent summary of the arguments pro and con, see pp. 301–307 of Rutledge: *Pre-Marital Counseling*, Schenkman Publishing Co., 1966
6. A. Rutledge: *Pre-Marital Counseling*, p. 186
7. *Ibid.*, p. 306
8. E. W. Burgess & P. Wallin: *Engagement and Marriage*, p. 204, J. P. Lippincott, 1953
9. L. M. Terman: *Psychological Factors in Marital Happiness*, pp. 327 ff., McGraw-Hill, 1936
10. C. Leuba: *Ethics in Sex Conduct*, p. 82, Association Press, 1948
11. I. L. Reiss: *Premarital Sexual Standards in America*, pp. 170 f., Free Press, 1960
12. E. M. Duvall: *Ibid.*, p. 87
13. L. Newman: *Talmudic Anthology*, p. 541
14. E. W. Burgess & P. Wallin: *Ibid.*, p. 371
15. *Current Medical Digest*, January 1965, p. 32
16. Kiddushin 2b
17. Sotah 2b
18. *Ibid.*, 25a
19. *Ibid.*, 47b
20. *Redbook Magazine*, April 1962
21. F. S. Caprio: *Marital Infidelity*, pp. 7, 11, The Citadel Press, 1953
22. R. Liswood: *First Aid for the Happy Marriage*, p. 195, Trident Press, 1965

CHAPTER 9
Both Sides of the Threshold

1. A. Rutledge: *Pre-Marital Counseling*, p. 162
2. *Boston Globe*, March 2, 1967

3. For fuller treatment see A. F. Guttmacher: *The Complete Book of Birth Control*, Ballantine Books, Inc., 1961
4. *The Nation*, October 5, 1964
5. Immanuel Jakobovits: *Jewish Medical Ethics*, Chap. XIV, Bloch Publishing Co., 1959
6. Dr. John Grover, Harvard Medical School, *Boston Globe*, January 20, 1967

Chapter 10
Old Voices–New Truths

1. I Corinthians 7:9
2. D. S. Bailey: *Sexual Relations in Christian Thought*, p. 14
3. *Ibid.*, pp. 23, 99
4. *Ibid.*, p. 63
5. Quoted by Robert E. Hall, M. D., in *The Nation*, October 5, 1964
6. Yoma 13a
7. Sanhedrin 39a
8. Maimonides: *Guide for the Perplexed*, 3:49
9. S. Glasner, in *Encyclopedia of Sexual Behavior*, p. 576, Hawthorn Books, 1961
10. Even Ha-ezer 76:1
11. Kiddushin 13a, Yevamot 52a
12. Pesikta Rabbati 17b
13. Responsa, Prague #199
14. Yoreh Dayah, Ch. 381, Sec. 6
15. A. B. Shoulson (ed.): *Marriage and Family Life*, p. 56, Twayne Publishers, 1959
16. Eruv. 100b
17. Nidda 31b
18. G. G. Scholem: *Major Trends in Jewish Mysticism*, pp. 105 f., Schocken Books, 1954
19. For the development of Catholic thought on contraception, see A. W. Sulloway: *Birth Control and Catholic Doctrine*, Beacon Press, 1959
20. F. A. Magoun: *Love and Marriage*, p. 293
21. *The Progressive*, September 1968
22. Raia Mehemna III: 34a
23. Zohar I: 187a
24. Yevamot 12b, Ketuvot 39a, Nedarim 35b, Nidda 45b
25. *Yearbook*, Central Conference of American Rabbis, 1927, p. 377

Chapter 11
Made in Heaven?

1. Zohar Chadash IV: 50b
2. Sanhedrin 22a
3. Ruth Rabbah 1
4. Pirke de Rabbi Eliezer 12:1
5. Ketuvot 61a
6. Shabbat 152
7. Hullin 84b
8. Baba Metzia 59a
9. *Ibid.*, 59a

10. Yevamot 62
11. Baba Metzia 59a
12. Ketuvot 62a
13. Kallah II
14. Zohar 233a
15. Zohar IV: 259b
16. Or Yesharim p. 109
17. Yevamot 65a
18. See article "Polygamy," *Jewish Encyclopedia, X:* 120, Funk and Wagnalls Co., 1905
19. Yevamot 37
20. Sanhedrin 22a
21. Song of Songs Rabbah I
22. E. M. & S. M. Duvall: *Sex Ways in Fact and Faith*, p. 98, Association Press, 1961
23. Deuteronomy 24:1
24. Yad: Ishut 14:8
25. S. Goldstein: *The Meaning of Marriage*, pp. 178 ff., Bloch Publishing Co., 1942
26. Leviticus Rabbah 9

Chapter 12
Generation to Generation

1. L. Newman: *Hasidic Anthology*, p. 45
2. Shabbat 10b
3. Sh'mot Rabbah 1:1
4. Intr. Tikkune Zohar 6a
5. Zohar II: 93a
6. Kiddushin 30a
7. *Ibid.*
8. Zohar Chadash to Sedrah Lech Lecha
9. Kiddushin 30a
10. Shabbat 119b
11. L. Newman: *Hasidic Anthology*, p. 45
12. Bereshit Rabbah 17:7
13. Zohar I: 50a
14. L. Newman: *Hasidic Anthology*, p. 118
15. *Ibid.*
16. *Ibid.*
17. Yevamot 6a
18. Kiddushin 31b–32a
19. Kiddushin 32a
20. Peah 15c
21. Zohar III: 93a
22. Montefiore & Loewe: *A Rabbinic Anthology*, p. 503, Macmillan & Co. Ltd., London, 1938. L. Newman: *Hasidic Anthology*, p. 304. A. Cohen: *Everyman's Talmud*, p. 183, E. P. Dutton & Co., 1949
23. Kiddushin 31b
24. Y. Kiddushin 61b

25. Niflaot Ha-Yehudi p. 45
26. Kiddushin 31a
27. Pirke de R. Eliezer 32
28. P. & H. Goodman: *The Jewish Marriage Anthology*, p. 46
29. Yalkut Shimon 95
30. A. B. Shoulson (ed.): *Marriage and Family Life*, p. 67
31. J. H. S. Bossard & E. S. Boll: *Why Marriages Go Wrong*, pp. 188 f.

CHAPTER 13
A House Divided?

1. J. H. S. Bossard & E. S. Boll: *Why Marriages Go Wrong*, p. 150
2. J. H. S. Bossard & E. S. Boll: *One Marriage, Two Faiths*, pp. 100 f., The Ronald Press, N.Y., 1957
3. M. Fine & M. Himmelfarb (ed.): *American Jewish Yearbook* 1963, pp. 18 f., Jewish Publication Society
4. *Ibid.*, pp. 30 f.
5. E. M. & S. M. Duvall: *Sex Ways in Fact and Faith*, p. 61
6. *Ibid.*, p. 62
7. C. Leuba: *Ethics in Sex Conduct*, pp. 127 f.

CHAPTER 14
Faith and Future

1. J. A. Pike: *The Next Day*, p. 95, Doubleday & Co., 1957
2. E. M. & S. M. Duvall: *Sex Ways in Fact and Faith*, pp. 88 f.
3. J. A. Peterson: *Toward a Successful Marriage*, p. 104
4. *Ibid.*
5. *Ibid.*, pp. 107 f.
6. Genesis Rabbah 8:9
7. Pirke de R. Eliezer Ch. 12
8. Kiddushin 6b
9. Berachot 30b, 31a
10. S. W. Baron: *The Jewish Community*, Vol. II, pp. 301–06, 315, Jewish Publication Society, 1942
11. S. Ganzfried: *Code of Jewish Law*, Vol. IV, pp. 6–13, Hebrew Publishing Co., 1927
12. For a discussion of what prayer can mean in the life of the modern Jew, see R. B. Gittelsohn: *Man's Best Hope*, Chs. 13, 14, Random House, 1961
13. *The New York Times*, January 31, 1965
14. For suggested translations of names as well as their origins and meanings, see Alfred J. Kolatch: *These Are the Names*, Jonathan David Co., 1948
15. F. A. Magoun: *Love and Marriage*, p. 420

15. Nishei Ha-Yehudi p. 13
16. Kiddushin 31a
17. Pirke de R. Eliezer 12
18. P. & H. Goodman: *The Jewish Marriage Anthology*, p. 46
19. Yalkut Shimoni 92
20. A. B. Shoulson (ed.): *Marriage and Family Life*, p. 69
21. J. H. S. Bossard & E. S. Boll: *Why Marriages Go Wrong*, pp. 188 f.

Chapter 13
A House Divided?

1. J. H. S. Bossard & E. S. Boll: *Why Marriages Go Wrong*, p. 156
2. J. H. S. Bossard & E. S. Boll: *One Marriage, Two Faiths*, pp. 100 f., The Ronald Press, N.Y. 1957
3. M. Fine & M. Himmelfarb (ed.): *American Jewish Yearbook* 1963, pp. 18 f., Jewish Publication Society
4. *Ibid.* pp. 30 f.
5. E. M. & S. M. Duvall: *Sex Ways in Fact and Faith*, p. 61
6. *Ibid.*, p. 62
7. C. Leuba: *Ethics in Sex Conduct*, pp. 127 f.

Chapter 14
Faith and Future

1. J. A. Pike: *The Next Day*, p. 96, Doubleday & Co. 1957
2. E. M. & S. M. Duvall: *Sex Ways in Fact and Faith*, pp. 88 f.
3. E. R. Peterson: *Toward a Successful Marriage*, p. 104
4. *Ibid.*
5. *Ibid.*, pp. 107 f.
6. Genesis Rabbah 8:9
7. Pirke de R. Eliezer Ch. 12
8. Kiddushin 30b
9. Berachot 30b, 31a
10. S. W. Baron: *The Jewish Community*, Vol. II, pp. 301–06, 315, Jewish Publication Society 1942
11. S. Ganzfried: *Code of Jewish Law*, Vol. IV, Ch. 6:13, Hebrew Publishing Co., 1927
12. For a discussion of what prayer can mean in the life of the modern Jew, see R. B. Gittelsohn: *Mark Each Hour*, Chs. 11, 12, Random [illegible], 1960
13. *The New York Times*, January 1[illegible]
14. For suggested translations of names as well as their origins and meanings, see Alfred J. Kolatch: *These Are the Names*, Jonathan David Co., 1948
15. B. N. Magoun: *Love and Marriage*, p. 420

Index